10/14/95

To Chinni,

A friend forever!

Howard N. Boxley

ORDINARY SOCIAL OCCASIONS, SANDCASTLES, AND STRUCTURAL REPRODUCTION

ORDINARY SOCIAL OCCASIONS, SANDCASTLES, AND STRUCTURAL REPRODUCTION

A Sociology of Everybody's Social Life

Howard Nathaniel Boughey

THE CASLON COMPANY

First published in 1995 in the United States of America by
THE CASLON COMPANY
Middletown, New Jersey

© 1995 by Howard Nathaniel Boughey

Library of Congress Cataloging-in-Publication Data

Boughey, Howard.
   Ordinary social occasions, sandcastles, and structural
reproduction : a sociology of everybody's social life / Howard Nathaniel Boughey.
     p. cm.
   Includes bibliographical references and index.
   ISBN 0-391-03938-5
   1. Social role. 2. Interpersonal relations. I. Title.
HM131.B658   1995
302—dc20

                                                                               95-6676
                                                                                   CIP

All rights reserved. No part of this publication may be
reproduced or transmitted, in any form or by any means,
without written permission from the publisher.

Printed in the United States of America

CONTENTS

	Acknowledgments	vii
	Overture: Sandcastles	ix
1	Social Occasions as Cellular Units of Everybody's Social Life	1
2	The Ingenuous Participant: Authentic Instrument of Sociological Observation	29
	Appendix: Exhibits A–R: Eighteen Interview Transcripts	46
3	Generic Agendas in Written, Spoken, and Tacit Formats: How Major Activity Modes Are Realized as Occasional Definitions of the Situation	111
4	The Display and Acquisition of Social ID during Live Occasions: How Institutional Structure Is Realized	169
	Epilogue	189
	References	191
	Index	197

ACKNOWLEDGMENTS

This book is dedicated to my most significant others, my wife, Dr. Nirmala Devi Cherukupalle, and my sons, Joshua Eric Boughey and Shawn Venkatesh Boughey, and to the memory of my intellectual godparents, Charles and Leonora Page.

Immeasurable thanks to those colleagues who lived up to the institutional relationship ID implicit in the term by unselfishly and honestly providing vital criticism to parts of this work at various stages of its development: David Brownfield, Jack Hewett, Malcolm MacKinnon, Doug Campbell, and Ed Silva. Shawn Boughey also displayed creativity and initiative in his invaluable research assistance.

OVERTURE: SANDCASTLES

Structure exists only as memory traces . . . and as instantiated in action.
Giddens, *The Constitution of Society*

All day long we play at the beach, digging up the commonplace grains of sand and piling, packing and shaping them into the structures we choose, the ones we know how to make together, whose shapes satisfy us.

Sometimes, close to the low tide line, we work to create *selves*, fearsome, noble, or pitiable structures intended to show something "off" to others who might pass by before the tide once again sweeps this part of the beach clean of pretension. Just a bit further up the beach we dig in pairs, interacting one-on-one to construct, reconstruct, develop, maintain and sustain *relationships*. Here is where sociologists begin to loiter to watch the action.

Far from the tide line but where there is still damp, packable sand to work with, we join progressively larger groups of diggers to design, decorate, repair and heap higher the great social *institutions* upon which we have come to rely for our sense of order, of permanent meaning, of certainty and predictability, of value and worth: the great structure of *kinship*, with its organizational components of families, lineages, ethnicities, and "peoples"; the *economy*, by which we make comparably meaningful our labors, our possessions, our monetarily measurable and countable transactions; the *polity*, through which we organize and give meaning to our power relations with legally established authority, with "the state," and all levels of government; *learning*, by means of which we institutionalize the intergenerational transfer of vital cultural information (primarily, information "how to" build and repair all the other sandcastles) and professionally create, restrict, apply, and sell knowledge; *religion*, by which we sanctify our mundane powers and activities; *friendship*, that most intimate of structures that protects our secrets and obligates us to keep our promises; *sport*, our citadel of idealism, altruism, and measured effort; and finally *art*, the institutionalization of every human being's longing for beauty, harmony, and perfect communication.

All of these great institutional structures emerge from the amorphous sand of the beach via our creative joint efforts, and when at last they stand before us, huge and intricate, they reflect back to us the profound and life-giving social meanings we have built into them. They sometimes appear to the sociologically unwary to "govern" our conduct, to be self-perpetuating, and to have "sui generis" origins. These of course are but some of the meanings we have built into the institutional devices, so that they will "work" for us as we intend them to.

Above all we try to make social structures appear permanent and unyielding, like Shelley's poetic kingdom of Ozymandias:

> I met a traveller from an antique land
> who said: Two vast and trunkless legs of stone
> Stand in the desert. Near them on the sand
> Half sunk, a shatter'd visage lies, whose frown
> and wrinkled lip and sneer of cold command
> Tell that its sculptor well those passions read
> which yet survive, stamp'd on these lifeless things
> The hand that mock'd them and the heart that fed
> And on the pedestal these words appear:
> "My name is Ozymandias, king of kings:
> Look on my works, ye Mighty, and despair!"
> Nothing beside remains. Round the decay
> Of that colossal wreck, boundless and bare,
> The lone and level sands stretch far away.
>   Percy Bysshe Shelley, "Ozymandias of Egypt"

But every morning when we arise, we pad on down to the local beach, pails and shovels in hand, fearfully and hopefully, to assess the damage done to yesterday's sandcastles by the night tides and the occasional storms of destructive activity by others, to discover how much we must rebuild today, and how much we may rebuild, perhaps for the better.

It is our joy and our despair as humans to realize that the sandcastle structures of our social lives are in a continual state of dissolution, and that only we, you and I writ almost six billion times, can perpetuate our life's meaningfulness.

1

Social Occasions as Cellular Units of Everybody's Social Life

Recently occurring "live" social occasions were the object of a lengthy and intensive empirical study. It principally found that if we take the time and trouble to look rigorously and systematically, we can see how ordinary people observably strive to reproduce normal social order and sensible social meaning, every day, over and over again. This finding has led to skepticism about the existence of permanent structures of social organization, or of fixed meanings inscribed deterministically into the brains and bodies of each generation of humans. Why? With regard to permanent structures, the effort that everybody observably expends every day to rebuild social meaning and social structure implies that these meanings and structures need rebuilding— that they are tenuous, fragile structures, like sandcastles subject to the predations of the next tide, rather than like solid edifices of brick and stone. As to fixed meanings and invisible inscription processes, the observability of conscious meaning construction and freely negotiated reality in live action contexts simply obviates these presuppositions.

Along with Lyman we have found that:

> continued performance of routine dramas—i.e., the dramas that are devoid of awesomeness, charisma, melodrama, histrionics, or theatricality—makes up the everyday life process and by their very unremarkability sews together the social fabric. (1990: 220)[1]

However, the "social fabric" evident in our data is persistently unraveling. Our examination of this "everyday life process" approaches social life as a distinct form of *life*, whose understanding begins with discovery of its fundamental principles of organization, those features that characterize it as a distinct form, and those structural elements and dynamics that enable it to live, to sustain its life. These principles are empirically instantiated in naturally occurring, live social occasions.

Thoroughgoing use of this approach allows us to clearly see that social life is constituted of a single great structure, normalcy, and a single great process, normalization. The substructures constituting social normalcy and the metabolic subprocesses contributing to its reproduction are observable features of episodes of live face to face interaction. These live episodes, Lyman's "routine dramas," reformulated here as "ordinary social occasions," display for our understanding the ways and means by which ordinary participants reproduce social structure. Empirical analysis of the events making up ordinary social occasions demonstrates in detail *how* we recurrently reproduce social structure, but the sandcastle metaphor helps to explain why we do it. Observably we seek normalcy in all our interactive doings, whether we call it that or meaningfulness or sanity or certainty or balance or coherence or ontological security. But chaos, incommunicability, and the senseless destruction of meaning are ever present threats. Structures of sense everlastingly decay, so if they are to be sustained to serve as sustenance for social life, they must be reproduced by all of us interacting together day by day to keep social life alive. "Definitions of situations" (Thomas, 1937), out of which meaningful social structure is composed, are perpetually in flux, requiring our assiduous efforts to preserve the appearance of either constancy or continuity. Our relationships, our institutions, all of the structural features of our social life are like sandcastles we've built on the beach, awaiting the inevitable tides and storms of change. As Sacks correctly pointed out, "being ordinary" in social life, "takes work," it is "a job that . . . people . . . may be coordinatively engaged in, to achieve that each of them, together, are ordinary persons . . . people take on the job of keeping everything utterly mundane . . . with every effort possible" (1984b: 414, 419).

As a first step toward empirical study of the process of reproduction of social structure, we decided to take Speier's advice (1973) to treat ordinary social occasions as living cellular units of social life,[2] the recurrent live contexts of meaning within which our actions achieve facticity and durability beyond their brief life spans. Definition of the social occasion as the ideal unit for the observation and analysis of activity characteristic of *everybody's social life* (the comprehensive field of study to which sociology is dedicated) began for us with the following negative question: "What is it that everybody's social life is *not* ? " Philosopher George Santayana's "four-word definition of a dog's universe, *"WHAT DON'T SMELL AIN'T,"* is a good example of the power of such negative thinking.[3] To see clearly what it is you want to see, it helps to clear away the clutter of irrelevancies. Having swallowed the answers to this terrible three-part question— "What is not everybody's?" "What is not social?" and "What is not life?"—we can then open our eyes like Alice on the other side of the looking glass and describe and analyze what remains to be seen within an intentionally restricted universe. This ground-clearing exercise, what phenomenologists call an "epoche," leaves the ordinary social occasion exposed in bas-relief as the ideal unit for sociological study.

What Is Not Everybody's?

A sociology of everybody's social life has to be about the social life of the entire human species, bar none, including all people now alive on earth (approaching 6,000,000,000), plus all who ever lived. Before we can say anything meaningful about species variants, like pre-moderns, moderns or post- moderns, it is important to develop, if we can, a clear picture of the social life the human species lives in common.

The first step is to ignore things too idiosyncratic to be everybody's (that heap of unrelated and unrelatable items that Pitirim Sorokin called "congeries" [1966: 414]) and point our noses, by successive approximations, in the direction of "human universals." This idea has long been out of fashion in the social sciences, but Donald Brown's recent anthropological work on human universals is a bright light on a grey horizon (1991). To seek out humanly universal patterns in the observable events of social life requires that we jettison idiosyncrasies. This exclusion cuts a great swathe across ripe fields of information about social life produced by historians, journalists, anthropologists, and fellow sociologists who are issue-oriented or otherwise parochial in their perspectives, and heaps all of it on the "congeries" pile.

What is not everybody's in most history books is description and analysis of events that happen once and only once. Historians line up preceding events as the cumulative causal nexus for the next, making each event studied necessarily unique as the "nth" in a linear series. By contrast everybody's social life observably consists of attempts to repeat events whose significance inheres more in their replication than in their uniqueness.[4] The universal historical fact is that every "civilization" "has" a history, spoken or written (and revised frequently), which is retold or reread by successive generations of members. However, your group's history is not necessarily my group's history, so no one History, no matter how authoritatively the official history, is "everybody's." Of greater sociological interest is how and for what purposes social groups fabricate and retell their histories. Ethnohistory, the study of how histories are produced and used to reconstruct the past and situationally define the present, can tell us more about everybody's social life than history can.[5]

Add to the "congeries" heap the contents of every day's newspaper and news broadcast. "Dog bites man," is not news because it is commonplace, ordinary, "normal." Inversions make news. "Man bites dog," however, which is the standard format of the news story, is intentionally not the standard format of everybody's social life. What sociologists should report, the most frequently repeated events of everybody's social life "as usual," would put the city editor to sleep. This is not a critique of journalism or "news." Consumers of news want precisely what is "new," what's different about what happened yesterday, what's extraordinary in the behavior of their "contemporaries," in Schutz's terms, who are outside their face-to-face "reach," but still inhabit the same space/time world (1967: 177ff.). What readers contrast with the news is their "stock of knowledge in hand" (another Schutz term) about how go the ordinary, business-as-usual activities in which they themselves participate.

It is this generalized format of standard operating procedures, necessarily shared by everybody who successfully engages in social life, shared in the sense of participation as well as the sense of knowledge and capability to enact it, which should be sociology's preferred focus of attention. Whatever the wise journalist designates as "not news" is likely to be of genuine sociological interest.[6] But in trying to develop authentic descriptions of banal, mundane, ordinary social activities, we have found that asking the standard, workaday five journalistic questions—what?, who?, when?, where?, and why?—can help reveal and explicate the internal structure of these sociologically meaningful, if non-newsworthy events.

Anthropologists' professed preoccupation with the "otherness" of the people they study consigns a hundred years of professional description of social life, directly observed or derived from the reports of participants ("informants"), to the "not everybody's" category. Unfortunately anthropological fieldwork derives from European colonists' and adventurers' travelogues and diaries, and has continued to the present predominantly as a "developed" world's view of the quaint inhabitants of the "undeveloped" world. To find balance we would require a hundred years of them writing about us. Excision of this imperialist bias from anthropology's contribution to our knowledge of everybody's social life leaves very little anthropological standing intact. The field is blinkered against perception of common human practices by theories of cultural relativism and determinism, which allows it to see only difference and the exotic, without ever having described the sameness and the ordinariness against which difference and exotica can be meaningfully contrasted. This is the theory underlying Brown's account (op. cit.), which nevertheless claims that some anthropologists are once again joining the search for "human universals" after a long hiatus.[7]

Add to the "not everybody's" category sociological writings on "social problems" and "social issues." None of these are problems or issues to all humans. They are as historically and culturally particular as the battles between kings that used to be the exclusive "stuff" of history: bareheaded women in Iran, democratic sentiments in China, teenage pregnancy in the U.S., overwork in Japan, gum chewing in Singapore, foreigners in Germany. However, all human collectivities do recognize some things to be problems and/or issues, and may well use standard procedures to define and "solve" social problems and constitute social issues.   These procedures, such as "moral entrepreneurship," and the promulgation of "scares," are part and parcel of everybody's social life, as analyzed by self-labelled "constructionists" like Joel Best (1989), Malcolm Spector, and John Kitsuse (1987), who find more of sociological interest in the means of construction and definition of social issues and problems and in standard reformist responses to them than in the content of the issues or problems themselves. This is the major merit of a strain of sociological research called "ethnomethodology," as described by its inventor, Harold Garfinkel (1967). Ethnomethodologists find that the methods, the procedures and "artful practices" that participants use to produce particular social meanings are more likely to be generalizable to all humans than are the specifics of those meanings. Construction of social reality from diverse "definitions of the situation" which Berger and Luckmann (1966) theorized, and which Garfinkel and Sacks (1972) began to study empirically, is a universal human process, whereas the localized, parochial realities thus produced are likely to be idiosyncratic.[8]

Too much of sociology has been narrow-mindedly parochial over the past hundred years, thus not informative about *everybody's* social life. The society-building work of females has been ignored or treated as insignificant by sexism-blinded sociologists, as "feminist sociologists" are only lately able to tell us. "The first difficulty is that how sociology is thought—its methods, conceptual schemes and theories has been based on and built up within, the male social universe (even when women have participated in its doing)" (Smith, 1974a: 7). This sociological sexism has led to almost a complete blank in the literature with regard to one of the most recurrent forms of social interaction, a foundational society-building activity mode, commensality, or mealtime interaction, which we try to restore to its deserved prominence in chapter 3, below. Women have been the major organizers and producers of this vital component of everybody's social life, and male-dominated sociology has ignored and trivialized it. To discover what is true about *everybody's* social life requires elimination from our field of view of the obviously idiosyncratic, the journalistically inverted, the historically specific, the anthropologically other, locally defined issues and problems, and theory and research on "mankind" from any parochial viewpoint, whether it be sexist, racist, imperialist or intellectually elitist.

WHAT IS NOT SOCIAL?

What is not social about everybody's life is the sum of: solitary activities, quasi-social "interludes," interior mental experience, "the individual" considered as anything but a social participant, and meanings attached to actions without reference to an interactive social context.

The only guaranteed equality in social life is this: every mother's daughter and son of us endures (and/or enjoys) a precisely allotted twenty-four-hour day of clock time which cannot be materially shortened or lengthened no matter how procrustean the bed in which we lie, nor how Canute-like we estimate our lordly power to be. This equally long day, however, is differently divisible by and for each of us into intervals during which we live alone and intervals when we live with others. Parkes and Thrift report survey findings on time allocation in thirteen countries showing average daily hours spent "all alone" (including sleep) ranging from 9.5 for employed men in Czechoslovakia to 16.4 for housewives in Bulgaria (1980: 168, 169).

That life we live when no one else is present, or in sleep, when we cannot interact consciously with others even if present, is not, in any concrete, interactional sense, social.[9] Everybody has a solitary existence, as an important part of "personal" life, but events which occur and actions we perform when we are alone cannot count as part of everybody's social life.[10] Some solitary actions are "prefabrications," the prior construction of elements of a future occasion's pattern of meanings, work done off-site to be erected, put in place and lived in or lived by at the occasion-site later on. They include such socially relevant but solitarily lived actions as attending to one's toilette, dressing, making up, rehearsing, studying, practicing, or doing research. These solitary prefabrications, such as the preparation of a research report to be delivered later cannot enter the range of observation as social actions until they are evidentially presented or alleged at a later social event. By saying that nothing that occurs in solitude can be considered in and of itself social, we join nineteenth-century sociologist Herbert Spencer in a classic exclusion: "Disregarding conduct that is entirely private, we consider only that species of conduct which involves direct relations with other persons" (Spencer, 1899). Our Santayanaist dog now has a Spencerian nose, "disregarding conduct that is entirely private."

INTERLUDES

But is all human action not performed in solitude "entirely social?" There is an intermediate ground on which we sometimes conduct ourselves which though not solitary, is not fully social either. Social psychologist Erving

Goffman characterized social life as "the realm of activity that is generated by face-to-face interaction and organized by norms of co-mingling—a domain containing weddings, family meals, chaired meetings, forced marches, service encounters, queues, crowds and couples" (1971: ix). Weddings, meals, meetings, marches and some kinds of encounters would appear to be eminently social affairs, but the last three items don't fit easily with the rest. "A couple" is clearly not an activity, but two participants presenting themselves in a friendly relationship ID. "A queue" or "a crowd" might be forms of activity as well as relationship, but not full-fledged social events. Goffman's offhand mention of such things leads us to seek a category of events that are "quasi-social." These are *social interludes*, events "between the acts" of everybody's social life, times when there are others physically present, but we are not quite socially engaged. Interludes include the passage of crowds "through" one another as they enter and exit subway trains; pedestrian traffic on urban streets; students moving through hallways to get to the next class; and the "interaction" between drivers on the highway.[11]

Everybody's everyday life is divided up into periods of solitude and of social engagement, punctuated by interludes of quasi-social activity. Our research strategy is to put aside solitude and interludes and focus first on that which is "strictly social." Sociological master Max Weber's working definition of "social action," while it is useful in many respects as a baseline, contains elements that are not strictly social, in particular, "subjective meaning," and "the acting individual": "Action is social," said Weber, "in so far as, by virtue of the subjective meaning attached to it by the acting individual (or individuals), it takes account of the behavior of others and is thereby oriented in its course" (1947: 72). Such actions must perforce be observable (though not necessarily observed, in any particular instance) by the others. Therefore everything that is not in principal observable is not social, including "subjective meaning."

When we do closely observe instances of social life, we can see meanings being attached to actions and courses of action, but such attachment is hardly ever observably done "by the acting individual." It is the others, toward whom and in concert with whom the action is oriented, who indicate verbally and/or nonverbally what the action means, who interpret it, judge it, "realize" it, and they do it intersubjectively, they objectify the meaning and make of it a public, exteriorized fact, sometimes an official, certified, documentary fact (see Smith, 1974b). Sociology's quarry should not be Mead's "I" and "me" (respectively, the self seen from inside, and the self regarded from the internalized standpoint of the other), engaged in my action, but rather an approach to understanding the emergence, in interaction, of the reality of "we" and "us," engaged in *our* action. For instance, when the kicker on a National Football League team boots the ball between the uprights and over the crossbar, the social meaning of the kick does not depend on what subjective meaning is attached to his act by the kicker. Only when the umpire thrusts both his arms straight up from the shoulder, the kick is "a field goal worth three points to be added to the score of the kicker's team."

We must argue strenuously against Weber's exclusive enshrinement of the individual actor. "The individual" is a social construct, raised, as "ego" to the level of an ideological icon in the mythology of modern industrial society, but a thing rarely seen to be acting alone in the reality of social life. Participants are most often seen to act as partners in relationship pairs, or as members, collaborators in some collective action, or as performers of sub-tasks in complex actions. At best, individuals can be seen to *conspire* with other participants to act socially, in agency-units made up always of two or more individuals. We conspire with tablesful of others to dine; with crews, teams, shifts, companies to work productively; with massed congregations to audience; with coteries, cliques and caucuses to confer; with teams, opponents, leagues, parties and juries to compete and judge in contests, and with one and onlys, double dates, gangs and our crowd to enjoy each other's company convivially. It is best to abandon "the individual" and "the self" as basic units of sociological analysis. Nothing substantively social is lost by this exclusion.[12]

If we excise emphasis on individual agency and interiorized events,[13] a more useful version of Weber's definition would be as follows: "Action is social insofar as social meanings are attached to it in observable ways by others toward whom it is acknowledged to be oriented." But this action has meaning only within its own meaningful context, as Weber also recognized, "For a science dealing with the true meaning of behavior, explanation requires: a grasp of the context of meaning within which the actual course of action occurs" (1962: 24). Contemporary conversation analysis, we must agree with Heath, has "cogently shown that an utterance and the action it performs can only be understood with regard to the context in which they occur" (1986: 9).

If actions are not social unless and until they are attributed social meanings within a meaningful social context, in Heath's terms, if "the character of an utterance, an action or an activity can only be determined, both by participants and analysts, with reference to its location within the local framework of action," (ibid) then utterances, actions or activities in themselves ought not be primary units any more than individuals. Rather, we should reach for a more concrete, empirically specifiable notion of this "context of meaning," this "local framework of action."

An ideal unit of observation and analysis is the *social occasion,* defined as:

"a gathering inside spatial boundaries defined by them of two or more persons identified by each other as participants, over a period of time whose intervals, precedents and antecedents they define, during which a named course of activity predominates, attached to which they display for attribution as normal and appropriate, explicit motives." [14] The social occasion is the living context within which by our own creative work we define where, when, among whom and for what reasons we live our social lives. Participation in social occasions makes up the material entirety of everybody's social life.

Individual selves, relationships, organizations and institutions are clothed with social meaning during occasional interaction, and "exist" as social entities only during and by dint of social occasions upon which they are invoked as elements of the definition of the occasional situation. Occasions are social participants' major meaning construction devices.[15, 16, 17] Everything about a social occasion, everything that can be said to be objectively "part" of it, is available, and is intentionally made available to participants' "naked senses," to use Goffman's phrase (1968: 297). So add to the "not social" bin everything that does not occur observably to the naked senses of participants in the context of a social occasion.[18, 19]

What Is Not Life?

Speier (1973) made the leap of seeing social occasions as events which should be provided by social scientists with "natural histories," ways of being described which reveal their character and structure as life forms. If it is to be a science of everybody's social life, sociology must be a "life science." The "life" of the phenomena under study needs clear differentiation from aspects which are not alive, and the form of life we are examining needs to be distinguished from other forms, such as mental and organic life. An important distinction between mental life and social life is that social life is completely overt, mental life unobservably covert, except for detectable neural brain activity, which we might call, with Giddens, "memory traces." Unlike organic life, which is continuous and materially dependent on its surroundings, or ecosystem, social life is intermittent and defines its own environment. It is composed of living cells, social occasions, plus the material and symbolic consequences of occasional life, these consequences or "leavings" being themselves not alive but representative of social life once lived and influential upon social life still to come. Analogous forms of organic life would be coral reefs, or trees, both of which have thin "skins" of living material stretched over dead matter which provides structural stability over time.

The social occasion is the ideal "social object" to study not only because it consists entirely of observables, but also because of its scale. The social occasion is neither a microsocial nor a macrosocial phenomenon, but rather it is life-sized, at the lived scale of social life. As Smelser says, "Neither micro nor macro theory is satisfactory. Action and structure must now be intertwined" (1988: 77; see also Hilbert, 1990; and Cicourel, 1981). Human scale is where materially observable activity produces symbolic structure, which in turn provides blueprints, but not determinants, for action. As Giddens puts it, "structure is both medium and outcome of the reproduction of practices" (1979: 69). For instance, the "historical constraints" we might experience in social life are "not available through a study of the institutional gloss of history, but only in the ongoing historical life process—which occurs at the level of human action or interactional (members') practices. An adequate interpretation therefore requires recovery of the detail of members' practices" (Rawls, 1988: 12).

Social life, like the living skin of a tree, depends on both "inner" and "outer" support systems which, while they are not social life itself, are nevertheless interdependent with it. Sub-occasional systems such as the organic life of humans, plus their interior mental lives, (thoughts and feelings,) are "inner" support systems upon which social life literally depends.[20] Supra-occasional systems like the nation state, the church, the family, or our friendship relationship, also have a kind of continuous existence. These are components of the non-living infrastructure of social life, entirely dependent for their continued existence upon the living of that life by participants in social occasions, but also critical for the continuity and health of occasional life, social life's life support system.   Relationships, organizations and institutions have no life of their own; they are the intentional byproducts of social life as we live it upon occasions, but at the same time we fashion them as "grammatical" infrastructure and integrative superstructures upon which social life can thrive and grow. These are the sandcastles in this book's title and "overture," constantly falling apart, constantly being rebuilt by all of us day by day, constantly being "reified," or mistakenly thought to have Ozymandian lives and powers of their own (see Maynard and Wilson, 1980). But language does not speak; religion does not worship; kinship does not nurture; the economy does not produce or consume, friendship cannot love, the polity cannot wield power, art cannot perceive beauty, learning cannot know, and sport cannot excel. Only we, as participants in live social occasions, can.

Rawls calls this distinction between social "life and its leavings," "two domains: (1) emergent interactive meaning and (2) retrospective institutional accountability frameworks" (1989: 15).

According to Berger and Luckmann's interpretation, this was also Marx's key distinction:

What concerned Marx was that human thought is founded in human activity ("labor," in the widest sense of the word) and in the social relations brought about by this activity. "Substructure" and "superstructure" are best understood if one views them as, respectively, human activity and the world produced by that activity. (1966: 6)

Braudel pioneers in delineation of the connections between the smallest scale activities and relationships of everyday life, and "those historical monsters, the world-economies" (1984: 71). The world economy is a concept first developed by Immanuel Wallerstein while, Braudel says, he was "looking for the largest units of measurement which would still be coherent." "Coherence is essential," Braudel asserts. "Without it there would be no unit of measurement at all" (70). The concept of the ordinary social occasion as the cellular unit of social life has emerged in the search for *the smallest* unit of measurement which would still be coherent, and it is deemed "cellular" because it is the smallest structural coherence which is in itself alive. At the largest coherent scalar level, where people build, inhabit, and rebuild "world-economies," Braudel reiterates the "sandcastles" theme in his concept of "the secular trend," which is "a process of destructuration: one coherent world system which has developed at a leisurely pace is going into or completing its decline while another system is being born amid much hesitation and delay" (85). At the cellular scale of social life, the level at which it is lived and can be most directly observed, we see the reciprocal of the secular trend—the process of renewal, of reconstruction, or better, social reproduction. As Schegloff puts it,

> the locus of order here is not the individual (or some analytic version of the individual) nor any broadly formulated societal institution, but rather the procedural infrastructure of interaction. (1992: 1338)

At this locus we can observe and analyze the production of "intersubjectivity" defined as a "convergence between the 'doers' of an action or bit of conduct and its recipients, as coproducers of an increment of interactional and social reality" (ibid.: 1299).[21]

Dorothy Smith describes the process of building living social structure on occasion and then leaving it lifeless behind us thus:

> people bring into being for one another a "structure" . . . which they inhabit temporarily and which drops away behind them; of course it is not made any way we see fit; what we put together in the past shapes the direction and framework of the future; what we build interlocks with what others build; we build what we know how to build with the materials that come to hand. None the less, we move into the future as into a building, the walls, floors, and roof of which we put together with one another as we go into it. It is an ongoing creation of and in action. (1990: 53)

Each occasion of "a class" engaging myself and my students comes to life at 2:10 p.m. on Tuesday. It lives, it pulsates with the organized life we give it, until 3 p.m., when we disperse. At that moment the life of that class occasion ends. But its leavings, its "retrospective institutional accountability frameworks," remain. There are grades on record, the university pays me a salary, the record of attendance and grades entitles students to a diploma, our careers go forward, the university continues to exist as an organization only because that class (and the many others isomorphic to it) has lived its fleeting life. The Institution of "higher" learning, a symbolic structure comprising all such universities, persists, not alive, but like a coral reef, or the woody center of the tree, as an amalgamation of dead leavings that once pulsed with life.

It is when it is being reproduced during social occasions that social structure is alive, and after that, as Giddens reasons, it "exists only as memory traces, the organic basis of human knowledgeability" (1984: 377). Additionally, via record keeping and architecture, we commemorate, commit to common memory, these live events as bits of structure to keep the memory traces available for the next live occasion when we choose to invoke them, and thus make them appear to have continued and substantial existence "across extended time-space, outside conditions of co-presence" (ibid.).

As Braudel demonstrates, cellular economic interactions are extended by networks of exchange to "world economies"; cellular kinship interactions are extended from families to "peoples"; cellular religious interactions are extended from congregations to "world cultures"; and cellular learning interactions like those with my students are extended to civilizations or world views, to cumulative knowledge bases.

It has been the scientific intention to focus upon the most recurrent phenomenon in the subject field that led to the idea of the ordinary social occasion as the cellular unit of social life. Speier was looking in the same direction in his early work, urging us to treat the observable reality of social life with all the rigor of a natural scientist:

> In the study of naturalistic activity the search for the invariant properties of cultural patterning takes precedence over other aims, in the same way that the whole science of biology appears to rest on the recognition of an invariant organizing principle for all life forms, the cell. (1973: 8)

We shall be on our way to an empirical sociology once we have recognized that the ordinary social occasion is the cell of social life, a phenomenon so repetitive that it demands replicative research. This realization builds also on the work of Kenneth Pike (1967) and Adam Kendon (1990). All that can be empirically known about social life is that which can be observed to occur upon social occasions and intersubjectively verified by accepted scientific procedures.

This might well leave out direct knowledge of consciousness, imagination, memory, emotion, intention, and purpose. Certainly many of these things can be known humanistically or spiritually, but because they cannot be directly observed nor intersubjectively tested, they cannot be known empirically. But there need be no conflict between an empirical, scientific sociology and one that operates with humanistic, phenomenological awareness of the meanings being transmitted between social interactants,[22] because there is so much about consciousness, imagination, memory, and the rest of "private experience" which participants make publicly observable to one another and thereby to an empirical sociology. Our empirical analysis will bring to light the specific procedures interactants use to overtly bring to life and publicly live out these features of their "inner lives" as elements of their social life, that life form that resides not within us, nor beyond us, but among us.

Observation, description and analysis of various forms and types of live social occasions is reported in selected instances in the substantive chapters below. This research program has taken as a beacon the following basic sociological question: *"What causes the meaningful organization of everybody's social life?"*

If we take everybody's social life to consist materially of participation in social occasions as defined above, then, continued controlled observation and careful analysis of such occasions via the methods described in chapter 2, below, thus far fails to disconfirm the following proposed answer: The sole observable cause of the organized character of social life as it is lived on occasion is the work that participants do to organize it. To the question, "what generates live social organization?", the direct empirical answer is, "participants make it happen." No other causal factors are directly observable, but must be inferred from often questionable evidence or deduced from grand theories. Are alternative, "invisible" causal explanations necessary? The more we observe naturally occurring social occasions, the more fully attributable their organization is to the meaning-conferral of participants. As the observed relationships between meaning-producing actions and elements of consequent structural organization accumulate, the necessity or probability of alternatives diminishes, and we are able to successively obviate competing explanations.[23]

Following the method of "authentic observation" outlined in chapter 2, we lay out for repeated inspection and rigorous analysis focused descriptions of how participants assiduously produced and integrated social meanings to constitute the meaningful contexts for their continuing interaction, the "live" ordinary social occasions in which they participated. The descriptions allow us to see how larger structures, like long term relationships and large scale institutions, are reproduced bit by bit by occasion participants and oriented to by them as objectively real social facts. Our instantial illustrations constitute a demonstration that at least in these cases evidentially, and therefore in all such cases hypothetically, the bulk of the observed organization is designed and implemented by participants acting in concert.

The eighteen such occasions each recounted by a participant under focused questioning presented herein as interview-transcription "exhibits," were selected from several dozen thus far recorded and analyzed using this method. Analysis of many more instances is needed, from the widest imaginable range of cultural and economic contexts, to prove or disconfirm these principles to be humanly universal.[24] Our "sample" is eighteen cells of living social interaction out of the billions that live, pass away, and leave their residues and memory traces every day. Our bravest hypothesis is that the truth about the social life represented in these instances, is much of the elemental truth about everybody's social life. It is proposed that these instances, like grains of sand on a beach, contain the morphological features that would make them generalizable to the extent of explaining the changing shapes, the internal structure, and even the origins and destiny, of the dunes. Of course these assertions invite disconfirmation.

Such as they are at this preliminary stage, the research findings presented here affirm the wisdom and capability of the common person. A corollary generalization that emerges is that, when asked appropriately, ordinary participants in ordinary social occasions can demonstrate that they know what they're doing, and, that they're doing it on purpose. Such findings begin to obviate conventional sociological notions of the overriding significance of unintended and unanticipated consequences (e.g., Merton, 1949). Standard-issue humans, by planning, crafting, and instituting social structure, demonstrate conclusively that they *can* do it, that they *know how* to produce social order, that the elegant, complex, multi-leveled and finely articulated structures of action and meanings we see and participate within are products of ordinary human capacity and competence.[25]

For Giddens, this is the issue of "knowledgeability:" "Everything which actors know (believe) about the circumstances of their action and that of others, drawn upon in the production and reproduction of that action, including tacit as well as discursively available knowledge" (1984: 375). Social occasion research thus far demonstrates that participants possess and overtly display and openly transmit to each other much more knowledge about how to reproduce structurally meaningful action than Giddens' and others' theories admit, and that they indicate to each other that which they tacitly know, making even tacit knowledge discursively available through analysis of such overt expressions.

Through procedures such as "routinization" as formulated by Giddens, and the "definition of the situation" of symbolic interactionists, through processes such as realization and identification, as detailed in the chapters below, occasional interactants create and express everything there is to know "about the circumstances of their action." This knowledge is reproduced simultaneously with the reproduction of meaningful social activity, which is always and everywhere *meant* activity.

Giddens theorizes "routinization" as characteristic of "the vast bulk of activities of day-to-day social life; the prevalence of familiar styles and forms of conduct, both supporting and supported by a sense of ontological security" (1984, 376). Are there ways in which "a sense of ontological security" or its lack can be made observable by social participants? The research reported below demonstrates that (and illustrates how) participants create and display a precisely appropriate degree of a sense of ontological security, among other things, to each other.

When we rigorously analyze a small sampling of that "vast bulk of activities," we find first of all that "familiar styles and forms of conduct" are not merely "prevalent," as if they were standing features of the environment surrounding social interaction. On the contrary, achieving "a sense of ontological security" is demonstrably the clear and conscious goal of participants in ordinary social interaction. Their major instrument for its achievement is the painstakingly enacted process of normalization, through which they establish, refurbish, and re-create the familiarity of styles and forms. This familiarity in turn provides the sought-for ontological security, (the sense of well-being, of sanity, of stable, sensible social reality), and participants show it, and state it, and publicly evaluate it.[26]

As Kendon formulates it, participants resolve their uncertainty about how others are likely to act "through the routinization of interactional situations and events . . . classifiable into types, and rules of conduct appropriate to each type come to be laid down in advance" (1990: 241). Our research is an attempt to inductively discover such classifications and to understand empirically how such rules "come to be laid down." Similarly, "definition of the situation" is not a frozen state of affairs or an established cognitive organization, as in a thesaurus of terms. It can be observed as both a fluid definition and as an active process, the defining of situations, as McHugh (1968) puts it. Once defined, it is evident that situations (better understood as social occasions) do not remain stable, like dictionary definitions changing only glacier-like over generations, but are volatile, and require constant re-definition to survive the chaos of advancing meaninglessness.[27]

In summation, these investigations accumulate live instances about which participants tell us how they have co-produced social organization, and how they have knowingly constructed live contexts of meaning and thus add empirical weight to two portions of a causal theory of social order: (1) that social organization is voluntarily constructed by social participants, observably, and (2) that ordinary human beings demonstrate the capacity to intentionally co-produce social structure by their own efforts.

To understand all of this as evidence for the "sandcastles" idea of the perpetual dissolution of social structure, one need make only one assumption about human nature: that everybody is naturally lazy, that is, resistant to the expenditure of unnecessary effort.[28] People observably construct intricate structures of social meaning, at great cost of effort, over and over again. If they didn't have to, the least effort assumption implies they wouldn't do it. So, why would they have to? Social structure dissolves. That is its only predictability. We are its daily custodians, its gardeners, its sculptors. Without our ceaseless efforts, it would disappear altogether, leaving behind that of which we are most terrified: chaos, meaninglessness, the void. And so we build and rebuild, day by day.

The theory that is argued and empirically grounded here to explain the structure and dynamics of everybody's social life is thoroughly humanistic: human participants are the creators of their own social life. They bring to life the organized interactive units (analogous to cells in biology), the observable living artifacts here labeled social occasions, and they fashion this life into multi-dimensional meaningful shapes and formats as an expression and as a satisfaction of their own self-determined preferences and their own interactively developed organizing skills and capabilities. Ordinary people regularly, and with enormous economy of effort, trace complex, multi-layered, intricate, beautiful, and functionally powerful patterns into their lives.

All of this artful effort is expended under essentially tragic circumstances. Permanence, certainty and security, are the perpetual goals of human creators of social structure, but dissolution is the only constant we experience. The fruit of our labors is constantly rotting on the vine, fulfillment always just out of reach, a basic theme of the humanities.

At the same time, the method proposed for the development, explication, testing and revision of this theory is thoroughly empirical, in the tradition of "hard science": Only that which is observable under conditions of controlled inquiry is acceptable as data; inferences from this evidence are made in clear steps open to public scrutiny, and formulated and presented in a manner which allows, nay invites, attempts at disconfirmation by any and all other students of social life. But this is a "Kantian" mode of science, according to Harre, wherein we treat the social and even the physical environment as a complex product of interaction between persons as active agents and the environment as a plastic construction that can be endowed with causal powers through the meaning-giving acts of agents. Environments do not exist in their fullness independent of the agents who enter them. They are part created by the way the individuals who enter them assign meanings to the people, activities, settings and social situations they find within them and even actually create. Then they are themselves affected by that which they have created. (1979: 143)

Thus this research is also an attempt to demonstrate that there need be no conflict between a humanistic and a scientific sociology. A valid sociology is necessarily both. Logical analysis of the empirical data reported below, nevertheless reaffirms fundamental humanistic postulates, such as art historian Erwin Panofsky's classic definition of "humanism": "the conviction of the dignity of man, based on both the insistence on human values (rationality and freedom) and the acceptance of human limitations (fallibility and frailty); from this two postulates result—responsibility and tolerance" (1955: 2).

Assuming that Rogers would see this work as "phenomenological sociology," we would see eye to eye that "the most important lesson inherent in the idea of phenomenological sociology is that the fulfillment of sociology as a social science and the fulfillment of its cultural responsibilities are complementary enterprises," because "what we study as sociologists are the origins, consequences, meaning, structure, and dynamics of the sedimentations of human activities" (1983: 161).

These broad affirmations emerge from the paying of sedulous attention to concrete instances of the smallest coherent units of social life, ordinary social occasions. The largest structural conditions for human social life are seen exemplified and illuminated in their smallest instantiations. And the dignity, wisdom and freedom of humans is again confirmed in our repeated finding that ordinary people routinely create the critical meanings and their interrelations that make up social structure written large, and reproduce that structure through their freely chosen actions. In Rogers' words, the research reported here is "the scientific illumination of social reality as a complex achievement of 'ordinary' commonsense people" (1983: 162).

This particular version of sociological research thus resolves three major dichotomies in sociological theory, case by case, instance by instance: It demonstrates that there is no necessary contradiction between science and humanism, between microsociology and macrosociology, nor between structure and action. In fact it shows that the most interesting and productive sociology can be done at the logical point where all three dichotomies intersect.

On the other hand, this research affirms only one side of a fourth major dichotomy, that between freedom and constraint in human social activity. All that we have been able to observe demonstrates the predominance of freedom, conscious choice, play, transcendence, creativity. It is a freedom that has been painstakingly, repeatedly built in to the action by the intentional meaning conferral of ordinary participants. Freedom is the healthy condition of ordinary social life which we all seek and work to reproduce; its many opposites are exceptions, aberrations, failures, emergencies, illness, catastrophe.

Consider the common terms for the involuntary versions of our six "modes of activity" (see chapter 3, below), which we assert based on the evidence are "normally" practiced voluntarily, as expressions of freedom and dignity, rather than by coercion or constraint:

Involuntary commensality = forced feeding;
Involuntary collaboration = slavery or penal labor;
Involuntary congregation = indoctrination as captive audience;
Involuntary communication = coercive interrogation;
Involuntary competition = gladiatorial combat or conscription;
Involuntary conviviality = rape.

Clearly the overwhelming bulk of social life is not involuntary like this. Why then would so many social scientists cling to theories of constraint, invoking norms, structures and forces as determinants of human actions? Why do they insist, against all evidence to the contrary, that what we do is out of our hands, beyond our reach to control, caused by cultures and structures, not willed by us, determined by forces and factors, not chosen by us? And why do they insist that there are fundamentally different kinds and types of humans, whose constraints and rules and operating procedures cause them to do different kinds of things?

Perhaps the truth is morally unbearable. If, as our findings and their logical consequences indicate, we are a single species with a universally shared capability for creating social life, and if all our actions are fundamentally voluntary, their meanings and consequences created by us in detail, intended and for the most part anticipated, then we must share and bear responsibility for the evil so many of us have so knowingly done.

One of the things we undeniably are as a species is willingly, knowingly, genocidal. We have conspired in great numbers to exterminate, enslave, or permanently degrade vast categories of our siblings. Our universally shared social life is filled with episodes perhaps capped, at least indexed, by the Holocaust. Hannah Arendt, the greatest social philosopher of our sorry century, has shown how even the most horrific of our activities could be and was normalized, day by day, turned into boring routines of torture, mass murder, and body disposal.[29] The banally evil Germans who systematically carried out the holocaust did it via a series of interactive occasions which were quickly defined and accepted among them as ordinary, using the same procedures of normalization we all use, the ones displayed in our eighteen little instances.

To accept the voluntary nature of our participation in social life is to accept responsibility for evil outcomes, and to accept the universality of the modes of action of our species is to accept membership with the perpetrators of humanity's worst crimes, so many of which are contemporary and continuing. It is more comforting, perhaps, to think that the devil (or norms, culture, structure, etc.) makes *them* do it. But then we must deny our magnificent creative powers, the freedom that allows us to use them destructively, and our membership in good standing with the likes of Aristotle, Shakespeare, Beethoven, Einstein, Gandhi, Martin Luther King, Mohammed, Jesus, Moses, Buddha, Mother Teresa, Marian Anderson, and the billions of other good folk. I prefer the hypothesis of social order created by all of us acting freely together as an expression of our species capabilities, including the bad actors among us, including the evil actions latent and potential within each of us. But even if I didn't prefer it, the observable facts demand it.

Our theoretical epoche has now appropriately situated the sociological point of view *outside* the individual mind or consciousness, where all events are empirically available to observation, but *inside* the frame of face-to-face live interaction, where the ongoing structuring of social life's cellular units, social occasions, takes place. The next chapter tackles the problem of how to translate authentic observation of such naturally occurring, live social events into useable data or evidence on which to establish basic sociological analysis.

NOTES

1. In the same article, Lyman (1990: 220) locates sociological interest in "routine dramas," what we here call "ordinary social occasions," within a variant stream of sociological thought which "unites the otherwise quite disparate sociologies of Thomas, Teggart, Turner, Gramsci, Schutz, Goffman, and Garfinkel. Taking notice of the significance of what they variously refer to as habits, routines, ritualized performances, behavioral presentations of self in public and private places, the Lebenswelt, the taken-for-granted world, and the old civilization,

these students of social order and its changes correctly perceived that the routinized charisma of everyday life, i.e., the drama in the routine, was . . . a permanently important focal subject matter of any sociology."
2. Through study of social occasions we find that nothing else but the activity of ordinary people causes social order or organization, breathes life into social structure, perpetuates and changes social reality. No outside forces, no natural laws self- actuating themselves, no deus ex machina, just us, doing what we as a species have learned how to do: live a socially meaningful life wherein the explicit purpose of our actions is to convey significance to others. This finding may be contentious because we ordinarily fail to give ourselves credit for our godlike powers to reproduce social life. As Hewitt states it, "That human beings are themselves the originators of the symbols by which they constitute their world does not mean that they see themselves as their creators. . . . The reality that people create often is seen by them as prior, as a solid set of facts that cannot be changed, and as exercising control over their lives" (1989: 266, 267). Direct observation of social participants reproducing social life empirically grounds the argument that we interactively create everything there is to know about social structure and social life, and guides us past the shoals of what philosopher Alfred North Whitehead called "the fallacy of misplaced concreteness" (1954: 75), the idea that our concepts are animate things, the erroneous notion, also called "reification," that, for instance, "Jazz came up the river from New Orleans" (see also Maynard and Wilson, 1980, for the best sociologically relevant statement of anti-reification). But reified concepts, such as "sui generis" norms and social structure, are only a part of the excess baggage to be jettisoned.
3. Most of what did "stick" in my education is similarly negative. As a callow fifties undergraduate I reluctantly learned two more negative things from Ernest Nagel in philosophy courses: in the Philosophy of Science, Nagel taught "What Science Is Not," i.e., it is not the only means to acquire valid knowledge, and it is never the last word on any subject, but always open-ended; and in epistemology, even more importantly, he taught "What Cannot Be Known," i.e., what cannot be scientifically known includes everything that is in principle unobservable, like people's thoughts, and undetected crimes. In graduate school there were more negatives to be learned. My demography/statistics professor at Princeton, Frederick Stefan, taught "What Cannot Be Counted," e.g., people who don't want to be counted by census takers; Marion Levy Jr., one of sociology's most cantankerous theorists, taught "What Cannot Be Taken Seriously by a Sociologist," e.g., most importantly for this exposition, anything that does *not* apply to "*any* society"; and my graduate mentor, the great sociological humanist Charles Page, taught "What Cannot Be Measured," e.g., the potential of any person or collectivity to do good or evil (because it is infinite). Later, as a junior colleague at the University of California during the tumultuous sixties, I was exposed to Aaron Cicourel, Harold Garfinkel, and their joint intellectual progeny, the "enfants terribles" of sociology who are called "ethnomethodologists." Despite myself, I learned from them the lessons of "What Cannot Be Communicated," otherwise known as the "Problem of Intersubjectivity," which limits sociology to study of observable interpersonal events.
4. Exceptions left standing in the field of history include the work of historians led by Fernand Braudel, who carefully sift the evidence of the past to find the repeated, commonplace, everyday actions of ordinary people which underly

and cumulate to become generally significant large scale historical trends and patterns (see Braudel, 1981, 1982, 1984).
5. History has great value as a source of knowledge, and as an instrument of moral instruction indispensable to the maintenance of orderly social life. It would be a far better world we live in if every statesman were to read Tuchman's *The March of Folly from Troy to Vietnam* (1984) before making that first fateful decision. The truths of history may be foundational for rational decision-making, but they are not useful scientifically because the events of interest do not repeat. Most facts of history are simply too historically specific to be everybody's. Therefore I agree with Nagel that "it seems most unlikely that a comprehensive social theory will be a theory of historical development" (1961: 465; see also Mayhew, 1983).
6. As a cub reporter on a newspaper myself, I was carefully taught to *exclude* the ordinary, the recurrent, the "standard" from news stories, and to emphasize the unprecedented.
7. The trouble with anthropology's consistent focus on "the others" or "them" rather than "us" is well illustrated by the following passage from Brown's own book. In a discussion of "componential analysis," as a method for the discovery of cross cultural universals in the underlying semantic components of a lexical domain, he says: "For example in the domain of address terms in English, comprising 'Mister,' 'Mrs.,' 'Miss,' and 'Ms.,' there are two semantic components: sex (male and female) and marital status (married, unmarried and undesignated). 'Mister' is defined as 'address term male,' 'Mrs.' as 'address term female married,' etc. In a similar domain among Brunei Malays, by contrast, a component of rank is not only present but ubiquitous: it has four gradations that must be kept in mind to use (the) terms. . . . The presence or absence of a rank component distinguishes English from Malay address terms, but the common presence of sex and marital status links them" (Brown, 1991: 163–164, 75, 76). Brown's work in compiling and interpreting the complete "domain of address terms" used among the Brunei was not matched by any such work among English speakers, apparently because Brown assumed he could "take it for granted." But the most superficial analysis of address terms as used in English would show that "Ms." did not exist, in the dictionary or in use, before about 1970 when feminists, rebelling against the ranking implications of marital-status-linked address terms for females, "Mrs." or "Miss" (both of which, the dictionary tells us, are derivatives of "Mistress") and marriage-neutral "Mr." (derived from "master") for males, giving men equal rank regardless of marital status, insisted that *all* females be addressed as "Ms." so that they might rank equally with men. Many anti-feminists came to equate insistence on "Ms." with an assertion of higher female rank. So, just as in Brunei, "four gradations" (of rank) "must be kept in mind to use" address terms, because in doing so, you may be indicating one of the following: (1) men rank above women; (2) women rank above men; (3) married women rank above unmarried women; or (4) women rank equally with men. Of course this assumes that the four terms cited are the only terms of address used commonly in English, the "complete domain." If we include the *absence* of "Ms." or "Mr."—("O'Leary, come here"), the use of first names, "Dr.," "Professor," "Boy," "Girlie," "Dearie," "Sir," "Your Honor," "Mr. President," "Governor," and "Colonel"—we can see just how ubiquitous rank is in the complete domain of English address terms. Maybe the ubiquity of rank in address terms is universal, but anthropologists'

antennae are tuned only to "them," so we may never know. Some anthropologists avoid the blinders of "otherness" by including all routinized practices, modern and ancient, northern and southern, "within the rich disciplinary field of ritual studies" (McLaren, 1986: 5). Anthropologists such as McLaren who study secular rituals broadly defined to include, for instance, the ritual format of classroom lessons in contemporary Canadian secondary schools, and Bocock (1974) who details modern ritual practices in modern industrial England, are engaged in the study of everybody's social life here proposed (see also DaMatta, 1979; Douglas, 1972, 1974; MacAloon, 1984; Meyer and Rowan, 1977; Moore and Myerhoff, 1977; Neiburg, 1970; Turner, 1969; and Visser, 1991).
8. The task of the sociologist then becomes discovery of "the formal properties of commonplace . . . actions 'from within' actual settings, as ongoing accomplishments" (Garfinkel, 1967: viii).
9. Hume, a model skeptic, goes further: "When my perceptions are removed for any time, as by sound sleep, so long am I insensible of myself, and may truly be said not to exist" (1738: 239). The corollary of this principle is a psychological extension of Cartesianism: "I am sensible of myself, therefore I am." Its sociological equivalent, embodied in the present research, is "I am sensible of the presence, ID, and meaningful actions of others, as they are of the presentation of mine, therefore we are."
10. Solitary actions are of particular interest to psychologists, and reported memories of experience while sleeping, called dreams, are to many psychoanalysts the most interesting phenomena one could study, but in the study of everybody's social life, they are of interest only when they are reported in subsequent social interaction, such as a therapeutic consultation.
11. Most of Goffman's attention in *Relations in Public* (1971) and many other works is directed specifically to such interludes in social life, social interaction "en passant," as it were (the one move in chess wherein pieces can affect one another while passing each other by—interactive, but not quite fully engaged). But these quasi-social times are not at the core of everybody's social life, they are, according to everyone's understanding of them, at the periphery. Later on, Goffmanic insights about the partial exceptions to the organizing principles of ordinary social interaction found in interludes will prove useful. But first, our goal is to discover the necessary and sufficient conditions for routine social life in full and as usual, the elements of those "periods of social engagement" making up the social life of everybody's ordinary day. Goffman's insights, in this and many other matters, provoke serious study of face-to-face interaction, but his researches themselves, as Lanigan (1990) demonstrates convincingly, remain "atheoretical." From beginning to end, the research reported herein attempts to link every empirical observation, every explication of a lived instance of social life with the furthest reach of theoretical generalization.
12. Here is where this version of sociology departs, not only from Weber, but more dramatically from social psychology and symbolic interactionism. "SI" is premised on the idea that "only individuals *act*. . . . Everything else—society, culture, social structure, power, groups, organizations—is ultimately dependent on the acts of individuals" (Hewitt, 1988: 5). The intent of this premise is admirable, to counter the reification inherent in claims that societies, cultures, structures, powers, groups or organizations can somehow autonomously act, have intentions, cause things to happen. Hewitt and others in the SI tradition also contribute an indispensable focus on face-to-face social interaction

as the empirical subject matter of social science. The problem is that few, if any, significant social acts are observably or interpretably "the acts of individuals." Only one kind of sex act, for instance, is the act of an individual, and it's not very social. Or, consider a handshake. Which individual's act is it? Interaction is inherently supra-individual, and cannot occur unless and until two or more individuals are engaged in the activity, their actions melded in every act. A speech act without a listener is not social, it is a solitary rehearsal or a less than "normal" "talking to oneself." To assume that "only individuals act" is to make officially invisible most social acts, which are not the acts of sole individuals, but the acts of *participants* (always plural) *in something* (always a social occasion). This distinction between the individual and the social participant also extends to the concept of "the self" as the primary social phenomenon. Developed by Symbolic Interactionists based on the philosophical ideas of George H. Mead (1934), the idea of the social self, like the individual, has limited usefulness in the study of everybody's social life. Only in particular circumstances is "self consciousness" or "self awareness" an important ingredient in a living context of social meanings, and even then it is almost completely unobservable, because it is interior to the individual, and purposely not expressed in most social contexts. Subjective interiority is excess baggage in the study of presentational social life, unfortunately retained and relied upon by social phenomenologists like Psathis, whose method, like ours, "basically consists of the examination of an occasion as a particular instance" (1989: 86). Psathas achieves valuable and useful findings about the space and time building activities of ordinary participants (op. cit.) and begins to move phenomenology's direct apprehension of interactive reality in a parallel direction with ethnomethodology's shift of focus onto observable social facts as they are produced and communicated among participants. But, rejecting a focus "only on that . . . which is overt and manifested in concrete, directly observable acts" (op. cit.: 29), he continues to rely on what actors "must be thinking," and thus fails to go far enough toward ethnomethodology's "exteriorization" of cognition, as Shrag indicates in his generally laudatory review of Psathas' *Phenomenology and Sociology*. The paradigmatic shift that ethnomethodology began and Psathas continues up to a point is neatly summarized by Shrag: "The epistemological modeling of cognition as a mental act (a legacy that continued to inform classical transcendental phenomenology) is transmuted into the articulatory and disclosive functions of skilled performances and social practices" (1991: 9). The shift is from what analysts can say about what participants must be thinking when they act based on what the analyst can see the participant overtly doing, to an analysis of what their overt acts are saying to interpreting fellow participants. Obviously, this requires us to ask "interpreting fellow participants" what other participants' acts said to them, or appeared to them to mean, or appeared to them to have been intended to mean (see chapter 2 for further discussion). The complete shift recommended by Shrag brings us "into closer proximity with the data themselves" (ibid.), the core goal of phenomenology, by focusing only on that part which is overt. Ethnomethodologists have not completed this shift, either, insofar a they still assert the "taken for granted" character of routine social meanings. Our research indicates that social participants take little if anything for granted, but work actively to consciously reinstate every routine. In this regard credit is also due the French sociological "founding father" Durkheim for warning against "psychological reductionism" and placing sociological thought on a foundation of externalized social facts rather than interiorized individual facts (1912). (For the moment we leave open the question of the adequacy or correctness of Durkheim's definition of "facts.") Too many contemporary sociologists appear to have forgotten this lesson, and continue to count the presumed or inferred states of mind of individuals as data about "the social." Social participants can be observed attributing meaning to each other's actions, but it is intersubjective meaning created in social interaction, not "subjective meaning" residing invisibly in the interiors of individuals. Interest in subjective meaning, to be studied via Weber's method of *verstehen*, as well as SI's focus on the interiorized contemplation of "the self" leads to a sociological dead end: the attempt to objectify subjective mental life. This should be relegated to a separate field of study, whose aim is the understanding of the human mind and emotions, and whose methods are appropriate to the aim, a field very much like psychology. Our central point here is to declare the realm of data of the field of psychology, once again as Durkheim did a century ago, "not social."

13. It is simply a mistake to try to study, at the same time and using the same methods, mental life and social life. How people attempt to display, regard and evaluate, via overt activity, what's on each others' minds is observable and immediately available to the analytical methods and theoretical logic of science; what people think of these displays, or feel about them, what they actually cogitate about each other is not. The mental life of other people is forever interior to them, beyond our direct empirical grasp, available as data only via tortuous chains of inference; their social life, which is also our social life, is presentational in its very essence, it is necessarily and intentionally observable from the "outside." We can readily observe social participants in the act of extending, repeating, amplifying and amending their actions until some other or others attribute meaning to it, and one of the most ubiquitous things we humans appear to be doing in the social presence of others is trying to be understood. When I hurl a hard spherical object in your direction, I do my best to insure that you understand that I am trying and intending to throw the ball to you and not at you. Otherwise, our social act of playing catch could not occur because, rather than colluding in a social construction of meaning, we would each be lost in the solitude of interior interpretations. Instead of catching it you might duck, and ask why I attacked you. At one with Moerman on this point, I find that "My empiricism is that of the art critic who cites the pigments and brush strokes of the paintings he interprets" (Moerman, 1988: xiii). However, I reject any interest in what the painter "must have been thinking," and focus instead exclusively on the question of what the painting most likely succeeds or fails to say, to me and to the art public.

14. The social occasion as a unit has various features in common with Murray's (1951) "event manifold," made up of behavioral "proceedings," Glaser and Strauss's (1964) "awareness context," with a variety of levels and directions of information input, Barker and Wright's (1950) "behavior episodes" situated by the analyst/observer within "behavior settings," and Goffman's (1961) "situated activity systems," whose every relevant feature is available to the "naked senses" of participants. The major difference is that whereas the units named above are primarily or exclusively observer/analyst constructs for the purpose of studying social behavior from an objective "outsider's" perspective, the social occasion, as defined, is primarily a user's construct. Participants observably

construct and use the meaning-complex of the social occasion as a context to unitize and integrate into wholes sets and segments of their own actions, and make them meaningful thereby to other participants, and only secondarily does it serve as a convenient unit of observation and analysis for the sociologist. Carucci (1989) comes close to our notion of the social occasion with his "contexts of interaction," as does Kendon (1990) with "focused encounters," but the emphasis in both of these usages is on the analysts' construction of the unit, and only secondarily on the participants' construction and use of it.

15. I first proposed and elaborated upon the social occasion as both the user's "natural" context of meaning and an ideal analyst's unit in Boughey, 1968. Adato, who uses the term "social occasion" in an almost identical fashion (he calls it "a socially structured situation as of which activities are specifically and integrally bound"), emphasizes that the occasion is primarily "a member's phenomenon . . . that which members are given to treat as a phenomenon in its own right, as having a real existence that transcends those practices on the part of members which upon closer scrutiny may be seen for how they serve in constituting the phenomenon *as such* (i.e., as transcendent and 'objective')" (Adato, 1972).

16. Speier uses "social occasion" in a similar manner to refer to these complicated organizational devices into which participants build temporal and spatial features (1973).

17. Why not call these units "situations" as many symbolic interactionists and social constructionists do? (see Berger and Luckmann, 1967; Blumer, 1969; Goffman, 1968; McHugh, 1968). For one thing, "situation," like "role," is one of those terms which have become so hopelessly overloaded with ambiguous and conflicting meanings that the only way to proceed is to start fresh with new terms. "Occasion" is fresh enough to carry a new set of unambiguous definitions without endless argument about its provenance, and previous usages. By definition, the "occasion" is first a user's concept and only secondarily an analyst's concept. Therefore the appropriateness of its theoretical use by an analyst can always be verified empirically by asking, "Is this what it means in practice to its naive (interpreting but non-analytical) participants?"

18. In addition, most uses of "situation" are more interiorized and individual-based, that is to say less social, than Goffman's, who "would define a social situation as an environment of mutual monitoring possibilities, anywhere within which an individual will find himself accessible to the naked senses of all others who are 'present', and similarly find themselves in one another's immediate presence" (1968: 297). Ordinary social occasions, as named and attended to by their participants, such as meals, work shifts, church services, seminars, court hearings, or parties, are more complex than Goffman's situations, but also more fully social, less individually based, and less interior. The key ingredient provided by Goffman is the centrality and overarching significance of the "naked senses" of participants.

19. Working from Goffman's (1971) diffuse typology of situations, gatherings, social occasions, and encounters, Giddens (1984) derives a definition of social occasions fairly compatible with the one developed here: "Social occasions are gatherings which involve a plurality of individuals. They are typically rather clearly bounded in time and space and often employ special forms of fixed equipment—formalized arrangements of tables and chairs and so on. A social occasion provides the 'structuring social context' (Goffman's term) in which . . .

a pattern of conduct tends to be recognized as the appropriate and (often) official or intended one." Examples cited by Giddens include "the work day in a factory or office . . . parties, dances, sports events." But whereas Goffman and Giddens go on from such a working definition to further theorize and specify the parts and particularities of social occasions based on unsystematic, catch-as-catch-can observations, taken-for-granted understandings about how things go in social life, and logical extensions of theoretical insights, we here draw the empirical line at precisely this point and say, let us observe, describe, and analyze living instances of this phenomenon before deducing one more thing about it. Here again we must agree with Speier, who says we must limit our formulation of sociological problems to those "in which conceptual terms clearly correspond to actual events in the social stream of life and are in fact responsive to those empirical events" (1973: 8).

20. It can also be argued and proven that the organic and mental lives of humans are dependent upon and critically shaped by their social life, but for that we have neither time nor space here and now. Let us agree for the sake of argument that they are interdependent with, but different from social life.

21. The departure here from the ideas of Schegloff and most ethnomethodologists and conversation analysts begins with insistence on the Weberian idea of "context." Talk, along with a host of other, non-verbal social behaviors, is co-determined in its specific meanings and its infrastructural formats or grammars, rules of use, by its actual uses as an instrument for producing social reality *and* by the situational context of its use. To understand the form of talk or conversation as something in and of itself, in other words, is not to be able to understand the meaning of the talk or the uses of the conversation on any observable live occasion of its use by interactants. Turn-taking is not the same kind of procedural infrastructure on any and all occasions. In fact, in Schegloff's most interesting substantive work (1979), he proposes that the structure of talk, and of turn-taking, during telephone conversations, is uniquely determined by the context of a telephone conversation as opposed to a face-to-face conversation. Talk itself is indeed too "micro" in its level of analysis. The live occasion at human scale is where the "procedural infrastructure of interaction," including many forms of talk but also many kinds of nonverbal meaning interchanges, comes into play, and can best be observed, analyzed, investigated as it lives. As Sacks said, "conversation is simply something to begin with" (1984: 26).

22. As phenomenological sociologist Schutz wrote: "I agree with Professor Nagel's statement that the social sciences, like all empirical sciences, have to be objective in the sense that their propositions are subjected to controlled verification and must not refer to private uncontrollable experience" (1962: 62). I also agree with Papineau that "there is no reason whatsoever to conclude that there is something reprehensible about science, that its application to the social realm is inherently supportive of systems of political domination and oppression" (1978: 183.)

23. A perhaps clearer statement of this principle is made by Atkinson and Drew: "The confusions of traditional sociology are inevitable so long as the search for descriptions and explanations of *the* realities underlying commonsensically available appearances of social order is preferred to an examination of *how* such appearances are interactionally produced, managed, recognized and used *as if* they were the facts of the matter by societal members in living their everyday lives" (1979: 20).

24. It still remains to be empirically validated that there are such things as "universal mutual-knowledge assumptions" or "interactional systematics . . . based largely on universal principles," as assumed by Brown and Levinson (1978: 288) and hypothesized here. The search for sociological universals is rather lonely at this point in the history of the discipline, as one of my finest teachers and fellow-travelers in this quest has also found: "Most of my colleagues have been too busy and too little interested in this sort of topic to give me detailed criticisms. Despite the protestations of my fellow sociologists, I find almost no one who is interested in what, if anything, can be said about *any* society" (Levy, 1989: xvii).
25. These ideas are related and beholden to the work of social phenomenologists like Schutz and ethnomethodologists like Garfinkel, but both groups adhere to a limiting principle about human capacity and knowledgeability which violates the truth of what we can observe—the idea that much if not all of the context of intersubjective bridge building between social interactants is *taken for granted*. Here we must part company. What they refer to as a "world taken for granted" is *not* taken for granted by participants but is observably painstakingly articulated, arranged, recreated upon every occasion of its enactment. We cannot sustain the presumption that they are taking it for granted when we see them making it real for each other, overtly, diligently, carefully. That which participants are observably taking into account, taking seriously, and taking care of, they cannot be said to be taking for granted.
26. See Schegloff (1986) and Lyman (1990) for two other approaches to seeing routinization as a basic society producing human procedure.
27. Garfinkel calls such sought-after situational definitions, social structure in the making, "the potter's object" (1988).
28. This is a restatement of Pareto's "Principle of Least Effort" (1935).
29. In *The Banality of Evil.*

2

The Ingenuous Participant: Authentic Instrument of Sociological Observation

THE SEARCH FOR A FITTING METHOD

Having identified ordinary social occasions as ideal units for the observation and analysis of social life *in vivo,* we then face the question of how best to observe them, how to "fix" our observations in time and space so that we and others can examine them repeatedly, and how to carry out the analysis such repeated examination makes possible. The problem is how to transform some of the living reality of a social occasion into data with a minimum of distortion, how to authenticate that data, and how to make it speak meaningfully to the theoretical sociological questions we are asking. These are the methodological considerations involved in choosing or custom tailoring a method of empirical inquiry.

After energetic review of the extant literature reporting sociological research we found nothing ready-made that fit our stated purposes, so it appeared necessary, not just to use some bits and pieces of innovative technique to get through the hard places, but by choosing appropriate components of established, tried and true research methods to cobble together an entire, integrated method of inquiry. The goal sought through collecting data about live social interaction is as Prus (1987) states it the ability to do "a generic processual sociology," but previous ethnographic work falls short of achieving a fitting method for this. We had to think through from the beginning what we would need to get us to where we wanted to go.

The major components needed were a method of observation designed to produce authentic and replicable data about live social occasions, and a method of analysis which would logically link this data to the elaboration and testing of theory. The whole had to be designed to allow sociological researchers to follow out all of the implications of Speier's explicit instructions on *How to Observe Face-to-Face Social Interaction* (1973). Speier writes as if only to introductory students in his Sociology class, telling them to do things that professional sociologists had not, and have not yet, done. We may take these directives, stated here as four new rules of sociological method, as foundational for a new sociology, if we don't mind acting "as" Speier's students trying to complete an assignment.

Four New Rules of Sociological Method

Rule 1

Speier tells us to *take "a natural history approach" to "social phenomena that are amenable to naturalistic observations, i.e., the ongoing stream of naturally occurring social activities"* (1).

Our collection of data must begin, according to this rule, with observational reports, descriptions of social life as it is lived. But what, precisely, is to be observed and described?

Rule 2

Use *"the method of instances; look at interactional events as instantial cases and ...try to account for their workings in each concrete case, always showing the tie between our abstract conceptions and conclusions and the concrete data on which they are based"* (25).

Our application of Rule 2 defines "social occasions" as instantial cases of holistic interactional events.

Rule 3

Further, we must *"derive problems from inspection of social data itself. The formulation of sociological problems has to be responsive to the data of observation"* (4).

Like Sacks (1984: 26), "We will be using observation as a basis for theorizing," and "from close looking at the world we can find things we would not, by imagination, assert were there." This is the original argument of empiricism against metaphysical speculation in fourteenth- and fifteenth-century Europe. Unfortunately many social scientists still don't "get it." The often heard argument that, after all, physicists must *infer* the existence of subatomic or supergalactic phenomena that cannot be directly observed, so why shouldn't social scientists rely on inference as well, is bogus.[1]

There are no justifiable grounds for social science reliance on inference alone to summon up the existence of essentially unobservable phenomena. Yes, science proceeds by making logical inferences, but only inferences *from* what has already been observed in a controlled manner, and only inferences *to* objects and processes that are defined as empirical, that is, as essentially observable. Rule 3 says let observations precede inferences in social science, let us confine ourselves to the at least theoretically observable, therefore empirical world, and let the observations begin.[2]

Rule 4

And finally, our ultimate analytical goal is to *answer the question, "How do members of the society methodically construct interactions into mutually organized social activity?"* (21).

This analytical goal only becomes visible after we have begun the rigorous observation and description prescribed in Rules 1, 2, and 3. The visible doing of social organization that demands to be seen and understood imposes itself upon the analyst once these methodological principles are taken up and implemented. Only then it becomes evident that the technology of order-construction used by ordinary participants during ordinary live occasions is the natural subject matter for a genuinely empirical and theoretical sociology.

A Method of Observation

The strategy employed was to implement Speier's four new "rules of sociological method," above, based on one of Sacks's "central findings":

> The detailed ways in which actual, naturally occurring social activities occur are subjectable to formal description [and these formally described singular occurrences] are generalizable in intuitively nonapparent ways and are highly reproducibly usable. (1984: 21)

Having chosen ordinary social occasions as the unit/scale of social activities to be studied, the problem became how to observe them as they "naturally occur," "live." Clearly it would require an "ethnographic" method to do this, an "ethnography" being any instrument for the observing and recording of living events.[3]

Speier's first rule above also means that as natural scientists we have to collect "raw" rather than "cooked" data, about "naturally occurring" rather than "staged" behavior. To do this we must use a truly ethnographic method. Direct audio and/or video recording, "participant observation" and informant interviews are the major established ethnographic methods for the collection of such data, but given the following limitations of all three of these methods, it has been found necessary to combine the best features of each into a single new methodological strategy.

Troubles with Participant Observation

The conventional "participant observer" cannot observe "uncooked," "natural" behavior because the contingencies of participation create a "double blind." (If the duck hunter's "blind" not only made his presence and intentions as a hunter invisible to the ducks, but also made the ducks invisible to his gun sights, the hunter would be similarly trapped in a double blind.)

The social scientist participant observer is doubly blinded by the contingencies of participation for the following reasons:

First, no social occasion is the "same" with one more participant present, particularly one who is acting as a "spy" (one whose primary motive for participation is to report back to other non-participants), as it would have been without. This is most drastically true in dyadic occasions, where the presence of a third party radically prevents any naturally occurring two-party interaction. Three of our eighteen instances, two-person occasions, would have been completely invisible to third-party participant observation.

As the size of the participant group increases, the effect of the presence of the spy theoretically decreases. But most of what is presented for observation in social occasions is how the other participants behave, not in general, but in particular toward you, the observer. So either what you see is heavily distorted by your known presence as a spy, or it is "cooked" by the false (non-spy) participant identity you are disguised in. In neither case can you observe "naturally occurring" interaction.

The second blindfold also makes "peephole" observation, whether through one-way mirrors or the use of hidden video cameras, equally unrevealing of the observable realities of social life. Only the ingenuously motivated participant can authentically perceive the intentionally presented meanings that comprise the life of social interaction.

An observer of a meal who is not there to dine, and to do her/his specific part to make it the kind of meal it is intended to be, cannot perceive the meaningful commensality of fellow diners; an observer of joint labor who is not there to do an assigned part of the work cannot perceive the meaningful collaboration of fellow workers (because they are not then collaborating with the observer); an observer of a gathering who is not there to join in with and become an indistinguishable part of the audience cannot perceive the meaningful congregation of fellow spectators; an observer of a conference who is not there to hear and be heard and to be seen hearing and being heard cannot perceive the meaningful communication of fellow conferees; an observer of a contest who is not there to contend cannot perceive the meaningful competition of fellow contestants (what can you understand about the actions of your opponents if they are not your opponents?), and an observer of a party who is not there to have and to give a good time cannot perceive the meaningful conviviality of fellow celebrants (because, to that observer, then, they are not fellow celebrants). In every case, if the meaning isn't mutually constructed and intentionally presented within a context which includes the meaningful presence of the observer, it is not there to be observed.

This is because the meanings of social actions are fundamentally presentational, they are intentionally conveyed to others with whom a sought-for alignment of perspectives is being forged. Both parties to any interaction must be engaged in trying to understand and acknowledge the actions of the other as part of this alignment process, for without appropriate, overtly expressed and genuine involvement, these meanings are not conveyed, they remain invisible to the "pure observer," be it spy, spy glass, or camera's dead eye. In social interaction, what you see is what you are authentically invited by the others to observe to be the case.

The number of sights and sounds available for observation at any moment, in or out of social engagement, is infinite. That which directs you toward selective observation of socially relevant meanings, the meaning structure of the occasion, is your paramount desire as a participant to participate appropriately, meaningfully, to convince fellow participants that your actions, your identifications, your timing, your movements and placements, and your displayed motives, are intentionally intersubjectively aligned with theirs to the degree and in the manner required by this specific occasion. Anyone not fully engrossed in this socially constitutive task cannot perceive the engrossment and the efforts of the others. Therefore the only eligible observer of "naturally occurring" social interaction is one who is "naturally participating," and this the conventional social science "participant observer" by definition is not.

TROUBLES WITH AUDIO/VIDEO TAPE

The fact that so much of naturally occurring social activity must be seen to be comprehended, and seen and heard by a motivated, engrossed participant, also rules out tape recording as an adequate method of observation and description. Sacks used taped transcriptions of conversations exclusively because of his commitment to "actual occurrences in their actual sequence," which parallels our commitment to an empirical, observation-based sociology. But as a result of being based exclusively on audiotape recordings as observations, his research, followed by three decades of followers' research, has been limited to the analysis of decontextualized talk, which is all that can be heard on an audiotape.

But Sacks did not intend this limit. He said, "my research is about conversation only in this incidental way: that conversation is something that we can get the actual happenings of on tape and that we can get more or less transcribed; that is, conversation is simply something to begin with" (1984: 26). Unfortunately, a closer look at tape recording reveals that we do not and can not "get the actual happenings" of conversation or any other live feature of naturally occurring social interaction on tape, and certainly not the cellular living whole of a social occasion.

Conversation is thoroughly determined in its structure and content by what speaking and listening participants are trying to do with it, by it, and through it within the context of their living occasion. Ripped out of this context by a tape recording, it is dumb, it can say nothing of its own meaning within a living context, and it doesn't even partially provide evidence of "the actual happenings," as Sacks and followers had vainly hoped. No "actual sequence" can possibly be observed exclusively through the instrument of audiotape, because there are inaudible moves within every interactional event which intersperse and simultaneously accompany the audible ones, and which codetermine the meanings of every audible utterance. A tape recording can tell us only some of what sounds were made and transmitted at the taped occasion. Nowhere on the tape can we find a single word of *what was heard to have been said* by any participant or team of participants, *what was received,* and the only talk that can possibly have social meaning is talk that was in fact heard by other participants as that talk coming from that participant, at that juncture in the ongoing interaction.

Heath, in his video analysis of patient-doctor interactions, moves one step beyond talk in itself as the content of social interaction by demonstrating that "speakers themselves engage in movement, gestures, posture shifts and the like actually within the course of talking," and these movements, in addition to utterances, "may be fruitfully investigated with consideration to their interactional organization and the local work they accomplish" (1986: 15).

But Heath is far too polite to the conversation analysts whose work his video analysis transcends. The visible gestural and positional and expressive actions Heath's interactants display on videotape as integrated, articulated, essential elements interspersed within any conversation are plainly and simply not present in the audiotaped evidence chain treated as an interpretable whole by conversation analysts.

Logically, we must conclude based on Heath's evidence that *none* of the utterances or utterance sequences analyzed by conversation analysts can be interpreted through audiotape analysis in any degree or fashion like the way they are interpretable by the actual participants, because each taped utterance is perforce analyzed outside of its most immediate material context of preceding, succeeding, and accompanying visible gestures, facial expressions and bodily positionings.

"Next turn" (see Schegloff, 1992) is not necessarily or even most often vocal, as Schegloff's own work on the initiation of telephone conversations (1979) and Heath's videotapes clearly and definitively demonstrate; therefore there can be no valid findings about turn sequences derived from audiotape evidence alone.

But what about videotape? Surely the "five hundred hours of video" showing "more than a thousand general-practice consultations recorded in a wide variety of practices throughout the United Kingdom" that Heath

(1986: 6) declares as his research's "corpus of data" should tell us all we need to know about "naturally occurring behavior in particular habitats such as the medical consultation." (ibid.: 3) (Exhibit J, below, tells us much more.)

Heath claims to advance the methodological agenda by developing "a way in which video can be used for the purposes of sociological inquiry and in particular to examine the interactional coordination of social actions and activity." Nevertheless, just as Heath's videotape research demonstrates the futility of audiotape research because massively essential behavior and meaning components of naturally occurring social interaction which appear on video are patently absent from audiotape, our interviews collecting the retrospective testimony of ingenuous participants demonstrate in a parallel manner the necessarily complete incomprehension by the videotape analyst of the lived reality of the social occasion that was supposedly filmed, but could not possibly have been captured on any number of films by any number of cameras focused and running at the scene.

Why not? We have explained that non-vocal or inaudible behavior, which is visible on videotape, can not be a part of audiotape evidence, and without it, the interaction can not make the same kind of sense to analysts that it made to live participants, so that audiotaped evidence can not begin to be true to the lived reality of occasional interaction. Now we ask, what is not and cannot be on videotape? Given that a videotape adds what there was to be seen on the interactive occasion to what there was to be heard, and therefore apparently corrects the inadequacies of audiotape, what essential elements of lived social reality are necessarily unavailable to the analyst of videotapes, no matter how cleverly shot? (On the failure of film to capture essentials of live social interaction, see also Sudnow, 1969; and Kendon, 1979.)

According to Heath, "the concern of the research was to identify the organization of particular action sequences and the structure of certain activities" by "scavenging through the corpus of video recordings to find additional instances." The result is Heath's selection of "fragments" of the videotapes chosen as "instances" of "a particular phenomenon." Somehow the tapes are meant to be film representations of the "wholes" of medical "consultations" (ibid.: 23ff.).

The basic flaw of the videotape is that it is a recorded view from a single camera's-eye perspective, which is the point of view of *none* of the co-present participants. Were these wholes and parts identified by Heath as "consultations," "instances," "fragments," "certain activities," or "particular action sequences" recognized, defined, enacted as such by either the doctor or the patient at any of the events that were filmed? The videotape cannot answer this question. Therefore Heath cannot know. What were the wholes and parts of the interactive occasion defined, created, and lived out by the participants? The videotape cannot tell us.

When and how did any one of the "consultations" begin or end? Was the camera running when it began, and did it keep running until after the end? What if, as is clearly indicated in Exhibit J, the "beginning" and the "ending" of the consultation both took place in another room outside the consultation room? Heath's camera was fixed in one place. No camera can orient itself to the whole and the parts of *the occasion,* as every natural participant must, to make minimal sense of it and perceive its meaning.

What did the doctor's actions look like to the patient? What did the patient's actions look like to the doctor? Parallel to the flaw in the audiotape, which although it speaks of what was said, is perforce mute about what was heard, the videotape contains no evidence of what was in fact seen by any participant, and it is only that which was in fact seen and heard that could have contributed materially to the meaning-making and meaning-understanding which constituted the live social interaction at the occasion. In fact the videotape is as blind as the audiotape is deaf to the empirical life signs of interactive social reality. The only instrument capable of observing and recording the live activity of a social occasion is a natural participant in that occasion's activity.

TROUBLES WITH INTERVIEWING

Determined to transcend "what's on tape" and what a "spy" can't see, and to describe the context of interaction on occasion as it naturally appears to participants, we are left with the observations of natural, ingenuous participants as the only authentic observational access to the truth about social life. The methodological solution to the "double blind" of participant observation, and to the blindness and deafness of audiovisual recording to the reality of social events as defined and experienced by participants is to ask a natural, actual occasion participant after the fact what happened, what the participant observed whilst ingenuously participating.

Of course this will also be a somewhat biased and necessarily limited account of what occurred, and we must deal systematically with these limits. Practically speaking, it was decided to try to combine "informant interviewing" with "authentic observation" and tape and transcribe the results for repeated review and analysis.

To produce such direct after-the-fact reports of what a participant observed to have happened, undergraduate sociology students volunteered to be interviewed by this professor about an ordinary social occasion in which the student had participated recently, no longer than a week prior to the interview. Volunteer student respondents were questioned during tape-recorded interviews held before a "jury" of the respondent's peers, the rest of the class.

The typed transcription of the tape was a week later distributed to this "jury," including the respondent, and together we evaluated it and judged whether it accurately reflected what we had all heard said during the interview, and we could and did refer to the tape recording itself whenever we had any doubts. The corrected transcription, judged as "accurate" as we could make it, became an "exhibit" in our class collection of data. Our standard was the level of accuracy of courtroom transcriptions: is all that was said in the transcript, are the statements there accurate renderings of the questions asked and the answers given in the interview?

The recorded accounts in our exhibits qualify as "explanatory speech" in Harre's terms, "the speech we use when we are talking descriptively about the prescriptions of our own culture, contributing to our own ethnography, so to speak," which must be distinguished from "accounting," the "speech we use to justify some action of one's to others within the culture." Harre goes on, "It may be that both call on the same material, but one is in the scientific mode and the other is a part of social action." This distinction can and must be maintained, I argue, even while we recognize that the interview in "the scientific mode" is also "a part of social action" (Harre 1979: 128).

The "exhibit" thus is our ethnographic instrument, recording sociologically "naive"[4] observations of a live, ordinary social occasion. For every transcribed exhibit presented here, there exists a collection of thirty or so people who once acted as a class of students, before whom this interview was conducted and recorded, and by whom it was studied as a transcript and checked for accuracy. Theoretically, any or all of them could be called once again as witnesses to verify the transcript, to testify that this is what was asked, and this is what the respondent answered.[5]

The interviews were designed with the methodological pitfalls and proposals brought forth by Pawson (1987) in mind, especially what he calls "the first principle of an alternative approach to data construction, namely to claim that sociological data should refer to what people do and not what they think" (1987: 302) and his methodological "Rule V," that "interviewers should adopt the role of conceptual tutors (but not hypothesis-disclosers) and respondents act as learner/informants" (1987: 325) in order to involve informants as cognitive equals in the socially interactive process of data construction.

The statements made in the data exhibits presented in this study can be verifiably attributed to the alleged speakers in the interviews, as indicated above. Further, there can be no doubt that these witnesses directly observed what was observable to them during the occasion. But if their reports are to empirically ground valid sociological analysis and theorizing, several methodological doubts remain about the completeness, veracity, and representativeness of their testimony.

These reports would certainly pass journalistic muster in terms of attribution, and legal tests of publicly legitimated witnessing, but scientific study requires more. In what ways, and to what degree, can the validity of the data be warranted? Shouldn't we suspect error in the respondents' answers based on faulty memory and/or lying, given the respondents' own reasons for presenting a "good" story? What is the likely relationship between what the respondents said happened and what actually happened at the time of the social occasion described?

Completeness versus Coherence

Following Speier's second rule, we have tried to produce through the student interviews coherent ethnographies of the workings of interactional events, ordinary social occasions, as instantial cases. They are not, and could not be, *complete* descriptions of the occasion's observables. Why not?

The "Rashomon effect" (a concept based on a 1947 Japanese film directed by Kirosawa in which each witness to a fatal event, including the victim in a seance, tells a different story about what happened and how) warns us that every participant experiences the same social event somewhat differently from every other, and given the dynamics of the reporting situation, will give a differentially biased account of what was observed. Therefore we can assume that if we had access to all of the participants in the occasions described instead of only one (our student informant), the combined account would include much more of what was actually observed, plus much more self-serving biased accounting. The combined account would thus be both more complete and more false. Further, *everything* that the single respondent observed over the course of the occasion, depending on how fine the level of description, would likely exceed our capacity to record and analyze. Reasoning thus, three methodological decisions were made:

1. Abandon hope for completeness and try for coherence instead, judging that whatever the single witness observed, however limited to one participant's perspective, may prove adequate as grounds for a coherent description of what one living occasion was for this one participant. If we questioned the witness carefully, we could perhaps hope to construct a description that might contain enough information to allow us to understand some of the occasion's structure and dynamics, some of the organization of its life, and subsequent analysis of the transcription could test this possibility. Our assumption was that any one witness had to observe enough about the occasion to have enabled that witness to participate naturally and adequately in it.

2. Maximize the conditions under which the single witness is likely to give a truthful account by minimizing the known sources of bias.

3. Focus the questioning and later analyses on those aspects of what the participant/witness observed which were likely to come under the purview of all participants, the things that all could have observed and all probably had to know to carry on the meaningful interaction that occurred. Following Pawson (op. cit.), we would "involve informants" as users of Harre's "explanatory speech" in explicating the *users'* meanings of the occasioned objects and processes.

In pursuit of coherence, via methodological decision 1, the interview questioning technique was crafted, "improving" it from interview to interview, as the reader may judge by reading the first three exhibits below, which happen to be the first three consecutive interviews conducted. The fifteen others included in this study are not sequential, but were selected from many dozens of interviews conducted under similar circumstances over the ensuing eight years of teaching the "same" course. What had the witness observed to be happening over the course of the recent occasion? How did all participants define and respond to these events?

The questions were directed in an open-ended "informational" format, based on the author's earlier experience as a journalistic interviewer. In a systematic but flexible and responsive manner, the informant was asked, what was the occasion, what did you call it, what happened, what did you and the others do, and do next, who else was there, how did it begin and end, how did you enter and exit, and what motives or reasons did you understand to be involved, in short, the journalist's "five w's"— what, who, when, where, and why. But as the reader will find, not all of these questions were actually asked in each interview. When the interviewer sensed that the ground had been spontaneously covered, the explicit question was skipped.

The strongest characteristic of the questioning was its responsiveness, rather than its directiveness. The reader of the interviews in Exhibits A through R below can perhaps perceive how intently the questioner was listeningto the respondent's answer. Almost always, the "next question" was based upon and materially shaped by the hearing and interpretation of the previous answer, and sometimes of an answer given much earlier in the interview. The objective was to elicit, through responsive questioning and probes, as unvarnished a description as possible of what the respondent had done and seen to be done while participating in the live occasion under review.

The consistent use of these five questions probably limited the reportage to what the respondent could remember about activity, identification, time, space, and motives, and there might be much more that occurred that a different questioning scheme would have revealed. At best, for all of these reasons, we can only claim to have collected valid data about some of what occurred upon specific occasions.[6]

Following methodological decision 2, above, the interviews were further crafted so as to minimize known sources of interview bias, broadly in two categories, unintentional error and motivated lying.

MINIMIZATION OF ERROR

Time elapsed, event trauma, and reporting trauma are the three major sources of error in eyewitness reports based on faulty memory, whether these reports are being made to journalists, social scientists, police officials, or in a court of law. The longer ago the event was witnessed, the more erroneous the report is likely to be. The more emotionally traumatic either the scene that was witnessed was, or the conditions of reporting are, the more erroneous the report is likely to be.

The first of these three sources of error, time elapsed since the event, we have tried to minimize by asking respondents to describe an ordinary social occasion in which they have participated yesterday, if at all possible, and in no case any longer ago than a week. When asked about more temporally distant events, respondents have generally claimed not to be able to remember many of the "details" we are especially interested in asking about.

Second, ordinary social occasions are precisely the least traumatic events in everybody's social life. There are emotionally upsetting aspects to them for all of us from time to time, but those are not the aspects we have been interested in asking about. What we are interested in is how social life goes on "as usual," and we generally associate traumatic events and experiences with the unusual, the disruptive, the times when things go wrong. Such traumatic events may well be interesting to study in and of themselves, but again, our priority is to take the "normal" before the "abnormal." Hence we have a "natural" inherent defense against this type of error.[7]

The third type of error we have also taken pains to minimize. Compared with the traumatic situation of reporting a crime to the police, whether as victim or bystander, or of testifying in a court of law in a case which has serious consequences attached to "whose story" is believed, the situation of recounting yesterday's breakfast in answer to a professor's questions in a classroom setting in which one is a student is bound to be less emotionally stressful or traumatic.

Further, we have avoided asking about activities such as sexual intercourse or the commission of crimes, which could be embarrassing for the student-witness to recount in front of a class of fellow students. It would be of great interest to have comparable descriptions of such occasions, but the increased stress this would cause in the interview situation, and the resulting error and distortion, would, we believe, outweigh any advantages.

MINIMIZATION OF LYING

Suppose we have minimized errors due to faulty memory of the witnessed events. We still face the problem, as in all testimony by witnesses to events, of lying. Here we are in no privileged position as social scientists: "lie detectors" just don't work, and even if they did build one that did, its use would destroy the cooperative relationship between researcher and respondents. Just like everybody else in everybody's social life, we have to estimate the balance between the reasons the speaker may have for speaking the truth as the speaker knows it, and the reasons the speaker may have for intentional falsehood.[8]

Before any of the interviews were held, lectures and discussions in the class, as well as text readings in sociological works, had all stressed the fundamental truth-seeking character of what we were about as professional sociologists, sociologists-in-training, and students of sociology. To try to reach an understanding of the truth about our social lives was then the official ethos of the occasions upon which the interviews were held. It is likely that student/respondents were strongly motivated to tell the truth in answer to my questions, and that this warrants the veracity and reliability of the data to some extent.

The lack of consequential outcomes to the testimony, such as one would expect in a court of law, would also tend to reduce the possible reasons for lying one way or another about what happened at yesterday's ordinary occasion. Again, the avoidance of potentially "embarrassing" occasions was also designed to reduce the reasons why a witness might "stretch" the truth.

Finally it must be left to the skeptical reader to judge whether the testimony dubbed "authentic" rings true or not. If you can believe what the students are saying in the exhibits, then you know for certain some of what they believe to have happened during eighteen recently-participated-in ordinary social occasions. The means by which to judge are provided in the form of the full, original transcripts, including all the questions asked and all the answers given, as Exhibits A through R in the text below.

Representativeness

The eighteen occasions described herein were selected as representative of some of the variety and uniformity found in one hundred and eighty such occasions described in similar interviews collaboratively produced over eight years. The hundred and eighty occasions are argued to be representative in specified ways of the billions of such occasions occurring worldwide every day among all members of our species, and constituting our social life. But what about the spokespersons for these instances? How representative of humanity at large could our eighteen respondents be?

We should discount the significance of the respondents' representativeness first by noting that the object of the research is not the respondents themselves, nor any of their individual personal or social characteristics, but instead the occasions in which they participated, which include as elements the personal characteristics of all the participants, ranging from two in Exhibit A to more than ten thousand in Exhibit G. Nevertheless, the reporters ought to come from diverse backgrounds if we are reaching for the potential of approaching human universality. In fact, drawing respondents from classes at the Erindale College campus of the University of Toronto provides extraordinary diversity in our small "sample" of occasion participants.

The western suburbs of Toronto, from which Erindale College draws most of its student body, has been for at least two decades a preferred secondary destination of immigrants to Canada from everywhere in the world. First, most new arrivals in Canada settle and make a living and a nest egg in the city of Toronto itself, and then, pooling resources and savings, large numbers of these families buy houses and settle again in and around Mississauga, and realize the ultimate dream of so many immigrant families by sending their children to University. In my classes, between 60 and 70 percent of the students have claimed to be the first member of their families in history to attend a post-secondary institution of education. Forty percent have been immigrants to Canada themselves, and another 40 percent the children of immigrants.[9]

The eighteen respondents recounting their observations herein thus reflect an extreme diversity of backgrounds, but as a sample, are of limited representativeness. None are younger than twenty, most are in their twenties, a few are in their thirties and forties. None are illiterate. None are from very poor backgrounds, though some are of the very rich. Almost all are women. But here is a simple list of each respondent's most significant background characteristic. In each of the eighteen interviews, the respective respondent is the child of a: Pakistani farmer; Polish military officer, retired; Hong Kong millionaire; Hungarian merchant; Ukrainian baker; French-Canadian civil servant; Ontario banker; Chinese government official; Ontario welfare recipient; Croatian accountant; Egyptian businessman; Ontario policeman; British single mother/secretary; African American football player; Nicaraguan peasant farmer; Greek shepherd; Polish restaurateur; Irish-Canadian factory worker.

Analytical Categories

The five journalistic questions repeatedly asked the respondents to get an apparently coherent description of the occasion have also been used as handy labels for categorical "bins" in which to sort the voluminous information collected. In the analytical work presented in the following chapters, we have separated out from the exhibits the testimony relevant to occasion participants' construction of the meaning of their activities, and of their occasion generated social identifications, or IDs, the what and the who questions. The time frames of their actions, the spatial settings they set up, and finally, their motives or displayed reasons for acting as they did, the when, where, and why questions are analyzed in a second volume to be published soon. In each of these categories, we have found common actions performed by participants whose consequences were to establish that sort of occasional meaning structure. We begin, in this way, to draw a general picture of the ways in which participants create the contexts for their meaningful actions, the live social occasions which are the cells of their social lives. This begins to fulfill Prus' call (op. cit.) for a "generic, processual" sociology.

What follows immediately below, then, is authentic observation of interaction at A's breakfast, B's lunch, C's dinner out, D's midnight, E's choir practice, F's move, G's Sunday service, H's football game, I's wedding, J's appointment, K's French class, L's confession, M's hearing, N's vote, O's waterpolo finals, P's barbecue, Q's pub night, and R's something.

NOTES

1. Physical science always starts with observation, exhaustive observation of everything within the phenomenal realm of interest that can be observed up to the limits of known observational instrumentation. Then, based on these painstaking and verified observations, inferences are made to phenomena—objects and processes—that logically must exist if the observations already made and the explanations based on those observations are to make sense, but there are no means of direct observation of these inferential phenomena currently available. Often such inferences lead to new methods of empirical observation, so that the inferred phenomena can be positively confirmed. It is also the case in physical science that the non-observed objects and processes that must be inferred, or

that can be presently known only by inference, are by definition *empirical* phenomena, their current non- observability notwithstanding. That is, they are always understood to be things that do leave tangible traces in the physical universe that *would* be seen or heard or tasted or smelled or touched if any of our five senses could be sufficiently enhanced. In other words they are in principle observables even if they cannot now be observed and must therefore be logically inferred until further and better observation becomes technically feasible. Everything else is consigned, by science, to the realm of the metaphysical, where, because phenomena are essentially unobservable, their existence and nature cannot be validated by science (see Nagel, 1957). Even if the *effects* of God's plan are observable, the plan itself, along with God, are not, and therefore must remain among metaphysical existences unconfirmable by science.

2. What is ruled *out* by Rule 3 is the inferential concoction of reified objects, substances or processes, such as phlogiston or norms, produced by an essentially metaphysical method, using the following recipe: presuppose social order (don't actually observe or describe it, define it into existence as "taken-for-granted"); then logically infer "norms" or something else to account for this order; after all, there must be norms, as a colleague argued, or how else could we explain orderly conduct? How else indeed. The outcome of following this recipe is the sociology of "Grand Theory" combined with "Abstracted Empiricism" that C. Wright Mills, we then thought, had laid to rest in 1959 in his scathing *Sociological Imagination*.

3. Also relevant were Irwin's warnings that non-ethnographic methods tend to distort social reality in non-random, "corrupt" directions because positivistic, quantitative research must be funded, and can be corrupted, by "powers that be" who have "a great stake in the continuation of present arrangements," and "have at their disposal a host of incentives they can offer social scientists: grants; high salaries; prestigious positions in academic, government, and private institutions, and celebrity.". . . "Without close, qualitative studies to contradict them, conservative theorists will continue to blame welfare recipients', heroin addicts' and ex-prisoners' failures entirely on their defective characters or employ other theories that are compatible with the interests of the powers that be.". . . "Good ethnographies, on the other hand, beseech us to develop theories and social policies that are consistent with subjects' humanity" (Irwin, 1987). The preference for ethnography over survey research or the study of official documents, the "documentary reality" discussed by Smith, is also not only a scientific choice but an ideological one because, as Smith says, the "knowledge" produced by non-ethnographic methods "preserves conceptions and means of description which represent the world as it is for those who rule it," rather than as it is for those who are ruled (Smith, 1974: 267). The latter, being "the many" should be sociology's primary focus, rather than the former, necessarily "the few."

4. "Naive" because, during the occasion observed, the observer/participant was not "knowing" as to the later reporting of what was observed in a different social context, so that the observing was not spying.

5. We acknowledge that we are speaking about one social event, the occasion being described, from within the context of another equally social event, the interview before the class, but this is necessarily the nature of social life, in which, as Garfinkel says (1988) there is "no time out."

6. It has been noted by anonymous critical reviewers that some of the interview transcript questions contain as many or more words spoken by the questioner as

by the student respondent. Partly, this is due to the fact that many rather wordy questions failed to elicit more than a "yes" or a "no," and these admittedly were not very successful questions. Also, the "responsiveness" of the questioning often entailed repetition of much of the previous answer by the questioner, in order to preface a probe seeking elaboration or clarification. But the comparative word-count method cannot possibly be argued to show, in and of itself, that the interviewer controlled the production, or fabricated the existence, of respondents' memories of what happened on the recent occasion being discussed. The student interviewees are not suggestible children being enticed to remember things that never happened; they are responsible young adults being guided to focus on some of the infinitude of memory of what happened, and to omit the rest. Compared to predetermined questionnaires, with their "one size fits all" questions, so many of which require only a one- word answer, or even a check mark, these interviews are extraordinarily flexible and responsive, allowing for revisions, emendations, and corrections by respondents, and providing a constant flow of *surprises* to the interviewer, which then generate serendipitous new directions of questioning. Any set of data collected by a social scientist is a text evidentiary of many different things, at many different levels at once, including the felling of trees to make the paper it's printed on. The fact that our interview transcripts, intentionally ethnographic exhibits, also display evidence that interviews took place as occasions of social interaction, and also reveal the focus and objectives of the interviewer in the questions asked, does *not* rule out the possibility, holus-bolus, that the interviews may also be relatively accurate depictions of some of what actually happened at the ordinary occasions being described via the interviews. There was certainly collaboration between interviewer and respondent to produce the interviews, and there may have been interviewer bias of which the interviewer was not aware, and as I find in rereading and analyzing the transcripts, there were definitely moments when the questioning likely led the respondent to answer in just that way. These are unfortunate distortions, but they cannot simply be edited out of the transcripts. Our data is our data, warts and all. Responsibility to the truth can be adhered to best by conscientiously discounting these biases and distortions, and by avoiding analytical reliance on respondents' statements that may have been "led" or "forced" for the interviewer. The remainder, we argue, is authentic data which is extraordinarily illuminating of the modes and means of production of everybody's ordinary social life.

8. Brannigan and Lynch (1987) detail the process of distinguishing between perjury and credibility as "interactional accomplishments" in everyday life in the courtroom. The goal of the prosecutor is to lead the judge, whose interpretation is definitive, to hear the defendant's testimony as "perjury."
9. Eighty percent of my students are women, which I speculate reflects the reputation of sociology as a major subject that won't help you get a high-paying job, thus discouraging male enrollment.

APPENDIX

Exhibits A–R: Eighteen Interview Transcripts

Exhibit A: "A's Breakfast"

LINE#/SPEAKER (QU = QUESTIONER; A = STUDENT A)

A-1	/Qu:	Could you tell me whether you have a meal at your home called
A-2	/	breakfast regularly and generally?
A-3	/A:	Yes, I do.
A-4	/Qu:	Did you eat breakfast this morning?
A-5	/A:	Yes.
A-6	/Qu:	About this morning's breakfast, first, who has breakfast with you?
A-7	/A:	Well it isn't so much having breakfast, as he sits with me, my
A-8	/	father sits with me while I eat breakfast.
A-9	/Qu:	And that, um, having breakfast, he just sits while you eat?
A-10	/A:	Well he usually drinks tea.
A-11	/Qu:	I see, so his breakfast is tea?
A-12	/A:	Yes.
A-13	/Qu:	Does no one else in the family have breakfast with you?
A-14	/A:	No.
A-15	/Qu:	Do the other family members have breakfast at a different time?
A-16	/A:	They do.
A-17	/Qu:	Why is that?
A-18	/A:	They leave earlier than I do.
A-19	/Qu:	What time do you have breakfast?
A-20	/A:	I have breakfast around eight.
A-21	/Qu:	Eight a.m. Why do you have it at eight a.m.?
A-22	/A:	Because I don't have to come here till about twelve.
A-23	/Qu:	But if you don't have to get to university until twelve, then you
A-24	/	don't have to eat breakfast till eleven, so why have it at eight?
A-25	/A:	I have lunch around eleven!
A-26	/	Both: [Laughter]

A-27	/Qu:	Do you make it a point to have your breakfast by eight o'clock?
A-28	/A:	Usually.
A-29	/Qu:	What time do you have to start preparing to have breakfast by eight?
A-30	/A:	Five minutes before.
A-31	/Qu:	Does your father know that you have breakfast usually at that time?
A-32	/A:	Yes, I would think so.
A-33	/Qu:	Then he comes and joins you?
A-34	/A:	He's already waiting.
A-35	/Qu:	So he is there having tea, waiting for you to make your breakfast?
A-36	/A:	Yes.
A-37	/Qu:	What is the activity that directly precedes making of breakfast?
A-38	/A:	Taking out the bread, butter and milk.
A-39	/Qu:	No, I mean before you prepare breakfast.
A-40	/A:	Coming down from upstairs.
A-41	/Qu:	All right, you wake up and get dressed, do your ablutions, and come
A-42	/	downstairs to make breakfast, is that right?
A-43	/A:	Basically, yes.
A-44	/Qu:	Do you need an alarm clock to wake you up?
A-45	/A:	No.
A-46	/Qu:	Just whenever you wake up, you . . . ?
A-47	/A:	No, when everyone wakes up they make enough noise.
A-48	/Qu:	So the rest of the family, their hustle and bustle, that's your alarm?
A-49	/A:	That's right.
A-50	/Qu:	Do they encourage you to wake up to have breakfast with them?
A-51	/A:	No, never.
A-52	/Qu:	When you have breakfast with your father having tea, do you converse?
A-53	/A:	Not very much, he usually asks me if I've got up.
A-54	/Qu:	Which is obvious, you did get up.
A-55	/A:	Then he'll say what time are you going in today, and I'll say
A-56	/	around ten. He'll say let me know an hour before, and I'll take you in.
A-57	/Qu:	And that's pretty much the routine conversation?
A-58	/A:	Basically, or he'll ask me to feed the dog before I go.
A-59	/Qu:	Right. Does he inquire as to whether you have slept well?
A-60	/A:	No.
A-61	/Qu:	About your health?
A-62	/A:	No.
A-63	/Qu:	About your studies?
A-64	/A:	Never.

A-65 /Qu: Never, then these are things that are never talked about. Other
A-66 /   than that little dialogue you just described, are there other
A-67 /   things that are discussed in your conversations over breakfast?
A-68 /A: Nothing special, just if there is any message that's been left by
A-69 /   my mother that I have to do in addition to what I usually do
A-70 /   when I get back.
A-71 /Qu: Would you say most of breakfast is silent, with little bits of talk?
A-72 /A: Usually listening to the radio and passing comments on what
A-73 /   the news is for the day.
A-74 /Qu: So the radio is on to the news, and eight a.m. is the normal news
A-75 /   time, so that's how you know you eat breakfast at eight?
A-76 /A: Yes.
A-77 /Qu: How long would you say breakfast lasts?
A-78 /A: Ten to fifteen minutes.
A-79 /Qu: And how do you know it's over?
A-80 /A: When I finish my tea, I get up and leave.
A-81 /Qu: Is that whether your father finishes his tea or not?
A-82 /A: Well he usually sits there for another couple of hours.
A-83 /Qu: I see, so he's there continuously, and when you finish your
A-84 /   breakfast you leave the room?
A-85 /A: Yes.
A-86 /Qu: Where is breakfast?
A-87 /A: In the kitchen.
A-88 /Qu: Is the kitchen an eat-in or does it have a breakfast nook?
A-89 /A: Yes, it's an eat-in kitchen.
A-90 /Qu: And what kind of table is it?
A-91 /A: A round one, with four chairs, glass top.
A-92 /Qu: When you prepare your breakfast, what are the foods you eat,
A-93 /A: normally? Just toast, an egg or cheese.
A-94 /Qu: And what do you do with them?
A-95 /A: I just put the food on the plate and take the plate over to the
A-96 /   table and sit down, and I wash up afterwards.
A-97 /Qu: Do you say anything when you get up to leave?
A-98 /A: No.
A-99 /Qu: Does your father say anything that would mark the end of the
         session?
A-100 /A: He usually wants to know when I'll be going. I'll tell him and
          leave.
A-101 /Qu: But you won't say, excuse me, I'm leaving or—
A-102 /A: No, it's very informal.
A-103 /Qu: Are there days that you don't have breakfast?
A-104 /A: Occasionally.

A-105 /Qu: Weekends?
A-106 /A: Yes, weekends. Usually the whole family is there.
A-107 /Qu: So what you are talking about here is weekday breakfast?
A-108 /A: Yes.
A-109 /Qu: What would be the exception on weekday breakfasts?
A-110 /A: He might be going into the office earlier, so I'll be by myself.
A-111 /Qu: Now this weekday breakfast, how long has this going on?
A-112 /A: For the past three years, while I've been in college,
A-113 /Qu: Is the breakfast that you now have everything it ought to be?
A-114 /A: Yes. I wouldn't want to change it.
A-115 /Qu: Is it the kind of breakfast you'd continue to have once you
A-116 / married and went to live in an apartment with your spouse?
A-117 /A: Yes, I think so.
A-118 /Qu: Would you say the fact that it always goes the same way is satisfying?
A-119 /A: Hmmm.
A-120 /Qu: Or have you just never thought of it in that way?
A-121 /A: Not really because its something I just do, and once its over,
A-122 / it's good to get on with the day.
A-123 /Qu: Would you miss it if you . . .
A-124 /A: Yes, I would miss it.
A-125 /Qu: What do you think you would miss?
A-126 /A: The nourishing effects.
A-127 /Qu: Of the food. Would it be equivalent to have some granola or something?
A-128 /A: No, it wouldn't do. I have to have my tea.
A-129 /Qu: Do you think any of the nourishing effects come from sitting
A-130 / calmly with your father and chatting?
A-131 /A: No, because I don't talk to him that much.
A-132 /Qu: Wouldn't he miss it?
A-133 /A: I think so.
A-134 /Qu: So maybe he is getting more pleasure out of having conversation
A-135 / with his child through breakfast?
A-136 /A: Probably.
A-137 /Qu: Okay. Thank you.

Exhibit B: "B's Lunch"

LINE#/SPEAKER: (QU = QUESTIONER; B = STUDENT B)

B-1 /Qu: B, do you regularly have a meal called lunch at mid-day?
B-2 /B: Always, I have to, I never eat breakfast.
B-3 /Qu: And where does this meal usually take place?

B-4	/B:	In the kitchen at my home.
B-5	/Qu:	Who is it that generally eats this meal with you?
B-6	/B:	My father and my little sister.
B-7	/Qu:	How is the food for the meal prepared?
B-8	/B:	We all make our own food.
B-9	/Qu:	Do each of you have a different kind of food?
B-10	/B:	Usually, yes.
B-11	/Qu:	Why is that?
B-12	/B:	My father is Polish and he likes his Polish food. My little sister
B-13	/	has a normal sandwich and I'm a vegetarian so I usually have salad.
B-14	/Qu:	So your little sister prepares her sandwich, your father cooks his
B-15	/	Kielbasa, or whatever, and you make your salad?
B-16	/B:	Exactly.
B-17	/Qu:	When do you start doing all this?
B-18	/B:	About ten minutes before we eat.
B-19	/Qu:	So all three of you are in the kitchen preparing at the same time?
B-20	/B:	Yes.
B-21	/Qu:	Does that get confusing? Do you get in each others' way?
B-22	/B:	Always. Every day [laughing].
B-23	/Qu:	But you try to all finish preparing at the same time so that the
B-24	/	three of you can bring your plates to sit at the table?
B-25	/B:	No, my father never sits down to eat, he stands and watches over us.
B-26	/Qu:	He stands while eating? And you and your sister are sitting at
B-27	/	a table in the kitchen?
B-28	/B:	Yes.
B-29	/Qu:	What kind of a table is it?
B-30	/B:	It's an oval table.
B-31	/Qu:	And where do you sit at it?
B-32	/B:	There is no set place.
B-33	/Qu:	How does your sister bring her food to the table?
B-34	/B:	Usually on a paper towel.
B-35	/Qu:	What does it consist of, other than a sandwich?
B-36	/B:	A glass of milk.
B-37	/Qu:	And yours?
B-38	/B:	A cup of tea always, and salad in a bowl, with a fork.
B-39	/Qu:	And your father has his food as a sandwich, or what?
B-40	/B:	A sandwich, and then his Kielbasa on the side, and some of those
B-41	/	huge pickles, and milk to drink, always.
B-42	/Qu:	What time does lunch occur?
B-43	/B:	Usually about 12:30, when my father gets home from work, my

B-44	/	sister gets home from school and I get out of bed.
B-45	/Qu:	What determines when lunch has to end?
B-46	/B:	I have to get to school by two, my father has to get back to work
B-47	/	for about 1:15, and my sister has to get back to school by 1:15 too.
B-48	/Qu:	Why do you have lunch at that time?
B-49	/B:	It's better than eating alone. I enjoy eating with my father and
B-50	/	sister. I just prefer it.
B-51	/Qu:	Is there a standard kind of conversation that goes on over the
B-52	/	course of these lunches, things that are talked about, people who talk most?
B-53	/B:	Yes, my father usually asks questions. We've got a very sports
B-54	/	minded family so he'll be talking football, hockey or baseball.
B-55	/Qu:	Does he also interrogate you and your sister about school, dates,
B-56	/	and how your life is going?
B-57	/B:	No, I think he's scared to ask. We keep it general.
B-58	/Qu:	Is there a lot of talking during lunch or is it pretty quiet?
B-59	/B:	There's lots of talking.
B-60	/Qu:	Do you and your sister also talk back?
B-61	/B:	My little sister and I talk the most. My father just opens up the
B-62	/	conversation, then my sister and I start talking and forget him.
B-63	/Qu:	Do you talk about the food?
B-64	/B:	No.
B-65	/Qu:	Nobody asks if your salad's good?
B-66	/B:	No.
B-67	/Qu:	Father doesn't refer to his sausage or sister to her sandwich?
B-68	/B:	Not unless she wants another sandwich and tries to get me to make it.
B-69	/Qu:	Who does the shopping for all these different foods?
B-70	/B:	My mother.
B-71	/Qu:	She has to make sure she has all the ingredients for three different
B-72	/	lunches in the refrigerator?
B-73	/B:	It depends. Normal lunches, my mother will shop for, but any
B-74	/	Polish food, my father gets his own.
B-75	/Qu:	Your mother doesn't have lunch with you?
B-76	/B:	No, she's at work during this time.
B-77	/Qu:	You said you skip breakfast, so lunch is your first meal of the day?
B-78	/B:	Yes, that's right.
B-79	/Qu:	How long have these lunches been going on?
B-80	/B:	Since I've been in university because in high school, I ate there.
B-81	/Qu:	So since they've started, these've been regular occasions?
B-82	/B:	Right.
B-83	/Qu:	Do you think your father enjoys them?

B-84 /B: He must. He keeps coming home.
B-85 /Qu: He could just as well take a lunch to his work?
B-86 /B: Yes.
B-87 /Qu: Does your sister have any choice in the matter?
B-88 /B: She could eat at school, but she comes home too.
B-89 /Qu: Do you think it's an important part of the solidarity of your
B-90 /   family that you get to eat and chat together regularly, during the day?
B-91 /B: Yes. It's about the only time I ever talk to my father.
B-92 /Qu: Why doesn't it happen at supper?
B-93 /B: Nobody eats supper together.
B-94 /Qu: Is your mother missed very much on these occasions?
B-95 /B: Not really.
B-96 /Qu: Its a time when two siblings have their father to themselves?
B-97 /B: It happens that way.
B-98 /Qu: Do you think this lunch routine will continue in future?
B-99 /B: No, because next year my little sister will be in high school and
B-100 /   won't be home for lunch and I don't know where I'll be.
B-101 /Qu: How do you know when lunch is ending?
B-102 /B: My father usually looks at his watch and leaves.
B-103 /Qu: He has to get back to work and your sister has to get back to school?
B-104 /B: Yes. She ends up asking for a drive.
B-105 /Qu: Who ends up cleaning up everybody's dishes after lunch?
B-106 /B: Nobody. We just take them to the sink and leave them there.
B-107 /Qu: Your mother usually cleans them at night?
B-108 /B: No, my other sister does them when she gets home from school.
B-109 /Qu: You've got another sister to clean up?
B-110 /B: Yes.
B-111 /Qu: "Cinderella!" [laughter]. I don't think I have it clear how the
B-112 /   eating starts. You're all there in the kitchen making up your food
B-113 /   and then you and your sister manage to get to the table some
B-114 /   how and your father's standing up. Does everybody start to eat
B-115 /   whatever they have whenever it's ready?
B-116 /B: Yes.
B-117 /Qu: Some families do grace and some say we'll all start eating at once...
B-118 /B: No. We're totally informal.
B-119 /Qu: I see. Thank you.

Exhibit C: "C's Dinner Out"

LINE#/SPEAKER: (QU = QUESTIONER; C = STUDENT C)

C-1	/Qu:	Could you tell me when was the last time you dined out?
C-2	/C:	Last Friday night.
C-3	/Qu:	How do you know that it was a Friday?
C-4	/C:	I'm sure 'cause I dine out every Friday with my family.
C-5	/Qu:	So where did you dine out?
C-6	/C:	Every week we go to the Jade Garden Chinese restaurant on Spadina Ave.
C-7	/Qu:	Who else goes?
C-8	/C:	Every week, I go with my brother, my sister-in-law, and my sister.
C-9	/Qu:	Do you all live in the same place?
C-10	/C:	No.
C-11	/Qu:	Okay, so how do you get together to go?
C-12	/C:	We meet at a coffee shop first, which is located by that restaurant.
C-13	/Qu:	Why did you meet there first?
C-14	/C:	Easier, 'cause it's close to where my brother and my sister's
C-15	/	offices. That's why, because all work in downtown.
C-16	/Qu:	Right, so what time do you schedule to meet?
C-17	/C:	Usually, any time after five.
C-18	/Qu:	Is that the standard time every week, so you don't have to make
C-19	/	special arrangements, just get there about five and you'll meet?
C-20	/C:	Yes.
C-21	/Qu:	So this last Friday, were you the first one there?
C-22	/C:	No, I was second, my brother was already there.
C-23	/Qu:	And how did you get there?
C-24	/C:	I drove my car from campus, and parked in front.
C-25	/Qu:	What was your brother doing when you went in?
C-26	/C:	Having his coffee, so I sat down at his table and ordered my drink.
C-27	/Qu:	Did he greet you, and did you engage in conversation?
C-28	/C:	Yes, we just usually talked about family things.
C-29	/Qu:	Then who arrived next?
C-30	/C:	My sister, so then we all waited for my sister-in-law.
C-31	/Qu:	How long did it take before she arrived?
C-32	/C:	Within thirty minutes.
C-33	/Qu:	And when your sister-in-law arrived, what happened?
C-34	/C:	We all got up to go to the restaurant, the Jade Garden.
C-35	/Qu:	And when the four of you got there, did anyone greet you at the door?
C-36	/C:	We go there every week, so the manager and waiters know we are coming.

C-37 /Qu: And then did someone show you to a table?
C-38 /C: Yes, the manager did, 'cause we know the boss there too, so
C-39 / everyone treated us nicely.
C-40 /Qu: Then the four of you sat down, and then what?
C-41 /C: Right, we looked at the menu and pick what we want, usually
C-42 / each of us pick one dish.
C-43 /Qu: Did the waiter come right away to take your order?
C-44 /C: Yes, and they stay around and talk to us.
C-45 /Qu: I see, so do they offer you a drink first?
C-46 /C: They know what we drink.
C-47 /Qu: So they just brought you the drinks?
C-48 /C: Uh-huh.
C-49 /Qu: Then you each ordered one dish, and then shared that all around?
C-50 /C: Yes, we put them in the middle of the table and shared together.
C-51 /Qu: And each has your own bowl of rice?
C-52 /C: Yeah.
C-53 /Qu: Did you have to ask the waiter for chopsticks?
C-54 /C: No, they were on the table already.
C-55 /Qu: And what was the conversation like while you were eating?
C-56 /C: Mostly things about family, all family talk.
C-57 /Qu: And these dishes you ordered, did each of you order the same
C-58 / thing all the time, or try something different every week?
C-59 /C: Something different every week, my brother usually orders
C-60 / seafood, so every week he will ask the waiter what's fresh on that day.
C-61 /Qu: When you finish the main dishes, are there other things you'll order?
C-62 /C: You mean desserts?
C-63 /Qu: Yeah.
C-64 /C: No, not really.
C-65 /Qu: Do you drink tea during the meal?
C-66 /C: Yes, I did, but the rest of them had pop.
C-67 /Qu: When you finished the meal, did the waiter bring in the bill?
C-68 /C: Yeah. But sometimes my brother will walk to the cashier and pay the bill.
C-69 /Qu: What happened last Friday?
C-70 /C: Uh. They brought the bill.
C-71 /Qu: They brought it to the table? Then who pays the bill?
C-72 /C: Always my brother.
C-73 /Qu: The whole bill? You didn't say this is my portion and that's yours?
C-74 /C: No, not for my family.
C-75 /Qu: Does he usually pay in cash or credit card?

C-76	/C:	Usually in card, American Express card.
C-77	/Qu:	So he paid by card, the waiter brought back the slip and he signed it?
C-78	/C:	Right. And he put the tip on the slip, too.
C-79	/Qu:	So there was usually no cash? How much would he tip?
C-80	/C:	Ten percent.
C-81	/Qu:	So, when the waiter gives him back the slip, you all get up to leave?
C-82	/C:	Uh, yup.
C-83	/Qu:	About how long did this meal take you?
C-84	/C:	Uh . . . about an hour.
C-85	/Qu:	So about an hour with slowly eating and a lot of talking?"
C-86	/C:	Yeah.
C-87	/Qu:	Do you plan to go someplace next, after the meal together?
C-88	/C:	No, 'cause last Friday I had to work on some assignment, so I drove home.
C-89	/Qu:	So what about the rest of them?
C-90	/C:	My brother gave my sister a ride home, she lives downtown. And
C-91	/	they went home afterwards—they live in Scarborough.
C-92	/Qu:	So each of you went separate ways. Were many families or groups there?
C-93	/C:	Yeah, quite a lot, a full house.
C-94	/Qu:	Did the waiter pay special attention to you because he knew you?
C-95	/C:	Uh-huh. Kind of 'cause he came to us a lot, sometimes the
C-96	/	manager and the boss came to us too.
C-97	/Qu:	Ah, they did. Well, okay, thank you, C.
C-98	/C:	You are welcome.

Exhibit D: "D's Midnight"

LINE#/SPEAKER: (QU = QUESTIONER; D = STUDENT D)

D-1	/Qu:	D, I want to ask you about the occasion of work you most recently
D-2	/	participated in, uh, what is your job, currently?
D-3	/D:	I do price changing in a grocery store midnights on Monday till 8:30 a.m.
D-4	/Qu:	So you work a full day.
D-5	/D:	Yes and we get two twenty minute breaks and an hour for lunch in between.
D-6	/Qu:	And how far from where you live is this grocery store?
D-7	/D:	Oh, only about a couple of miles away.
D-8	/Qu:	And how do you go?

D-9   /D: I drive my car there.
D-10 /Qu: On this Monday night, when did you start preparing to get ready to go?
D-11 /D: Oh, I usually start about 11:30.
D-12 /Qu: Yes?
D-13 /D: Well, actually I usually have about a two hour nap before, and
D-14 /   I get dressed in my grubby clothes and I drive to work.
D-15 /Qu: Is this preparation for going to work and staying up all night?
D-16 /D: Yes, definitely.
D-17 /Qu: Grubby clothes, you mean something like jeans and a sweatshirt?
D-18 /D: Yes, right.
D-19 /Qu: Where do you park when you drive to work?
D-20 /D: Right in front of the store.
D-21 /Qu: Then you go right in at midnight?
D-22 /D: Yeah, the doors are open.
D-23 /Qu: How do you indicate that you've arrived on time?
D-24 /D: Well, not everybody is exactly on time. We just sort of walk in.
D-25 /Qu: You don't have to punch in?
D-26 /D: No.
D-27 /Qu: All right. Is there a boss there supervising you at that time?
D-28 /D: Yes, there is a night crew chief who's there.
D-29 /Qu: Does the crew chief welcome you or indicate he knows you're there?
D-30 /D: Oh, yeah.
D-31 /Qu: And what if you arrived five or ten minutes late?
D-32 /D: Oh, they don't get upset.
D-33 /Qu: What if it was a half hour late?
D-34 /D: They get a little upset. But if I tell them in advance it's no problem.
D-35 /Qu: If you were as much as an hour late, would you lose an hour's pay?
D-36 /D: Yeah, I might.
D-37 /Qu: Then you're paid by the hour?
D-38 /D: Yup, by the hour.
D-39 /Qu: How many working hours are you paid for?
D-40 /D: Well, I work two midnights a week, so that's sixteen hours.
D-41 /Qu: From midnight to 8:30 a.m., and you get paid for eight of those hours?
D-42 /D: Yes.
D-43 /Qu: And you said there are two twenty-minute breaks and a one hour. . . ?
D-44 /D: Well we bend the rules a little; we should get two fifteen-minute
D-45 /   breaks and a half hour for lunch and we get paid for the breaks,

D-46	/	but not the half hour. So that works out to eight hours.
D-47	/Qu:	Right, you take an extra half hour for lunch.
D-48	/D:	Yeah, we work extra hard to make up for it.
D-49	/Qu:	And the night crew chief goes along with this?
D-50	/D:	Yeah, he does.
D-51	/Qu:	Uh, you entered the store at midnight and then, where did you go?
D-52	/D:	Well, we go and we make coffee, and then we drink our coffee.
D-53	/Qu:	How many of you are working then?
D-54	/D:	There's seven guys and myself, so there's eight of us.
D-55	/Qu:	Eight including the night crew chief?
D-56	/D:	Yes.
D-57	/Qu:	The first thing you do when you all arrive is someone makes coffee?
D-58	/D:	Yes.
D-59	/Qu:	Do you usually make the coffee?
D-60	/D:	No, usually the guys make it.
D-61	/Qu:	So you all drink a cup of coffee, and what do you do after that?
D-62	/D:	Then I go into the office and get my papers organized. Like,
D-63	/	finding all the price increases, and getting all that organized.
D-64	/Qu:	Where is the office in relation to the rest of the store?
D-65	/D:	Near the main entrance. You walk in the front and it's right there.
D-66	/Qu:	All right. And do you work in the office then?
D-67	/D:	No, I work in the store. I start off in the office to get my papers.
D-68	/Qu:	And is there any equipment involved?
D-69	/D:	No, not really.
D-70	/Qu:	I mean, like, what do you put the labels on with?
D-71	/D:	Oh, sorry, a price gun.
D-72	/Qu:	A price gun. Do you determine what prices will shoot out by setting it?
D-73	/D:	The little knob.
D-74	/Qu:	The little knob, and do the papers that are there indicate to
D-75	/	you which items and prices you should be responsible for price changing?
D-76	/D:	Yes, well, I go in there and I find out, like several papers come
D-77	/	in, I take the ones that show exactly what I'll be doing, what I have to do.
D-78	/Qu:	So you lay out the night's work pretty much in advance?
D-79	/D:	Yes.
D-80	/Qu:	Are the seven other employees doing the same kind of work as you do?
D-81	/D:	No. They're stocking shelves.

D-82 /Qu: There are the crates of things that they are taking out?
D-83 /D: They are out in the back, but only one guy brings it all in the front.
D-84 /Qu: The others are in front, taking things out and putting them on shelves?
D-85 /D: Right.
D-86 /Qu: Do you have to price those things as well?
D-87 /D: No, I only do the increases. I pull everything off the shelf, peel off
D-88 / old labels, put on new ones and put it back on the shelf.
D-89 /Qu: I see, you have to take off the old labels, not put one over the other?
D-90 /D: No, I can't do that, it's against the law.
D-91 /Qu: I see. What about items going on shelves that haven't been priced yet?
D-92 /D: I have nothing to do with them. The boys in the night crew do that.
D-93 /Qu: Are you being paid the same as those guys?
D-94 /D: They're on full time and I'm on a part time basis so I'm getting less.
D-95 /Qu: What about the ranking of the work you do, is it considered the same?
D-96 /D: Oh yeah, the guys that are part time night crew, I get paid same as them.
D-97 /Qu: You've been working let's say four hours, then you take your break?
D-98 /D: Two hours, then in another two hours. It works out every two hours.
D-99 /Qu: Every two hours you get some kind of break?
D-100 /D: Right.
D-101 /Qu: So you walk down the store and pull off the things that need
D-102 / changing, change them, and put them back, and you do this for two hours, about?
D-103 /D: Right.
D-104 /Qu: And then what do you do? Does everyone take a break then?
D-105 /D: Yeah. They announce "It's two o'clock," and everyone goes to
D-106 / the front of the store, gets something to eat, grabs a coffee, and
D-107 / we sit around and talk. When we feel like going back to work we get up and go back.
D-108 /Qu: When you eat on break, do you eat anything that's in the store?
D-109 /D: Oh, I don't know if I should say this, we do it but we're not
D-110 / supposed to. But there's so much stuff in there, you can't tell what's missing.
D-111 /Qu: The crew chief participates too, so there's nobody snitching

	on you?
D-112 /D:	Well, he is a workaholic so he doesn't usually take any breaks at all.
D-113 /Qu:	I see.
D-114 /D:	But, he doesn't mind. I'm sure the management knows and they
D-115 /	don't seem to say anything either.
D-116 /Qu:	Okay, so you finish your break and chatting and you go back
D-117 /	to work. While you're working, are you talking to anyone else?
D-118 /D:	Oh, yeah. If one of these guys is in my aisle, I'll talk to him.
D-119 /Qu:	Chatting back and forth?
D-120 /D:	Yes.
D-121 /Qu:	Does this crew chief ever come around and make you speed up,
D-122 /	or criticize the speed that you work?
D-123 /D:	No cause what I do is a favor for them, they don't say anything to me.
D-124 /Qu:	How's that?
D-125 /D:	Well there is only two girls in all of Toronto doing this. All the
D-126 /	the other guys have to do this themselves. So our store is
D-127 /	privileged. I'm doing all the stuff that they don't want to do.
D-128 /Qu:	Why don't they want to do it?
D-129 /D:	Because who wants to pull things off the shelf, pull little stickers
D-130 /	off, put new ones on, put them on the shelf? It's very time consuming.
D-131 /Qu:	Is that considered to be more difficult work than hauling cans
D-132 /	and putting them up on the shelf?
D-133 /D:	Yes, it's fiddly. You're spending hours, peeling off labels.
D-134 /Qu:	And that's considered tedious?
D-135 /D:	Yes, to them it is.
D-136 /Qu:	Is it tedious to you? Would you rather be putting things on shelves?
D-137 /D:	No, I wouldn't.
D-138 /Qu:	So as far as you're concerned, it's not any more difficult?
D-139 /D:	No, I wouldn't be working if I thought it was.
D-140 /Qu:	Do you enjoy doing it?
D-141 /D:	Yeah, I enjoy doing it.
D-142 /Qu:	Do you ever get the sense that it's not worth it?
D-143 /D:	No, the money is really good.
D-144 /Qu:	The money is good, you feel the job is good from that point of view?
D-145 /D:	It's not just the money; I was part time in the store for six years,
D-146 /	and this is really a change. I've only been doing this for four months.

D-147/Qu: This job. So it's a more interesting job and at better pay.
D-148/D: Yeah, it's different.
D-149/Qu: Do you get very routine about it without thinking about it?
D-150/D: I try not to because then I would get very bored with it.
D-151/Qu: So how do you avoid that?
D-152/D: I do different things. Like I don't have a set order for doing
D-153/ things. Like I do one thing then I do another thing.
D-154/Qu: So you try and make it interesting for yourself.
D-155/D: Yeah. Like when I first started, I was doing the same things over
D-156/ and over again. Now I try and change so it doesn't get too monotonous.
D-157/Qu: You can break the monotony by moving to different parts of
D-158/ the store or doing different kinds of items?
D-159/D: Yes.
D-160/Qu: Are you thinking about what you're doing, or something else?
D-161/D: No, I'm too tired to think about anything.
D-162/Qu: Are you day dreaming or something?
D-163/D: Yeah, well there's music playing so I'm usually singing to myself.
D-164/Qu: I see, and that makes it go by faster?
D-165/D: Oh, yeah!
D-166/Qu: That eight hours, in the middle of the night, does it seem very long?
D-167/D: No, time goes by quickly, like I'm going in there and coming right out.
D-168/Qu: Right, so when you get to the end of the work day, do you usually
D-169/ stand around and chat with the other employees for a while?
D-170/D: Yes. We go over to the restaurant next door for a coffee or two.
D-171/Qu: Then you go home? And what do you do when you get home?
D-172/D: Yes I go home, take a long hot bath and then go to bed for a few hours.
D-173/Qu: You have to sleep right away?
D-174/D: Yes, I have a night class Tuesday night so I usually sleep till two
D-175/ or three in the afternoon. Then I go to my class. That way
D-176/ I haven't had a complete night's rest and I can get to sleep when I get home.
D-177/Qu: Is it an advantage to get your work over with at this time of night?
D-178/D: Yes, I'm too busy during the day to have to do that during the day.
D-179/Qu: So you really haven't cut into your days?
D-180/D: No, I haven't, and I need my time during the day.
D-181/Qu: So in a sense you've got your time and some money, too.
D-182/D: That's right.
D-183/Qu: If anybody said to you that the job is alienating, would you

APPENDIX: EXHIBITS A-R ■ 61

D-184 /   understand what they were talking about from having done it?
D-185 /D: What do you mean by "alienating"?
D-186 /Qu: That it turns you into less than a human.
D-187 /D: Lot's of people say that. But I would disagree with that because
D-188 /   I only work two days a week. Now, the guys that are doing that
D-189 /   full time, I could see them being like that. Their social life is
D-190 /   limited. They socialize mainly with themselves because they are
D-191 /   off during the day when everyone else is working.
D-192 /Qu: I know, I've worked nights myself. You're sort of separated from
D-193 /   the day working population. But people say certain kinds of
D-194 /   repetitive work is alienating, it doesn't require much imagination
D-195 /   or ability, that it "dehumanizes" you and turns you into a machine.
D-196 /   That's the critique some have of that kind of job. What would
               you say to them?
D-197 /D: No, not this. As a cashier, it was like that. That's why I stopped.
D-198 /Qu: During work, is there lots of chatter back and forth between the
               crew?
D-199 /D: Oh yes. We are all nice and close and we can hear each other.
D-200 /   There's lots of yelling and screaming going on.
D-201 /Qu: You're not working under the eye of the public, like as a cashier?
D-202 /D: That is right. There's nobody watching every move you make.
D-203 /Qu: Do you feel confined at all in the store for those eight hours?
D-204 /D: No, not at all.
D-205 /Qu: Do you come to feel that the place is yours somehow?
D-206 /D: Yes. I've been at that place so long, it's practically a second home.
D-207 /Qu: The other people that work there, are they people that you would
D-208 /   socialize with if they weren't working in that store?
D-209 /D: Yes. I do socialize with them. There is a lot of people there that
D-210 /   I'm good friends with, some have left and I'm still in contact with
D-211 /   them, so we've become very close.
D-212 /Qu: Thank you.

Exhibit E: "E's Choir Practice"

LINE# /SPEAKER: (QU = QUESTIONER; E = STUDENT E)

E-1   /Qu: E, when did the choir practice we're going to talk about occur?
E-2   /E: I went to the last practice, Tuesday last week, at seven at night.
E-3   /Qu: And do they run regularly at seven on Tuesdays each week all
               year?
E-4   /E: Unless maybe Christmas or so and they reschedule if there are

		problems.
E-5	/Qu:	What organization sponsors the choir or of which the choir is part?
E-6	/E:	It's part of Saint Nicholas Ukrainian, the Catholic church I attend.
E-7	/Qu:	Is it the choir that sings in the church at Sunday services?
E-8	/E:	No, we have two choirs, the choir that I've joined is just young
E-9	/	girls, we sing, on occasions, but the other choir sings regularly, Sundays.
E-10	/Qu:	Does this choir have a name?
E-11	/E:	It's called "Wesnivka," which means, in Ukrainian, "little flowers."
E-12	/Qu:	So that is symbolic of the fact that the members are young ladies?
E-13	/E:	Yeah.
E-14	/Qu:	And when did you first join this choir?
E-15	/E:	Uh, it was three weeks ago, I've been to two practices.
E-16	/Qu:	And you are a long time member of this church congregation?
E-17	/E:	Yeah, I've always wanted to join the choir, I heard from a friend,
E-18	/	she told me when the practices were, I decided to go and find
E-19	/	out if I liked it or not.
E-20	/Qu:	When you first went, did you have to, audition or, uh—
E-21	/E:	No, she just asked me what type of a singer I am, or, what
E-22	/	category I go, I said, "I think I'm an alto," she said, "Well, why
E-23	/	don't you just sit with the altos and see if it works out or not."
E-24	/Qu:	Who is this otherwise unnamed "she"?
E-25	/E:	Uh, well, the conductress, she's uh, her name is K—.
E-26	/Qu:	Is her sole position in the church, conductress of the girls' choir?
E-27	/E:	Uh-huh.
E-28	/Qu:	And where did this rehearsal last Tuesday night take place?
E-29	/E:	Uh, in a, under the school, on Queen and Bellwoods.
E-30	/Qu:	Is that attached to the church building?
E-31	/E:	Uh, well it's close by.
E-32	/Qu:	It's a school building under the auspices of the church?
E-33	/E:	Right.
E-34	/Qu:	And did you say under the school?
E-35	/E:	Yeah, well, in the basement of the school.
E-36	/Qu:	And how did you know where to go for the choir practice?
E-37	/E:	I've gone to Ukrainian school, so I knew, and my friend told me where.
E-38	/Qu:	How far is it from your home?
E-39	/E:	Quite a way, I live in the West End, and that's like in downtown

area.
E-40 /Qu: So when did you have to leave, to get to the seven o'clock practice?
E-41 /E: I had to leave at six, I took the street car which took me to another
E-42 / street car and then, I just walk across the street and I'm there.
E-43 /Qu: What did you do just prior to leaving your home Tuesday night?
E-44 /E: Um, just got ready for the rehearsal.
E-45 /Qu: How did you do that?
E-46 /E: I ironed my pants and, uh, I dressed, and I curled my hair and that's it.
E-47 /Qu: What time and from where had you gotten home?
E-48 /E: From school, from university, at about 5:30.
E-49 /Qu: The way you dressed for school was not all right for choir practice?
E-50 /E: No, it's more dressy.
E-51 /Qu: Is this a "dress code" or requirement? How did you learn of it?
E-52 /E: The first time I wasn't sure what the other girls would be wearing,
E-53 / so I wore dress pants, I'm glad I did cause a lot of them dress up.
E-54 /Qu: So from your observation of how the others dressed you decided
E-55 / that was the appropriate level of dress?
E-56 /E: Uh-huh.
E-57 /Qu: Was there anything you had to take with you?
E-58 /E: No, uh, I just brought some money, that's all.
E-59 /Qu: Uh-huh, did you gargle or clear your throat?
E-60 /E: Uh, I brushed my teeth.
E-61 /Qu: To have a clean fresh mouth for singing?
E-62 /E: Right.
E-63 /Qu: So you got on the street car, and got there by seven?
E-64 /E: I was there early.
E-65 /Qu: Was anyone else there yet?
E-66 /E: Oh, there were a lot of girls.
E-67 /Qu: Already there waiting early?
E-68 /E: Right. I saw my friend there, we started talking, and she intro-
E-69 / duced me to other people, I've seen in church, but I didn't really know them.
E-70 /Qu: And how many girls are there in the choir?
E-71 /E: There are fifty, but at practices I've been to, the most was thirty-five.
E-72 /Qu: Do you feel right appropriately part of this group in terms of
E-73 / all the characteristics that you noticed about the others?
E-74 /E: I wasn't sure at first, but with time I'll become like one of them.
E-75 /Qu: Uh-huh. Are you the right age? What's the age range?

E-76 /E: Oh, yeah. I think it's 17 to, the oldest I know there is 28 years old.
E-77 /Qu: Middle class?
E-78 /E: Oh, yeah, and upper, wealthy.
E-79 /Qu: What clues could you see to indicate that some were wealthy?
E-80 /E: Um, well, just their clothes I would say, and jewelry.
E-81 /Qu: Very fancy garb, eh? Could you afford to dress like that?
E-82 /E: Uh, if I really wanted to, sure.
E-83 /Qu: Were there leaders among them, in terms of old hands, or
E-84 / established members compared to other newcomers like
E-85 / yourself, perhaps, or younger girls, does there seem to be any pattern of a, more dominant or . . . ?
E-86 /E: There were a few handing out notes so, that one girl I know,
E-87 / she's been in there for ten years already.
E-88 /Qu: Uh-huh.
E-89 /E: And maybe during that time she got to know the conductress real well.
E-90 /Qu: What do you mean, "handing out the notes"?
E-91 /E: Uh, well, sometimes we get new notes, and, uh, . . .
E-92 /Qu: Sheet music?
E-93 /E: Yes.
E-94 /Qu: And so the conductress would give it to them to be the monitors?
E-95 /E: Yes.
E-96 /Qu: And, what kind of space is this in the basement of the school building?
E-97 /E: Oh it's quite, a quite a big room.
E-98 /Qu: And is it only used for things like singing?
E-99 /E: No, when I went to Ukrainian school we had lunch down there
E-100 / and it was used for many things, even a gymnasium.
E-101 /Qu: And how is it arranged for the choir practice?
E-102 /E: There are two rows of chairs in a semicircle, a piano in the
E-103 / front and a table for the conductress, to keep her purse and other sheet music.
E-104 /Qu: When you got there, you assembled outside for fifteen minutes?
E-105 /E: Yeah, outside in the hall, standing there and talking.
E-106 /Qu: And when did the conductress arrive?
E-107 /E: Uh, it was about ten to seven when she got there.
E-108 /Qu: Um, and did she go right into the room when she arrived?
E-109 /E: Yeah.
E-110 /Qu: And then everyone more or less filed in?
E-111 /E: Right.
E-112 /Qu: And where did she go to, inside the room?

E-113 /E: To the table in front, and there's this little room she went in
E-114 / there to hang up her coat.
E-115 /Qu: I see, what did other people do with their coats?
E-116 /E: There's chairs at the back of the room, right, and everybody puts
E-117 / their, their purses and coats there.
E-118 /Qu: Then where did she go, after she put her coat away in the back room?
E-119 /E: Oh, she came back to the, the table.
E-120 /Qu: And stood there in a, um, a disposition of readiness?
E-121 /E: Uh-huh, and then the girls all took their seats.
E-122 /Qu: How did they seat themselves?
E-123 /E: The altos sit on the left, and the sopranos sit on the right of the
E-124 / room, and so everybody in between soprano and alto sit in the middle.
E-125 /Qu: Is there a category between soprano and alto?
E-126 /E: They divide it like, first soprano, second soprano, and first alto,
E-127 / alto, second alto.
E-128 /Qu: You had been there before so you knew you were to sit among the altos?
E-129 /E: Right.
E-130 /Qu: Which altos?
E-131 /E: Well, the first time I sat with the second but I think I'm going
E-132 / to switch to, ah, first alto, cause second alto was too low.
E-133 /Qu: What happened after everyone got seated?
E-134 /E: The conductress was asking how our weekend went, or whatever, and—
E-135 /Qu: She chit-chatted?
E-136 /E: Yeah, she chit-chatted then she said get your sheet music out
E-137 / for one song and she would stand and start singing, and, uh,
E-138 / the girl on the piano would start playing and she would sort of say, okay, let's start.
E-139 /Qu: Ah, there was a girl on the piano? [laughter].
E-140 /E: Well, sitting, playing the piano.
E-141 /Qu: And who is she? A member of the choir?
E-142 /E: I don't know, I never asked; I think she is a member.
E-143 /Qu: The pianist. And it's the same pianist who starts you off every time?
E-144 /E: Uh-huh.
E-145 /Qu: She has sheet music on the piano. Do you think there has been
E-146 / some prefabrication between the pianist and the conductress;
E-147 / does she have to say page so and so, you know, bar such and such?

E-148	/E:	I think maybe, like she has known what they were going to play first.
E-149	/Qu:	Um, but hasn't sheet music been handed out in the meantime?
E-150	/E:	Oh, we've had this from the week-before.
E-151	/Qu:	Ah, but you mean you've had, you brought it with you?
E-152	/E:	Yeah.
E-153	/Qu:	When I asked before what did you bring with you, you said nothing.
E-154	/E:	Um, I was thinking about the first time I went.
E-155	/Qu:	Right, and the second time you went, you brought your sheet music?
E-156	/E:	Right, uh-huh.
E-157	/Qu:	Um, okay, then what happens, um, you sing?
E-158	/E:	Uh-huh.
E-159	/Qu:	And are you rehearsing for a particular concert or performance?
E-160	/E:	Yeah, we're going to England to perform in April, I don't know
E-161	/	if I'm going 'cause I'm new, I don't know if I'll be able to sing in the choir.
E-162	/Qu:	Uh, that is if your voice will qualify?
E-163	/E:	Right, so I just have to wait and see.
E-164	/Qu:	Oh, how do you feel, insecure or fairly optimistic about that?
E-165	/E:	Oh, a little bit insecure, because I've never sung before, so . . .
E-166	/Qu:	You can hear your voice in relation to the others? Whether you
E-167	/	are croaking or harmonizing.
E-168	/E:	Yeah. I think I'll get there with time.
E-169	/Qu:	You blend fairly well so far. Do you sing a particular piece
E-170	/	and then, uh, take a break of some kind and then, uh, sing another?
E-171	/E:	The few times I've been there, we hadn't taken a break. It's just
E-172	/	from 7 till 9. During the song, if she doesn't like something,
E-173	/	she'll say, "Okay, stop," and then she'll go to the section, she
E-174	/	feels haven't sang, uh, fairly well, and then she'll sing, and then tell them to sing.
E-175	/Qu:	So she has to sing in every range while she's conducting, you get
E-176	/	the sense she's monitoring very closely the blend of each section.
E-177	/	Is she a very dynamic and, uh, personable person?
E-178	/E:	Oh, yeah.
E-179	/Qu:	She draws the interest and the enthusiasm of the group to her?
E-180	/E:	Yeah, she's very nice.
E-181	/Qu:	Is she a hard taskmaster, tough on the choir?
E-182	/E:	Yeah, I heard before that she was really tough, like, if she wouldn't
E-183	/	like the way you sang, she'd say, "Okay, we have to do it till we

APPENDIX: EXHIBITS A-R ■ 67

E-184 /   do it right," keep them for an extra hour, but the few times that
E-185 /   I was there I didn't notice that.
E-186 /Qu: Do times she stops you have to do with hitting the right notes, or
E-181 /   the right timing, or intonation or articulation, some or all of
          that?
E-188 /E: Yeah, some of all of that, I noticed a few times, like either the note
E-189 /   isn't right or we don't keep up with the other sections.
E-190 /Qu: Orchestration of sections with each other, is that a major
          problem?
E-191 /E: Right.
E-192 /Qu: She conducts with her hands the way an orchestra conductor
          conducts?
E-193 /E: No, just once in a while. She sings along, but quietly because
E-194 /   she wants to hear us.
E-195 /Qu: Right, how do you begin all at the same time, does she use her
          hands?
E-196 /E: I think, then, she uses her hands, and to cut it off.
E-197 /Qu: And the pianist is also keeping time?
E-198 /E: Uh-huh.
E-199 /Qu: Ah, are these religious songs?
E-200 /E: Some are religious, but some are Ukrainian folk songs, in
          Ukrainian.
E-201 /Qu: Um, what do you find rewarding about going there and doing
          that?
E-202 /E: I'd like to be in that group, when I heard them sing they sounded
E-203 /   really nice, so I think being in the group, I'd feel pretty good.
E-204 /Qu: Can you articulate what about being in that group would please
          you?
E-205 /E: They are well known, I want to get into something Ukrainian
E-206 /   like that, socializing with the other girls would be good too.
E-207 /Qu: What about the singing itself. Do you take great pleasure in it?
E-208 /E: I like singing, because I took piano lessons and I would hum
          along.
E-209 /Qu: You get a good feeling when the singing is harmonious and you
E-210 /   are a part of it? You are enjoying it?
E-211 /E: Oh yeah, uh-huh.
E-212 /Qu: Of these three motivations, which is the most predominant?
E-213 /E: I think, being in a Ukrainian choir.
E-214 /Qu: Participation in celebrating the ethnic community? And that
E-215 /   would rank above the socializing aspect, or being a member of
E-216 /   that group of girls, and the pure joy of singing part of it?
E-217 /E: Well, that's what I think.

E-218 /Qu: How do you make this assessment, can you think of anything that
E-219 / you've observed or heard that would lead you to think that?
E-220 /E: It seems they all want to continue being Ukrainian, I noticed
E-221 / a few that were at Ukrainian school, and so that is sort of part of it.
E-222 /Qu: Hmm. Now, how did this occasion end?
E-223 /E: Nine o'clock, she says okay, choir practice is finished. Sometimes
E-224 / she asks people to stay after. The people that have to stay, stay,
E-225 / and the rest leave.
E-226 /Qu: Thank you.

Exhibit F: "F's Move"

LINE#/SPEAKER: (QU = QUESTIONER; F = STUDENT F)

F-1 /Qu: I want to ask you about an occasion in which you participated,
F-2 / in which members of your family helped to move some goods. Is that all right?
F-3 /F: Yes.
F-4 /Qu: Now, first of all, when did this occasion take place?
F-5 /F: Last Saturday.
F-6 /Qu: Could you just tell me what it was in your own words?
F-7 /F: My sister was moving out of her house, back home so she needed
F-8 / some help moving furniture, and things, clothing. She got a mov-
F-9 / ing company to move really large things but the smaller items we helped her move.
F-10 /Qu: Who is "we"?
F-11 /F: My brother, his friend and my sister's husband and myself.
F-12 /Qu: So altogether that's five of you. How was this joint move arranged?
F-13 /F: My sister asked my brother and me to help her move. My
F-14 / brother's friend works for a truck company so he has access to
F-15 / large trucks. She asked if he would help her out, so he was given a call.
F-16 /Qu: So your sister gave your brother's friend a call?
F-17 /F: No, my sister gave my brother a call, in turn he gave his friend a call.
F-18 /Qu: And did your sister ask you directly?
F-19 /F: She was up at the house so she asked me. She came in the
F-20 / morning and said, "Are you going to help me move today?"
F-21 /Qu: Saturday morning. And prior to that you didn't know anything about it?
F-22 /F: Well I knew about it but I hadn't really offered my services as

		yet.
F-23	/Qu:	Did you offer your services when she asked you?
F-24	/F:	Of course.
F-25	/Qu:	Was a specific time arranged to make the move?
F-26	/F:	Yeah, it was to be ten thirty in the morning.
F-27	/Qu:	Did the friend with the truck have to be consulted?
F-28	/F:	Yes, that's when he could get the truck. And that would be the
F-29	/	most convenient time because after that my brother and his
F-30	/	friend and my sister's husband were going to the Argo game.
F-31	/Qu:	So before the Argo game but after when he could get the truck?
F-32	/F:	Yes.
F-33	/Qu:	Did he donate the truck because of his friendship with your brother?
F-34	/F:	Actually he is a friend of my sister's as well, a friend of the family.
F-35	/Qu:	The other four were getting ready when your sister asked you join?
F-36	/F:	Yes.
F-37	/Qu:	Was that because they saw they would need another pair of hands?
F-38	/F:	No, what they were moving I couldn't help with. It was the small
F-39	/	things like her clothes that I could carry in and help her with.
F-40	/Qu:	Did you go with them in the truck to load up?
F-41	/F:	No, my sister stayed home, the guys brought the stuff and left the
F-42	/	truck in the driveway with the things in it. I took in what I could
F-43	/	and had to stay around the house while they were at the game
F-44	/	so that someone could keep an eye on the furniture and the valuables in the truck.
F-45	/Qu:	So the moving didn't get finished before they went to the game?
F-46	/F:	No, they didn't finish it.
F-47	/Qu:	And then your job was to . . .
F-48	/F:	Take in what I could and keep an eye on the rest because no
F-49	/	one else was in the house at the time.
F-50	/Qu:	So you spent about how much time carrying things in?
F-51	/F:	Probably about fifteen minutes.
F-52	/Qu:	And then a period of time being on surveillance, just being on hand . . .
F-53	/F:	About four hours I would suppose.
F-54	/Qu:	And then your sister arrived, and did she start carrying things in?
F-55	/F:	No what we did, we figured the guys wouldn't be back for quite
F-56	/	a while and it looked like rain so I called a friend of mine who
F-57	/	works for a moving company and so he came over and helped us.
F-58	/Qu:	You and your sister and your friend carried the rest of the things in?
F-59	/F:	That's right.

F-60 /Qu: And when the original three movers got back from the game?
F-61 /F: They said, "Oh, where's all the furniture? How did it get in?"
F-62 /Qu: So you explained it to them. Why did your friend help?
F-63 /F: Well, he's an old boyfriend. He would help me out whenever he could.
F-64 /Qu: And you were asking him to help carry your sister's things in,
F-65 / not your things. So your sister was the beneficiary of this work
F-66 / by her sister and brother and husband, her brother's friend and her sister's friend?
F-67 /F: It was my other sister's husband.
F-68 /Qu: Oh. But the married sister wasn't involved. So your other sister's
F-69 / husband helped your sister to move too, partially helped, anyway.
F-70 /F: Mmm-hmm. Yes.
F-71 /Qu: Was anyone to blame for having left the stuff half moved in?
F-72 /F: Yeah, I was mad at that because I had plans to go out and I figured
F-73 / when the guys got back I would carry in what I could, they
F-74 / would take in the larger pieces and that would be it. But they
F-75 / pull up and say, "The furniture's here, let's go." I called my sister
F-76 / and said "What's going on here? Who's going to look after the
F-77 / truck? I'm supposed to go out." She says, "Can you do stick
F-78 / around until I get there?" So I said okay. She didn't get there till 4:30 and my plans were ruined.
F-79 /Qu: Did you feel obligated to do this because she was your sister?
F-80 /F: The way it is in our family is if you need a favor I'll do it.
F-81 /Qu: And she would do the same for you, you could expect?
F-82 /F: Yes, I would hope so.
F-83 /Qu: So when was the move completed?
F-84 /F: About five. But the guys didn't come back from the game until about seven.
F-85 /Qu: Did anything follow, a joint activity related to the moving?
F-86 /F: Yes, there were a few related arguments after that.
F-87 /Qu: What were they all about?
F-88 /F: Well, I was mad that my brother would leave the truck in the
F-89 / driveway and expect me to look after it all day. Who did he think
F-90 / was going to move it in? And my sister was kind of angry because
F-91 / one of her mirrors, a hand made stained glass mirror, got bro-
F-92 / ken. She wasn't too pleased about that.
F-93 /Qu: So that was the evaluative aftermath of that work. Was anyone
F-94 / concretely rewarded for having done any of this work?
F-95 /F: In material things? No.
F-96 /Qu: Was it either a thank you or whatever?
F-97 /F: It was a little of both. A thank you and whatever.

F-98 /Qu: Okay, thank you very much.

Exhibit G: "G's Sunday Service"

LINE#/SPEAKER: (QU = QUESTIONER; G = STUDENT G)

G-1 /Qu: I want to ask about the most recent religious ceremony you attended.
G-2 /G: Yes.
G-3 /Qu: First of all, what is the name of your Church?
G-4 /G: The Chinese Alliance Church of Toronto.
G-5 /Qu: What is the Church's religious denomination?
G-6 /G: Christian, interdenominational Protestant.
G-7 /Qu: Where is the meeting place for the Alliance Church?
G-8 /G: It's a church building on First Avenue in Broadview, in Toronto.
G-9 /Qu: Okay, when was the last time you attended a ceremony there?
G-10 /G: Last Sunday, the Sunday service.
G-11 /Qu: And, uh, how did you know that the Sunday service was going to happen?
G-12 /G: Because it is happening on every Sunday.
G-13 /Qu: And what time does it start?
G-14 /G: Eleven o'clock, but first we have fifteen minutes for singspiration.
G-15 /Qu: "Singspiration?" What's that?
G-16 /G: Just everybody singing hymns for inspiration before the service starts.
G-17 /Qu: Is it written anywhere that first comes "Singspiration?"
G-18 /G: Yes, a mimeographed bulletin, it's the first thing on the program.
G-19 /Qu: Did you actually go to the singspiration?
G-20 /G: Yes, I did.
G-21 /Qu: You intended to arrive at 10:45. How did you prepare?
G-22 /G: I woke up about ten o'clock, dress up, do the washing and go by subway.
G-23 /Qu: Did you dress in a special way?
G-24 /G: No, just as usual, as I would for school on weekdays.
G-25 /Qu: Did other people attending dress up more formally?
G-26 /G: Some of them are, and some don't.
G-27 /Qu: Did you travel on the subway to church alone or with someone?
G-28 /G: With my friends. I stayed in my friends' house during the weekend.
G-29 /Qu: So how many of you boarded the train together to go to church?
G-30 /G: Five, including me.
G-31 /Qu: What was the nature of your conversation on the journey?

G-32 /G: Well, just talking what we are going to do after the service.
G-33 /Qu: Right. What kind of things would you plan to do?
G-34 /G: Ah, we are going to have our lunch and then go shopping.
G-35 /Qu: When you arrived at the church building, was anybody already there?
G-36 /G: About forty other members, families who came earlier for Sunday school.
G-37 /Qu: Where do you enter the church?
G-38 /G: The main entrance, going in to the hall.
G-39 /Qu: Does it have a sign on the door, to say what it is?
G-40 /G: No, but there is a sign on top of the building.
G-41 /Qu: Is anyone from the public at large welcome to join the service?
G-42 /G: Yes.
G-43 /Qu: Do people often drop in?
G-44 /G: Not really, not on Sunday service but on evangelistic meetings.
G-45 /Qu: But Sunday service by and large it's only members who go?
G-46 /G: Yes.
G-47 /Qu: When your group entered, were those already there seated in chairs?
G-48 /G: Benches, in rows, with an aisle down the middle.
G-49 /Qu: What's at the front of the hall?
G-50 /G: A stage, a microphone, an altar, and an organ.
G-51 /Qu: Was there somebody playing the organ?
G-52 /G: Usually is.
G-53 /Qu: Were people seated in separate little family groups, or all together?
G-54 /G: All together, but in family groups, too.
G-55 /Qu: And how did you and your friends seat yourselves?
G-56 /G: As a group, all on one bench.
G-57 /Qu: By the time everyone had arrived, how many people were there?
G-58 /G: About one hundred and fifty.
G-59 /Qu: Has that pretty much filled the hall? Are all the benches full?
G-60 /G: Yes.
G-61 /Qu: And what happened next?
G-62 /G: We say prayers by ourselves.
G-63 /Qu: For how long?
G-64 /G: For about two minutes.
G-65 /Qu: And what happened at the end of that two minutes?
G-66 /G: We look at the program they handed us at the door, to see what's first.
G-67 /Qu: And what is first?
G-68 /G: Singspiration.

G-69 /Qu: And after that, what begins the service proper?
G-70 /G: We have a prayer by the chairman. Every Sunday, there's a new chairman.
G-71 /Qu: How is he selected?
G-72 /G: I don't know.
G-73 /Qu: And, would there be a prayer book out of which he reads?
G-74 /G: No, no, just in his own words, and we follow him.
G-75 /Qu: In his own words, but, how did you follow him?
G-76 /G: Just say amens, whenever you want.
G-77 /Qu: So people say "amen" whenever they feel it's appropriate?
G-78 /G: Yes, exactly.
G-79 /Qu: Is it a personal prayer, to describe his own spiritual experience?
G-80 /G: No, it's for all, for the church, just in his own words.
G-81 /Qu: What did the chairman pray for last Sunday?
G-82 /G: For the evangelistic meeting we are going to have this coming Sunday.
G-83 /Qu: He prayed that it would be a successful meeting?
G-84 /G: Yes.
G-85 /Qu: What, exactly did he say? Ah, did he speak in English?
G-86 /G: No, he spoke in Cantonese.
G-87 /Qu: In Cantonese. So it wouldn't help if you quoted him here [laughter].
G-88 /G: He hoped others, not only members, come to the evangelistic meeting.
G-89 /Qu: Let's go back for a minute. When you were on the train to church,
G-90 /   with your friends, did you speak in English, or in Cantonese?
G-91 /G: No, sometimes we spoke in English, sometimes we spoke in Mandarin.
G-92 /Qu: So, is everybody there trilingual in English, Mandarin, and Cantonese?
G-93 /G: Yes.
G-94 /Qu: When the chairman finishes his prayer, would you say "amen" in English?
G-95 /G: Yes, they did, it's more or less the same, "amen" is "amen."
G-96 /Qu: Okay, the last "amen" is said, then what happened?
G-97 /G: We're going to sing some gospel songs, from the hymnody.
G-98 /Qu: Is the song title in the program?
G-99 /G: Yes, and then the organist would start up the theme.
G-100 /Qu: Is the hymnody written in Cantonese?
G-101 /G: Each song is in English and Cantonese, both.
G-102 /Qu: Do you stand up to sing?
G-103 /G: Yes, we do, when the piano starts playing.

G-104 / Qu: So everyone stands up to sing, with the hymn book in hand?
G-105 / G: Yes that's right.
G-106 / Qu: Where were the hymn books situated?
G-107 / G: There's enough for everybody, just on the bench.
G-108 / Qu: Then you open it up to the number on the program, and start
G-109 / to sing. Is the singing in Cantonese and some in English?
G-110 / G: Yes, some are singing in Mandarin, too [laughter].
G-111 / Qu: That's really interesting! But it's not Mandarin in the book, is it?
G-112 / G: But the Chinese is the same, it's how you speak the characters.
G-113 / Qu: Is there harmony musically speaking? Do people sing in harmony?
G-114 / G: No, it's unison.
G-115 / Qu: Unison musically, but multi-lingual, interesting. Does everyone
G-116 / sing loud and lustily or are they dragged along like in some churches?
G-117 / G: They sing very loud.
G-118 / Qu: People really sing with enthusiasm. Ah, that's nice.
G-119 / G: Yes [laughter].
G-120 / Qu: You sing all the verses of a song, the music stops and everyone sits?
G-121 / G: Yes.
G-122 / Qu: What does it say next on the program?
G-123 / G: We're having a choir up on the stage, who will present a song, too.
G-124 / Qu: Did they get up from their seats and go up on the stage?
G-125 / G: They've been there all along, and went to their seats after the song.
G-126 / Qu: Does the choir sing in Cantonese?
G-127 / G: Sometimes they will sing in English.
G-128 / Qu: But they all sing in the same language when they sing?
G-129 / G: Yes.
G-130 / Qu: So the choir finishes its song and they sit down. Then what happened?
G-131 / G: The chairman will come up again and say, "Give the time to the pastor."
G-132 / Qu: Introduce the pastor. Is he ordained, a pastor by occupation?
G-133 / G: Yes, I think so.
G-134 / Qu: Does he wear a robe of any sort?
G-131 / G: No, just a suit with tie.
G-136 / Qu: Yes. All of us pastors have ties [laughter]. So what does he do?
G-137 / G: He will give out the message.
G-138 / Qu: Does it take very long?

G-139 /G: It's about forty-five minutes.
G-140 /Qu: In what language does he speak?
G-141 /G: In Cantonese.
G-142 /Qu: He lectures in Cantonese for forty-five minutes. Does he quote the
G-143 / Bible and interpret biblical passages?
G-144 /G: Yes, he does.
G-145 /Qu: Does everyone carefully listen to what he's saying, or not?
G-146 /G: Not everyone is listening. Sometimes, we are very sleepy [laughter].
G-147 /Qu: Yes.
G-148 /G: Because that's too long.
G-149 /Qu: Your attention goes off. Luckily, they don't ask questions [laughter].
G-150 /G: No, we always look at our watch.
G-151 /Qu: Uh-huh. The demeanor of the congregation, during the forty-five-
G-152 / minute message, are they keeping the children quiet, whispering?
G-152 /G: No, they're usually very quiet. Some are falling asleep [laughter].
G-153 /Qu: Then what happens? How does he end his message?
G-154 /G: He prays.
G-155 /Qu: Okay, do people say amen to his prayers as they did to the chairman?
G-156 /G: He just say "amen" at the end, and then give the announcements
G-157 / about what happened this week.
G-158 /Qu: And then?
G-159 /G: Uh, the pastor will come up again for the blessing.
G-160 /Qu: And after the blessing?
G-161 /G: Just before the end we have the last hymn. Oh! Before the hymn, we
G-162 / have an offering.
G-163 /Qu: Ah, the crucial part that you left out [laughter]. How does it work?
G-164 /G: The ushers pass around the red velvet bags.
G-165 /Qu: Do people put cash into those bags?
G-166 /G: Yes, most put in cash, in an envelope.
G-167 /Qu: With the program you are given an envelope?
G-168 /G: I keep some at home so I put the money in before the service.
G-169 /Qu: So they put money in envelopes, and then they collect it at the back?
G-170 /G: Yes, then comes a hymn, and then the blessing.
G-171 /Qu: And where does the pastor go after the blessing?
G-172 /G: He went to the exit, and he says good-bye to us.
G-173 /Qu: Shakes hands with each person as they come out?

G-174/G: Yes, and just some greeting.
G-175/Qu: Do people stand outside and make plans for the weekend and such?
G-176/G: Yes, they do. And me and my friends go downtown for lunch.
G-177/Qu: Okay. Just off the top of your head, why do you go to service?
G-178/G: Because I go every week.
G-179/Qu: Ah, and because you go every week, you go every week?
G-180/G: Yes.
G-181/Qu: That's fine. Thank you very much.

Exhibit H: "H's Football Game"

LINE#/SPEAKER: (QU = QUESTIONER; H = STUDENT H)

H-1   /Qu: I understand you attended a sporting event recently?
H-2   /H: Yes, I did.
H-3   /Qu: Could you tell me what it was?
H-4   /H: It was a football game between the Argos and the Calgary Stampeders.
H-5   /Qu: When was this, and how were you made aware that you were going?
H-6   /H: A week and a half ago. My father always buys season tickets and
H-7   /   when he can't go he gives them to whoever wants them.
H-8   /Qu: So how did it happen in this specific instance?
H-9   /H: A couple of days before my dad confronted me with these
H-10 /   tickets and said, "There's a football game on Saturday and I can't go, do you want them?"
H-11 /Qu: How many tickets were there?
H-12 /H: Two.
H-13 /Qu: And were there other possible candidates he could have given them to?
H-14 /H: Yes. My sister, my uncle; I guess I was just the first one he came to.
H-15 /Qu: Okay, so what did you say?
H-16 /H: I said sure I'll take them.
H-17 /Qu: You took the tickets. What did you do next with regard to the game?
H-18 /H: I phoned my boyfriend, Ken, to see if he could go, and he said yes.
H-19 /Qu: What did you ask him exactly, did he know the time and day of the game?
H-20 /H: No, he asked me and it says on the tickets the time, the date,
H-21 /   where we sat and where we entered.

H-22	/Qu:	What arrangements did you make to go to the game?
H-23	/H:	I asked Dad if I could take the car and asked Ken to drive
H-24	/	cause I couldn't even make it down to the C.N.E. stadium.
H-25	/Qu:	When did you ask your dad for the car?
H-26	/H:	The same day he gave me the tickets. I said, "Okay, if I'm going
H-27	/	to the game I'll need the car." When I called Ken I told him I'd pick him up.
H-28	/Qu:	What time was all this supposed to happen.?
H-29	/H:	One o'clock. We were late, we didn't really get going till about 12:30.
H-30	/Qu:	By getting going you mean you didn't get to his place till 12:30?
H-31	/H:	Yes.
H-32	/Qu:	Did you dress in any particular way beforehand?
H-33	/H:	No, just jeans and a shirt, oh, and a sweater.
H-34	/Qu:	So, okay, then you went and picked him up and he drove.
H-35	/H:	To the stadium at the C.N.E.
H-36	/Qu:	Okay, and where did you park?
H-37	/H:	Oh, we parked at the Ontario Place lot and walked over.
H-38	/Qu:	And how far a walk is that?
H-39	/H:	Oh, about a quarter or half a mile.
H-40	/Qu:	So about a ten-fifteen minute walk. You approached the stadium
H-41	/	on foot. Where did you enter the stadium?
H-42	/H:	The gates are numbered and your ticket says which one to go
H-43	/	through in relation to what section you're to sit in, we were gate 11.
H-44	/Qu:	So you got into the stadium and found the game had already started?
H-45	/H:	Yes but we already knew it would have. So we went and found
H-46	/	our section and our seats which are all numbered and on your ticket.
H-47	/Qu:	Were all the seats around you full?
H-48	/H:	Oh, yes.
H-49	/Qu:	Was there a big crowd? How many people were there?
H-50	/H:	Well over ten thousand, I'd guess.
H-51	/Qu:	Were they all yelling and screaming a lot?
H-52	/H:	Oh, yes.
H-53	/Qu:	What was the first thing you saw occurring once you were seated?
H-54	/H:	The Argos had the ball and they were making their way to the goal line.
H-55	/Qu:	Did you recognize the different colors of uniforms of the two teams?
H-56	/H:	Yeah, the Argos are blue and white and the Stampeders are red

		and yellow.
H-57	/Qu:	And, um, could you make out the details of the different plays?
H-58	/H:	Well we were close enough but I'm half blind, I can hardly see
H-59	/	where the ball is.
H-60	/Qu:	Do you have a pretty good working knowledge of the game of football?
H-61	/H:	Fairly, yeah, first downs and stuff like that.
H-62	/Qu:	So you don't need someone to explain to you what's happening?
H-63	/H:	Well, the odd time I'll ask Ken, "Hey what did he do that for?"
H-64	/Qu:	So you can ask Ken because he knows.
H-65	/H:	He played football, he pretends he knows anyway; he fools me [laughter].
H-66	/Qu:	Okay, is the game played in sections?
H-67	/H:	Quarters they switch sides, half time a little marching band comes out.
H-68	/Qu:	In between the halves there's a band that comes out?
H-69	/H:	Yeah, this one was from Ohio, a high school band, they were really good.
H-70	/Qu:	And what else happens during the half time?
H-71	/H:	Everyone gets up to get something to eat and go to the bathroom,
H-72	/	go out to the car to get their mickey, everyone gets up anyway to stretch.
H-73	/Qu:	Did you go to get food or . . .
H-74	/H:	No, we wait until the little boys come around and sell things.
H-75	/Qu:	So during half time you didn't go anywhere?
H-76	/H:	No, you can't move, everyone's packed together.
H-77	/Qu:	And no alcoholic beverages sold there so people go to their cars
H-78	/	and get whatever they want?
H-79	/H:	Yeah, right.
H-80	/Qu:	Is that supposedly illegal?
H-81	/H:	Oh, yes. We saw some guy get arrested when we were there too.
H-82	/Qu:	Oh, really, what was he doing?
H-83	/H:	He was further down in front, and all of a sudden we saw
H-84	/	five policemen come up and grab him. Maybe they saw him with a bottle or something.
H-85	/Qu:	So you think that he was arrested for alcohol?
H-86	/H:	Yeah, well he seemed pretty wasted when he came up the stairs.
H-87	/Qu:	Um, other than breaking the law by drinking alcohol, were
H-88	/	there other rules of decorum that you could see being either broken or observed?
H-89	/H:	Well there was one sort of heckler, he was drunk too, but he
H-90	/	was commenting on every single play, "oh you goof," "oh this,"

H-91 /		"oh that"; people were getting aggravated and the police took him away, too.
H-92 /Qu:		What were they getting aggravated by, using obscene language, too loud?
H-93 /H:		No, it's just so jerky, you just don't do that.
H-94 /Qu:		What do you do?
H-95 /H:		Well you can cheer and everything, and some people do heckle,
H-96 /		but not constantly, you don't comment on every single play.
H-97 /Qu:		He was over the line. Would not cheering be over the line in
H-98 /		another direction, sitting there primly in your seat like at a church service?
H-99 /H:		No, no, there are quite a few wives that go probably because of
H-100/		their husbands' tickets, don't understand what's going on and just sit there.
H-101/Qu:		Do they talk to each other?
H-102/H:		Well it's, "What did he do? Oh, good. Clap." Not like the guys.
H-103/		There are some women that are really into it too, but not many.
H-104/Qu:		Who won the game?
H-105/H:		The Argos, a good game, at the last minute they scored a touch
H-106/		down, and everybody was up on their seats and cheering; it was good.
H-107/Qu:		Have you watched other games on television?
H-108/H:		Yes.
H-109/Qu:		What is the difference between that and going to the game as you did?
H-110/H:		You can get right in with the fan participation, there's no comparison.
H-111/Qu:		How much did your tickets cost?
H-112/H:		Probably around ten dollars each.
H-113/Qu:		Were those the least or most expensive?
H-114/H:		They're around the middle, they range from seven-fifty to fifteen.
H-115/Qu:		Did you get the impression that the teams were aware of the crowd?
H-116/H:		Yeah, on interceptions and things where the team gets excited
H-117/		and so does the crowd, I think they feel it a lot; I never used to
H-118/		think it made much difference but you hear them comment how important fans are.
H-119/Qu:		The fact it was the home crowd stimulated the Argos to higher efforts?
H-120/H:		Yes, I guess.
H-121/Qu:		Were there any out-of-town fans for the other team?

H-122/H: Just scattered, when it's Hamilton there is a big section of them
H-123/ and there are verbal battles, but not that many Calgary fans.

H-124/Qu: Do you think they were squelched because it was an all Argo crowd?
H-125/H: Oh, yes.
H-126/Qu: Did people carry pennants or wave banners or anything like that?
H-127/H: Oh yeah, throwing toilet paper and waving little banners, and horns.
H-128/Qu: Were a lot of people there dressed in Argo colors?
H-129/H: No, but you can tell a lot of the men used to play football in
H-130/ school because they wear their football sweaters, it's really funny.
H-131/Qu: What happened when the gun sounded for the end of the game?
H-132/H: We missed that too, its such a screw up getting out of that place,
H-133/ so when we saw the Argos were obviously going to win, we got started out.
H-134/Qu: Were there other people avoiding the rush and leaving early?
H-135/H: Oh, yeah, cause its not worth it getting caught in the traffic.
H-136/Qu: From the time you got there till you left, how much time had passed?
H-137/H: Three or four hours.
H-138/Qu: And during that time you stayed mostly in your seats?
H-139/H: Yes.
H-140/Qu: Where were your seats in relation to the field?
H-141/H: Near the middle, thirty rows up, with fifty or sixty rows behind us.
H-142/Qu: Right in the middle of the crowd. Was the sound pretty overwhelming?
H-143/H: Yeah, it was great. It's a real thrill, being in that crowd.
H-144/Qu: Okay, thank you very much.

Exhibit I: "I's Wedding"

LINE#/SPEAKER: (QU = QUESTIONER; I = STUDENT I)

I-1 /Qu: We're going to talk about a wedding you attended recently, all right?
I-2 /I: Okay.
I-3 /Qu: Whose wedding was it, and what was their relationship to you?
I-4 /I: It was my boyfriend's friends' wedding, they were no relationship
I-5 / to me, they were just friends that I had met through my boyfriend.
I-6 /Qu: Okay, and you knew them as friends also?

I-7	/I:	Yes, but I didn't know them very well, not at all.
I-8	/Qu:	So you were attending as it were, via your boyfriend's involvement
I-9	/	with them as close friends of his?
I-10	/I:	Right.
I-11	/Qu:	Okay, uh, where was this wedding to take place?
I-12	/I:	The church part was someplace in Mississauga, I don't know
I-13	/	exactly, and the reception was at the Skyline Hotel, at the airport.
I-14	/Qu:	Just about the church part, how did you know where and when?
I-15	/I:	My boyfriend informed me of everything.
I-16	/Qu:	Did he receive a printed invitation?
I-17	/I:	He was part of the wedding party as an usher. So he was asked,
I-18	/	and I was asked too, and then they sent us an invitation.
I-19	/Qu:	Uh, were you asked to be a part of the wedding party also?
I-20	/I:	No.
I-21	/Qu:	And, uh, when were you supposed to arrive for the ceremony?
I-22	/I:	The church part?
I-23	/Qu:	Yeah.
I-24	/I:	The ceremony was at two on Saturday afternoon, and we were
I-25	/	supposed to be there at about fifteen minutes before two o'clock.
I-26	/Qu:	Okay, and how did you dress for this occasion?
I-27	/I:	I had a dress, a very nice, looking dress, formal dress, I don't know.
I-28	/Qu:	And your boyfriend had to wear a tuxedo?
I-29	/I:	Yeah, a tuxedo.
I-30	/Qu:	And you dressed up to his tuxedo?
I-31	/I:	Kind of. Yeah.
I-32	/Qu:	Did you have anything special done with your hair, or your makeup?
I-33	/I:	No, I just washed my hair and placed a flower on the side of it.
I-34	/Qu:	Where did you get the flower?
I-35	/I:	I had bought one before for another wedding, so I wore the same flower.
I-36	/Qu:	And, uh, you and your boyfriend arrived, uh, fifteen minutes before?
I-37	/I:	Yeah, with another couple. My boyfriend's brother was also an
I-38	/	usher, and his girlfriend came with us.
I-39	/Qu:	Whose car did you go in?
I-40	/I:	His girlfriend's.
I-41	/Qu:	So she drove you to the wedding. What happened when you got there?
I-42	/I:	We got to the church fifteen minutes early like we were supposed
I-43	/	to and we waited, the bride and groom were late, so, everybody

I-44	/	was just waiting for the bride to come.
I-45	/Qu:	Who was everybody?
I-46	/I:	All the rest of the ushers and usherettes that were there early
I-47	/	so they could prepare themselves to walk down the aisle and stuff like that.
I-48	/Qu:	Who else showed up?
I-49	/I:	The best man, the maid of honor, and just guests, friends
I-50	/	and relatives of both the bride and groom.
I-51	/Qu:	Did the guests seat themselves on opposite sides of the aisle as
I-52	/	his relatives and friends and her relatives and friends?
I-53	/I:	Yes, but the ushers were ushering the guests to their seats, they
I-54	/	would ask, "Whose side are you on?"
I-55	/Qu:	"Whose side are you on?" The battle begins! [laughter].
I-56	/I:	So everybody was waiting for the bride and groom to come, as
I-57	/	soon as the guests came they were seated and ah, the ushers and
I-58	/	bridesmaids got their act together and waited for the bride,
I-59	/	and did their procession down the aisle, the priest was ready, everything went ahead as planned.
I-60	/Qu:	Where was the groom when the bride got there?
I-61	/I:	Sitting down at the front, where the priest was, and then the
I-62	/	bridesmaids came with their ushers and then the bride came
I-63	/	with the two little girls and two little boys.
I-64	/Qu:	Was there music?
I-65	/I:	The organ was playing "Here Comes the Bride" in the background.
I-66	/Qu:	Did the bride's father accompany her and "give her away"?
I-67	/I:	Yeah, the father gave her to the groom, he took her and they
I-68	/	went and faced the priest.
I-69	/Qu:	At which point the priest pronounced the standard service?
I-70	/I:	First he said a normal mass, a Sunday Mass, and then he said
I-71	/	"Do you take so and so," and all that stuff, then the thing about the rings.
I-72	/Qu:	Did they exchange rings, back and forth?
I-73	/I:	Yeah, then he said, "I now pronounce you husband and wife."
I-74	/	And that was it, that was the end.
I-75	/Qu:	Does he kiss the bride?
I-76	/I:	Yeah, and then they allowed for the bride to kiss her mother
I-77	/	and father. And mother-in-law and father-in-law, and shook
I-78	/	hands with the ushers and bridesmaids, then they went back,
I-79	/	shook the priest's hand, they signed the wedding certificate, or
I-80	/	whatever they call it, and that was it, and there was no throwing of confetti in the church or outside.

I-81	/Qu:	Nobody threw rice or anything like that?
I-82	/I:	The priest wouldn't allow it. He stated after the wedding, he
I-83	/	didn't even wait one second, "Please, no throwing of confetti!"
I-84	/Qu:	So the bride and groom proceeded down the aisle and out of the church?
I-85	/I:	Yeah, then the ushers and bridesmaids and then the rest of the guests.
I-86	/Qu:	And the bride and the groom, were they waiting outside?
I-87	/I:	Yes, they were having pictures taken.
I-88	/Qu:	And everybody congratulating them before going off to the reception?
I-89	/I:	Right, and then an hour and a half of photo sessions with the
I-90	/	bride and groom and ushers and the immediate families.
I-91	/Qu:	That's longer than the ceremony took [laughter].
I-92	/I:	Yeah, the ceremony was only about an hour.
I-93	/Qu:	Thank you very much.

Exhibit J: "J's Appointment"

LINE#/SPEAKER: (QU = QUESTIONER; J = STUDENT J)

J-1	/Qu:	I want to interview you about a recent visit to your doctor. First
J-2	/	of all, can you tell me something of how it got set up?
J-3	/J:	I have every six months an appointment, so I made this one in May.
J-4	/Qu:	How did you remember it for so long?
J-5	/J:	The nurse gave me a little doctor's card, I kept it in my wallet,
J-6	/	and I open my wallet every day and so the card faces me.
J-7	/Qu:	When was the appointment for?
J-8	/J:	Two-fifteen on Tuesday.
J-9	/Qu:	Did you have to leave off work or school?
J-10	/J:	Yes, I left work early at one o'clock.
J-11	/Qu:	Did you dress or otherwise prepare yourself that morning for
J-12	/	the fact that you were going to the doctor later that day?
J-13	/J:	No, because I wore a skirt and blouse to work so I was presentable.
J-14	/Qu:	You would have felt it appropriate to dress presentably for the doctor?
J-15	/J:	Yes.
J-16	/Qu:	How did you go from work to your doctor?
J-17	/J:	I drove in my car, and parked near his office.
J-18	/Qu:	What did you do when you got to the office?
J-19	/J:	I entered, introduced myself to the secretary, who was new,

J-20	/	I had not met her before, and then I waited until the patient was out.
J-21	/Qu:	What did you say to the secretary?
J-22	/J:	My name and that I was there for my appointment, and she had
J-23	/	it written down that I was to be there at two-fifteen.
J-24	/Qu:	And then what did you do?
J-25	/J:	I sat down in the waiting room and read a magazine.
J-26	/Qu:	And what ended your reading and waiting?
J-27	/J:	The doctor entered with his patient, they booked a new appoint-
J-28	/	ment, and then I went into the office with the doctor.
J-29	/Qu:	His inner office . . . is that where he has his desk and such?
J-30	/J:	It's the examination room and his office.
J-31	/Qu:	And then how did the two of you station yourselves in that room?
J-32	/J:	He sat behind his desk and I sat directly in front of his desk.
J-33	/Qu:	Did he ask you to sit down or did you just take that seat?
J-34	/J:	He didn't say, he just pointed to the chair and I sat myself down.
J-35	/Qu:	Then what happened?
J-36	/J:	He took out my file, read what I told him the last appointment,
J-37	/	and then he asked how I had been the last few months.
J-38	/Qu:	And what did you reply to him?
J-39	/J:	I had been fine, no problems.
J-40	/Qu:	Then what did he say?
J-41	/J:	He asked me what was my summer job and if I was returning
J-42	/	to school in fall and then he started asking health questions
J-43	/	because he was ready to do an examination. He said I could go
J-44	/	behind the curtain and undress into the white gown. So I did, and then I announced that I was ready.
J-45	/Qu:	And what happened then?
J-46	/J:	I was sitting on the table, and he came around to test my heart.
J-47	/Qu:	How was he dressed at this time?
J-48	/J:	He had the white medical garb over a suit.
J-49	/Qu:	During the examination, did he speak with you, or did he seem
J-50	/	to be communicating with your physical state directly?
J-51	/J:	Yes, both, directly and he asked questions.
J-52	/Qu:	Like, "Does this hurt?" And he told you when to breathe, and so on?
J-53	/J:	Right.
J-54	/Qu:	Did you feel any sense of embarrassment, or threat, at all?
J-55	/J:	No, not at all.
J-56	/Qu:	What happened next?
J-57	/J:	After he did the complete physical, he said I could get dressed.
J-58	/Qu:	During the course of the examination, did he tell you any

		conclusions?
J-59	/J:	Yes. He said that everything had gotten better from the last time.
J-60	/Qu:	What did he do next?
J-61	/J:	He left me to get dressed. When I had gotten dressed and back
J-62	/	out, he was still writing on my file.
J-63	/Qu:	Then what happened?
J-64	/J:	I sat down near his desk, and he announced he was pleased with
J-65	/	what he found, asked if I had any questions; I didn't. Then he
J-66	/	began to tell me what he wanted me to do next, like procedures
J-67	/	to do. I had to go to the hospital for blood tests, he told me
		those procedures to follow.
J-68	/Qu:	Okay, and that was the end of the conversation?
J-69	/J:	Yes, then we walked back out to the waiting, and he wished me
J-70	/	well in starting school.
J-71	/Qu:	He walked out with you, as he had walked out with the previous patient?
J-72	/J:	Yes.
J-73	/Qu:	Was there someone waiting in the waiting room?
J-74	/J:	Yes, there was an elderly gentleman waiting.
J-75	/Qu:	Okay, did you go right out the door or did you go to the nurse?
J-76	/J:	To the nurse because she had to give me a form to get these blood tests.
J-77	/Qu:	How were you paying for this visit? By Ontario Health Insurance Plan?
J-78	/J:	Oh, we skipped that. When I first got there I had to give the
J-79	/	nurse my new OHIP number because I was not on my father's anymore.
J-80	/Qu:	And that was payment. Then when you got the blood test
J-81	/	information from the nurse, you left?
J-82	/J:	She told me I had to phone in November to book another
J-83	/	appointment for January, and that was it, and I went back to my car.
J-84	/Qu:	Thank you very much.

Exhibit K: "K's French Class"

LINE#/SPEAKER: (QU = QUESTIONER; K = STUDENT K)

K-1	/Qu:	I want to ask about the class you attended most recently before this.
K-2	/K:	That was this morning, ten to twelve, French 423.
K-3	/Qu:	Where was it held?
K-4	/K:	In room 281 in the North Building.

K-5	/Qu:	Is it one of your required subjects?
K-6	/K:	Yes, I'm specializing in French.
K-7	/Qu:	So it's a four hundred course which means it's an advanced class?
K-8	/K:	Yes, supposedly.
K-9	/Qu:	Um, and what did you do before going to that class?
K-10	/K:	To go to school, I left my house and caught the bus, got to
K-11	/	Islington subway, another bus to campus, to the cafeteria, got
K-12	/	a coffee, waited until ten o'clock and then I walked up to class.
K-13	/Qu:	And how often does this class meet?
K-14	/K:	Once a week, on Thursday.
K-15	/Qu:	Was there anyone already there when you arrived?
K-16	/K:	Yes, I was the last one to arrive.
K-17	/Qu:	How did you know that?
K-18	/K:	I glanced around the room, and it's only a small class, there are
K-19	/	only ten people in it.
K-20	/Qu:	Was the professor there?
K-21	/K:	No, not yet. She always comes late, that's why I took my time going up.
K-22	/Qu:	Do you have a particular seat that you usually sit in?
K-23	/K:	Generally, yes. It's an oval table and I sit at one end, directly in
K-24	/	front of the prof.
K-25	/Qu:	So she sits at the other narrow end of the oval?
K-26	/K:	Right. And the others sit along the sides.
K-27	/Qu:	What did you bring with you for this class?
K-28	/K:	Books, pencils and papers. We're doing one play right now,
K-29	/	so that's the text I brought, and my notebook.
K-30	/Qu:	Do you dress in any particular way to go to these classes?
K-31	/K:	No, not really, just very normal attire, casually.
K-32	/Qu:	Had you prepared in advance for the class in any way?
K-33	/K:	I just re-read some of the sections that she had asked us to re-read.
K-34	/Qu:	Was there any conversation before the teacher arrived?
K-35	/K:	Yes, in little groups, in twosomes and threesomes, and then
K-36	/	there were a few oddballs. I spoke to the girls closest, who I have lunch with.
K-37	/Qu:	The teacher arrived at the door of the classroom and what did she do?
K-38	/K:	She wished us the time of day and went to her seat. In French
K-39	/	she said, "Bonjour."
K-40	/Qu:	Does she conduct the class in French, and expect you to speak French?
K-41	/K:	Yes, apart from any whispers, they're in English.

K-42 /Qu: Then what happened after she took her seat?
K-43 /K: She started to take her things out of her briefcase, and then she
K-44 / went into her lecture. Oh! Tell a lie, there were two presenta-
K-45 / tions today, so somebody else started off the class.
K-46 /Qu: How did they know they were to start?
K-47 /K: She said, "We're to have two presentations today. Kim, would
K-48 / you like to start?" And Kim went ahead with her presentation.
K-49 /Qu: When she said, "Kim, would you like to," did Kim have a choice?
K-50 /K: No, she didn't. It was just a form of politeness, I guess.
K-51 /Qu: In fact it was a command?
K-52 /K: Yes, but in French you wouldn't say that. The French language is
K-53 / supposedly more polite than the English.
K-54 /Qu: Did Kim move her location in the room?
K-55 /K: No, she stayed where she was and then she pulled out her
K-56 / papers and started her presentation.
K-57 /Qu: How long did it last?
K-58 /K: About ten minutes.
K-59 /Qu: Did you and other students take notes on that?
K-60 /K: No. Well, we listened and took notes when appropriate.
K-61 /Qu: When she was finished what happened?
K-62 /K: The professor asked for any questions, and there weren't any,
K-63 / so we went along to the next presentation.
K-64 /Qu: When you speak to the professor in class, how do students refer to her?
K-65 /K: We refer to her as Madame C.
K-66 /Qu: And how does she refer to you?
K-67 /K: As Mademoiselle R. By your last name.
K-68 /Qu: Hmm. So did she actually say, then, "Kim, would you like to start?"
K-69 /K: She did. That's odd! Maybe she knew her from another class
K-70 / or something, because she addresses me as Mademoiselle R. Maybe she doesn't like me.
K-71 /Qu: Maybe there's a special naming relationship with Kim?
K-72 /K: Yeah, maybe, because I've really only heard her say Kim.
K-73 /Qu: What happened next?
K-74 /K: After the first one the second girl did her presentation.
K-75 /Qu: How was she introduced, do you recall?
K-76 /K: She's a married lady, so she's "Madame Evans."
K-77 /Qu: And then was there another request for questions?
K-78 /K: Yes, but this time the professor had a question, and then she lectured.
K-79 /Qu: Did you all take notes?

K-80 /K: Yes, we tried to but she goes at an awful speed.
K-81 /Qu: Very fast?
K-82 /K: Yes, but she repeats everything ten times over and she more or
K-83 / less refers to old essays by students and critics. She never seems
K-84 / to have her own notes and her desk is scattered with these old essays or books.
K-85 /Qu: How long did this last?
K-86 /K: For another, I'd say, forty minutes and then we took a break.
K-87 /Qu: How was this break announced?
K-88 /K: She looked at her watch and said, "We ought to stop for a break now."
K-89 /Qu: Did she congregate with the students outside?
K-90 /K: No, she goes straight to her office, probably to hang up her coat.
K-91 /Qu: How long does the break last?
K-92 /K: About fifteen minutes, then we start again just like before the break.
K-93 /Qu: Is there any kind of roll call?
K-94 /K: Oh yes, just before break she shouts out the names from index cards.
K-95 /Qu: How is the end signaled?
K-96 /K: She tells us what we'll be doing the following week. She starts
K-97 / folding up her papers and putting away her books, then we
K-98 / leave, except for the "eagers" who stay behind to talk to her, just one or two.
K-99 /Qu: Okay, thank you.

Exhibit L: "L's Confession"

LINE#/SPEAKER: (QU = QUESTIONER; L = STUDENT L)

L-1 /Qu: You said you'd tell us about an occasion you participated in recently?
L-2 /L: Last Sunday, it's called a confession, I went to church to confess.
L-3 /Qu: Did you tell anybody you were going?
L-4 /L: Yeah, my parents made me go actually. The day before, they said
L-5 / tomorrow we're going to church and we have to go to confes-
L-6 / sion because it's Easter season or Lent, I don't know.
L-7 /Qu: And what church is this?
L-8 /L: Croatian Martyrs. It's Catholic.
L-9 /Qu: How often do you go?
L-10 /L: Church almost every Sunday and confession, I guess Christmas and Easter.

L-11	/Qu:	So Sunday Morning you got ready. Did you have breakfast at home first?
L-12	/L:	No, I didn't have time because I woke up late.
L-13	/Qu:	What time was late?
L-14	/L:	We had to be at mass at 9:30, so confession was before that. My
L-15	/	parents wanted to be early because there is a lineup. So we had
L-16	/	to be there by about nine so left around quarter to nine which
L-17	/	meant I had to be ready by 8:30. I got up around 7 and I should of gotten up around 6:30.
L-18	/Qu:	Okay, and did you dress special for this occasion?
L-19	/L:	I dressed up more than I would for school, like a skirt and a blouse.
L-20	/Qu:	And who constitutes your family?
L-21	/L:	My father, my mother, my little brother and myself.
L-22	/Qu:	So the four of you had to drive to church?
L-23	/L:	My father drove, then he parked in the church parking lot
L-24	/	and we all walked in together.
L-25	/Qu:	Describe the church building.
L-26	/L:	It's brown brick, there's two entryways, one you go downstairs
L-27	/	and you have a banquet room for weddings and parties, and
L-28	/	another entryway, there's a hall, and there's two sets of large
L-29	/	doors. Then you enter and there's a big church about four
L-30	/	times the size of this room, and there's an altar at the front, doors
L-31	/	to the right and there's little rooms and that's where you go in for confession. You line up in front of them.
L-32	/Qu:	And how many people were on that line?
L-33	/L:	When we got there, five people in front of us, but it accumu-
L-34	/	lated to maybe fifty people behind us. My dad didn't get in line
L-31	/	because he had confessed the week before, so it was my brother, myself, and my mother.
L-36	/Qu:	How long did each of the people ahead of you take?
L-37	/L:	About five minutes each, I was watching my watch.
L-38	/Qu:	Your brother went in? Did he tell you what he said, before or after?
L-39	/L:	No, it's private.
L-40	/Qu:	What did you do when he came out?
L-41	/L:	I open the door and walk into this little cubicle, as big as a bathroom.
L-42	/Qu:	Is there a place to sit down?
L-43	/L:	You kneel. There's a little bench where you kneel and there's
L-44	/	a mesh in front of you, behind it there's a priest and he's sitting down.

L-45 /Qu: How big is this mesh?
L-46 /L: About two by two feet, just big enough to cover where you are
L-47 / kneeling, so the priest can't see you; he can, but he doesn't really

L-48 / look. You can see him, but the mesh you can sort of see through, but not really.
L-49 /Qu: You're kneeling facing him through the mesh, and he's facing you?
L-50 /L: No, he's sort of facing the wall, so you're facing his profile, like.
L-51 /Qu: And so then you speak directly into this mesh, into his ear?
L-52 /L: Yeah.
L-53 /Qu: What did you say to him?
L-54 /L: In Croatian, so I have to translate: "I'm here to confess my sins,
L-55 / last time I was here was Christmas." He says, "Go on, tell me what
L-56 / you did," and you tell him, you go by the Ten Commandments.
L-57 /Qu: You tell him in detail which commandments you broke?
L-58 /L: Yeah. Like I made my parents mad often, once, or frequently,
L-59 / you don't say how many times or exactly what you did.
L-60 /Qu: So its how many times you violated each commandment. What does he say?
L-61 /L: Each one he doesn't say anything, he waits till you tell him everything.
L-62 /Qu: Ah-ha. And does he say, "Is that everything?"
L-63 /L: Yeah. Then he asks you if you pray regularly, and according to
I-64 / the sins you told him, he tells you why its important not to do
L-65 / that, why you should do certain prayers, and that's it. Then he
L-66 / tells you to say a little prayer to confess your sins and he mumbles something in Latin.
L-67 /Qu: So he tells you prayers you have to say?
L-68 /L: Depending on what you said, how many Hail Marys and Our
L-69 / Fathers to say. Then he asks you if you understand. You say yes
L-70 / or no, usually yes. Then you just say good-bye and that's it.
L-71 /Qu: And who speaks last?
L-72 /L: He does. He just says, "Peace be with you," and that's it.
L-73 /Qu: Do you know how long yours lasted?
L-74 /L: Yeah, about three and a half minutes.
L-75 /Qu: Shorter than most. Does that mean you had fewer sins to confess?
L-76 /L: Not necessarily. They could take longer because they may not
L-77 / have known how to say it in Croatian as fast as I do.
L-78 /Qu: Is there anything you're supposed to confess you don't think is sinful?

L-79 /L: No.
L-80 /Qu: By your own standards these are legitimate to confess. Is it your
L-81 /   feeling it helps you to get these things off your mind to confess
            them?
L-82 /L: No, I don't see the purpose of it.
L-83 /Qu: So it doesn't relieve guilt, and his explanation of why you
L-84 /   shouldn't do them isn't really educational at all?
L-85 /L: And I know why I shouldn't, so . . .
L-86 /Qu: So in that sense it's purely ritual gesture for you?
L-87 /L: Yeah. I think to satisfy my parents.
L-88 /Qu: When you are married and have kids, will you make your kids
            do this?
L-89 /L: Yeah.
L-90 /Qu: Why?
L-91 /L: Just for tradition. I don't know, same reasons my parents make
            me go.
L-92 /Qu: Okay, thank you.

Exhibit M: "M's Hearing"

LINE#/SPEAKER: (QU = QUESTIONER; M = STUDENT M)

M-1   /Qu: Tell us about a court session in which you recently participated?
M-2   /M: It was through my summer job. I was an investigator for Simpsons
M-3   /   store and we caught some shoplifters for theft over two hun-
M-4   /   dred, so we've gone to court. They were charged, there
M-5   /   was one court hearing on September 5th, it's been remanded
            to November 13th, I think, we're going back.
M-6   /Qu: On this September 5th occasion, when was the session supposed
            to begin?
M-7   /M: At two o'clock, it was on a Friday.
M-8   /Qu: Were you going to be paid for the hours you spent in court?
M-9   /M: Yes.
M-10 /Qu: And, um, were you supposed to make any preparations before
            you went?
M-11 /M: I went up to our security office and re-read our sheets, they're
M-12 /   called dope sheets, that we had written down our case on, to
M-13 /   familiarize ourselves with what happened, who was involved, and
            brought them with us.
M-14 /Qu: Ah, "we," were you to go as part of a team of investigators?
M-15 /M: Yes, with another girl, it was our case, we worked together and
M-16 /   we went to court with it.

M-17 /Qu: Did you dress in any particular way in order to go to court?
M-18 /M: They like, Simpsons likes us to get dressed up, so I wore a suit.
M-19 /Qu: Did they tell you specifically that you should dress up?
M-20 /M: No, but it was rumored throughout the department that they
M-21 / liked you to be presentable, the guys in suits and ties and the
M-22 / girls in dresses or suits.
M-23 /Qu: Okay, and, um, you went to the office and met then your partner there?
M-24 /M: Right.
M-25 /Qu: Had the miscreants been arrested? Were they in jail?
M-26 /M: No, out on bail, I guess. They had been arrested in May, and
M-27 / we had to wait over three months for court, I guess.
M-28 /Qu: They were expected to come to court that date of their own free will?
M-29 /M: Right.
M-30 /Qu: How many defendants were there?
M-31 /M: There were five charged.
M-32 /Qu: And where was the courtroom?
M-33 /M: In old city hall, it was courtroom 22. So it was right across
M-34 / the street from Simpsons.
M-35 /Qu: Ah, so you could just walk across the street.
M-36 /M: Right.
M-37 /Qu: How did you know it was going to be in courtroom 22?
M-38 /M: The sergeant from 52 Division phones in all our cases and we
M-39 / have a great big calendar with the names of the investigators,
M-40 / the date, the police officers, and the court room.
M-41 /Qu: The names of the police officers involved?
M-42 /M: Yes, we had officers arrest the girls for us, do the "stop" anyways.
M-43 /Qu: What was the scene when you arrived at courtroom 22 at two o'clock?
M-44 /M: We walked up to the door and the three police officers who were
M-45 / on shift the night we had our case, were waiting outside.
M-46 /Qu: Were they in uniform?
M-47 /M: No, they were in suits. And the crown attorney was waiting for us also.
M-48 /Qu: Did you know him from before?
M-49 /M: No, I had never seen him, but the other girl had, so she knew him.
M-50 /Qu: Was anyone else waiting in the hall?
M-51 /M: Yes, the defendants, just two of them, were sitting across the hall
M-52 / on the other bench, just waiting to go in.
M-53 /Qu: And were they talking to each other?

M-54 /M: No, they were pretty quiet, they weren't saying too much.
M-55 /Qu: What about the rest of you?
M-56 /M: We sat on the benches and waited because something was going
M-57 / on in court. We were running late, so we just chatted until we were called in.
M-58 /Qu: You and your partner?
M-59 /M: Yes, and one policemen was sitting beside me, and the crown
M-60 / attorney was running around, they were trying to lower the
M-61 / charges, and he was trying to get things organized for that.
M-62 /Qu: I see. Did the defendants have a lawyer?
M-63 /M: They did, he showed up for a couple of seconds and left again.
M-64 /Qu: Uh, weren't there supposed to be five of them did you say?
M-65 /M: Only two showed up, one came late, one was pregnant when we
M-66 / stopped her, supposedly having her baby that week, couldn't be
M-67 / there, and one they had a bench warrant for, she had disappeared.
M-68 /Qu: And how were you called in?
M-69 /M: The policemen walked in, said, "Come along." No one came out and told us.
M-70 /Qu: And where did you go in the courtroom?
M-71 /M: We went and sat at the back of the court.
M-72 /Qu: What was the arrangement of the room?
M-73 /M: There was the place where the judge sits and two court stenog-
M-74 / raphers and the policemen were sitting, there was that railing
M-75 / along the front with policemen sitting in front of it, on the left,
M-76 / and then there were three sections of benches. We were sitting
M-77 / towards the right and the defendants sat behind the policemen
M-78 / up on the left side. And there were other people sitting there waiting for other cases I guess.
M-79 /Qu: Was the judge present at that time?
M-80 /M: No, he came in after, from the side door. There was a man who
M-81 / announced the judge was coming in, please rise, the judge, or
M-82 / your honor, or something, I can't really remember exactly.
M-83 /Qu: So you all stood up?
M-84 /M: Yes, we stood up, and he came in.
M-85 /Qu: What did the judge look like?
M-86 /M: He had a black robe on, an older man in his fifties, grey hair, glasses.
M-87 /Qu: Did he appear distinguished?
M-88 /M: He looked bored actually, he sat down and riffled through his papers.
M-89 /Qu: Did this standing up and sitting down impress people, you

M-90 /   think? I mean does it add to the dignity or importance of the judge?
M-91 /M: Probably, I would think so.
M-92 /Qu: Were you watching the defendants during all of this?
M-93 /M: Yes, because we were trying to remember what names went with
M-94 /   what person because we hadn't seen them for a few months, just
M-95 /   to try and get everything straight.
M-96 /Qu: So you compared notes back and forth in terms of which one was which?
M-97 /M: Right, we were missing so many, we weren't sure what had
M-98 /   happened to the other ones, because no one had told us yet what had happened.
M-99 /Qu: So you didn't know at that point about the pregnancy and the warrant?
M-100/M: At that point we didn't know.
M-101/Qu: What happened next?
M-102/M: The judge asked them to come forward to plead guilty or not
M-103/   guilty, then the crown talked to the judge because so many
M-104/   being missing, he wanted to change the trial date, not have it
M-105/   that day, so there was a conference between the lawyers and judge,
M-106/   and a decision was reached. They talked to us, too; the crown
M-107/   attorney said we could either go through with the hearing and
M-108/   a trial if a trial developed, plus another hearing and trial for the
M-109/   others, or else do it all at once, wait to get them all together. We decided wait and do it all at once.
M-110/Qu: What had the ones who were there pleaded?
M-111/M: One pleaded not guilty, and one pleaded guilty, and one girl
M-112/   was going to plead guilty to theft under two hundred, but not to theft over.
M-113/Qu: So the attorneys took your decision back to the judge?
M-114/M: Right, and told him, and he made a decision, he agreed.
M-115/Qu: What did he say?
M-116/M: As the witnesses are willing to come back and there was no
M-117/   problem with defendants or attorneys, he would remand the date to November 13th.
M-118/Qu: Was the deal struck to allow her to plead guilty to a lesser charge?
M-119/M: Our crown attorney said he was getting pressure from his office
M-120/   to lower the charges, we went back to our wholesalers to find
M-121/   out the cost of the goods without markup, it was still over, so I
M-122/   think they're think they're going to have to go with that, it

	seemed that way.
M-123/Qu:	What was the appearance of the defendants?
M-124/M:	All dressed up, not like we had seen them before. Two of the
M-125/	girls had the same dress on [laughter].
M-126/Qu:	When they were stealing in the store they were dressed sloppily?
M-127/M:	Very.
M-128/Qu:	And now they looked like solid citizens?
M-129/M:	Right.
M-130/Qu:	How about the crown attorney?
M-131/M:	He had a brown three-piece suit.
M-132/Qu:	And the attorney for the defendants?
M-133/M:	He had a suit on.
M-134/Qu:	So this ended with the judge putting it off for a later date?
M-135/M:	Right, we were all to come back November 13th at ten in the morning.
M-136/Qu:	When you left, did the judge leave the courtroom?
M-137/M:	No, he stayed, there were other cases waiting, I think.
M-138/Qu:	So what did you and your partner do?
M-139/M:	We walked out with the police officers, talked for a while in the
M-140/	hallway, and then went back to Simpsons, just checked in and went home.
M-141/Qu:	Okay, thank you very much.

Exhibit N: "N's Vote"

LINE#/SPEAKER: (QU = QUESTIONER; N = STUDENT N)

N-1	/Qu:	I'd like to ask about when you recently participated in an election.
N-2	/N:	I voted in the Mississauga municipal election last Monday.
N-3	/Qu:	How did you know where and when to vote?
N-4	/N:	Um, a little card in the mail tells you where your polling station
N-5	/	is, and what time it's open, about a week before the election.
N-6	/Qu:	How far from your home was the polling station?
N-7	/N:	About a five minute walk, at a community school.
N-8	/Qu:	Who was to be elected?
N-9	/N:	We were electing a councilor and an educational trustee or whatever.
N-10	/Qu:	A member of the school board and a member of city council?
N-11	/N:	Yes.
N-12	/Qu:	Did you have any knowledge or familiarity with any of the candidates?

N-13 /N: With one for councilor, she lives in our area and I know her daughter.
N-14 /Qu: And were you concerned that she should be elected?
N-15 /N: I thought she should be.
N-16 /Qu: Were you concerned about the other office—the school board office?
N-17 /N: No, I didn't, I didn't know who was running.
N-18 /Qu: Did you plan to vote for both anyway?
N-19 /N: Uh-huh.
N-20 /Qu: On what grounds?
N-21 /N: I guess I just like to exercise my right to vote.
N-22 /Qu: What time did you plan to go to the poll?
N-23 /N: Um, after eleven o'clock.
N-24 /Qu: Were you at home that day?
N-25 /N: No, I was at school from nine to eleven.
N-26 /Qu: Ah, so you went from school. How did you travel?
N-27 /N: I took a bus, and then about a three-minute walk.
N-28 /Qu: Where was the polling place in the school?
N-29 /N: In the gym; they tell you that on the little card.
N-30 /Qu: And how did you know where the gym was in the school building?
N-31 /N: I went to that school, it was my public school.
N-32 /Qu: And what was the scene when you entered the gym?
N-33 /N: There were a few desks arranged with people sitting at them.
N-34 /   They had a desk where two sat with a list of names and addresses
N-35 /   of voters and a little desk to the side with a cardboard box, sort
N-36 /   of a blockade, where you sit behind while voting. Oh, as soon
N-37 /   as you go in there's this guy demonstrating a new technique for
N-38 /   voting. They had little machines you slip the card in and he would
N-39 /   show you how. Because I had never used that before. It was usually just with a pencil and you mark it.
N-40 /Qu: So he shows you how to use it, and then what?
N-41 /N: He asked where I lived, what street, and he told me which table
N-42 /   with lists to go to, I told the lady my name and what street I live
N-43 /   on, she crossed out my name and she gave me my ballot and I went and sat down.
N-44 /Qu: What was the ballot like, and what did you do with it?
N-45 /N: It was a computer card. I inserted it in the machine, and then
N-46 /   I flipped the page and punched a hole opposite the candidate
N-47 /   you are voting for; the second page was the educational trustee
N-48 /   member, and I did the same thing, and then the rest was for separate schools.
N-49 /Qu: How did you select which trustee to vote for in the trustee

		election?
N-50	/N:	I just picked one out, at random.
N-51	/Qu:	Whereas in the first election . . . ?
N-52	/N:	I knew who I wanted.
N-53	/Qu:	All right, and then you take the ballot out of the machine?
N-54	/N:	Yes, there's a cover for it, you slip it in and hand it back to the
N-55	/	lady and she folds it and puts it in the box.
N-56	/Qu:	This box, it has a key?
N-57	/N:	Right, it's locked, she can't open it up.
N-58	/Qu:	Okay, and then what happened?
N-59	/N:	Then I left the room, walked out of the school, and went home.
N-60	/Qu:	Did you find out later who won the election?
N-61	/N:	The next day, my dad told me. My candidate for councilor
N-62	/	won, but I still don't know who won the educational.
N-63	/Qu:	And you don't really care?
N-64	/N:	No.
N-65	/Qu:	How did your dad find out the results? Was it in the newspaper?
N-66	/N:	I don't think so. I think one of the neighbors phoned and told him.
N-67	/Qu:	Okay then, thank you very much.

Exhibit O: "O's Waterpolo Finals"

LINE#/SPEAKER: (QU = QUESTIONER; O = STUDENT O)

O-1	/Qu:	I would like to ask about a competition you participated in recently.
O-2	/O:	It was last week, the finals for women's innertube waterpolo.
O-3	/Qu:	Could you elaborate on that?
O-4	/O:	It's an interfaculty competition between colleges of the university.
O-5	/	Six people on a team, like waterpolo, except we are in tubes.
O-6	/	There's two rules: you can't physically touch someone or pos-
O-7	/	sess the ball for longer than ten seconds and you of course try to score.
O-8	/Qu:	How do you score?
O-9	/O:	Well you're in the tube, you have the ball, and you try to get it
O-10	/	to your team members and of course in the opponent's net.
O-11	/Qu:	Can you throw it in?
O-12	/O:	Yeah, if you can get it past the goalie.
O-13	/Qu:	How big is the net?
O-14	/O:	The same size as a waterpolo net, a bit smaller than a hockey net.

O-15 /Qu: How much distance is there between the faces of the two nets?
O-16 /O: Half the length of an Olympic pool 60 feet, and width is 25–30 feet.
O-17 /Qu: You say you played in the innertube waterpolo finals?
O-18 /O: There is two preseason games and four season games. You have
O-19 / to play two games a night so eight games and the ones that win
O-20 / the most games go to the finals. We were in first place going into the finals.
O-21 /Qu: So your team made the finals. How many players on your team?
O-22 /O: Six girls and two subs.
O-23 /Qu: Eight female students of Erindale College?
O-24 /O: Yes.
O-25 /Qu: How did you become a member?
O-26 /O: I played last year. People told me to sign up because it's a lot of
O-27 / fun. It is a lot of fun but girls don't really know about it.
O-28 /Qu: Is there any competition to get on the team?
O-29 /O: No, because there is so few people that know about it.
O-30 /Qu: Do you enjoy this sport?
O-31 /O: Yes, I love it. You get to meet all the colleges from downtown.
O-32 /Qu: Relative to any sport you've played is it intensely competitive?
O-33 /O: It is very competitive and it's physically demanding.
O-34 /Qu: What do you mean by that?
O-35 /O: We had a lot of pressure on us. We won the last three years,
O-36 / two girls that were really good in the past graduated last year.
O-37 / We wanted the championship back this year.
O-38 /Qu: This final game, where did it take place?
O-39 /O: Downtown campus athletic complex, a physical ed. building downtown.
O-40 /Qu: This is a room with a swimming pool?
O-41 /O: Yes, and about ten rows of spectator seats the length of the pool.
O-42 /Qu: How many can be seated in them?
O-43 /O: I would say about 200.
O-44 /Qu: How many fans were there that evening?
O-45 /O: Three [laughter].
O-46 /Qu: What time was the game scheduled for?
O-47 /O: Eight o'clock at night.
O-48 /Qu: What time did your team arrive?
O-49 /O: Around 7:45, we went into the locker room, put on bathing suits,
O-50 / and took our towels out with us.
O-51 /Qu: Are the bathing suits all the same color?
O-52 /O: No.

O-13 /Qu: Is there any way in which the two teams are recognizable?
O-54 /O: Yes, usually one team gets to wear caps, usually whoever arrives first.
O-55 /Qu: Is there any advantage to wearing caps?
O-56 /O: No, it's a disadvantage because the caps fall off.
O-57 /Qu: So when you put on your bathing suits and went out to the
O-58 / pool with your towels, was the opposing team already there?
O-59 /O: Yes, because they played before as well.
O-60 /Qu: Who were the opposing team?
O-61 /O: Pharmacy, from the Pharmacy School at U. of T.
O-62 /Qu: They also had six players and two subs?
O-63 /O: They had lots of players, about twenty players.
O-64 /Qu: So they wore caps?
O-65 /O: Yes.
O-66 /Qu: Is there an umpire or referee?
O-67 /O: Yes, two, on both sides of the pool, paid officials, from the phys.
O-68 / ed. department, with whistles and keep score on clipboards. In
O-69 / the finals there is one more girl who is seated at a table who writes it down.
O-70 /Qu: How do they start the game?
O-71 /O: Both sides are at the edge of the pool in their tubes when the
O-72 / referee blows her whistle and she throws in the ball to the center.
O-73 /Qu: In the pool each player has a tube, does the goalie have a tube?
O-74 /O: No.
O-75 /Qu: How do you propel the tube?
O-76 /O: Swim backwards, arms and legs, everybody has their own style.
O-77 /Qu: Can you touch anybody's tube?
O-78 /O: Yes, you can grab the tube and dunk her, tip her out, but you're
O-79 / not supposed to touch somebody physically, only the tube, but
O-80 / of course they do, gouge with their nails underwater where the referees can't see.
O-81 /Qu: Ouch!
O-82 /O: Yeah, it gets pretty bloody, the pool turns pink.
O-83 /Qu: What happens when they get dunked?
O-84 /O: You can't touch the ball if you are not in the tube; if you're
O-85 / dunked out, you must let go and whoever gets to the ball has possession of it.
O-86 /Qu: And who sees to it that you don't hold the ball for over ten seconds?
O-87 /O: The referee is counting; if you foul, the other side gets the ball.
O-88 /Qu: Is there a time period?
O-89 /O: We have two twenty-minute continuous halves.

O-90 /Qu: What happens when a team scores a point?
O-91 /O: You give the ball back to the referee and you go back to your side.
O-92 /Qu: Then you start again. Do you play strategies like certain players
O-93 /   are your offense and certain players are your defense?
O-94 /O: We play man-on-man to try to stick to one person, or we have
O-95 /   three moving up and two staying with the goalie to be defense, zone or man.
O-96 /Qu: And the other teams have their own different strategies?
O-97 /O: Yes.
O-98 /Qu: Are there coaches?
O-99 /O: Yeah, the downtown people have coaches, ours is an experienced
O-100 /   player who tells us what to do.
O-101 /Qu: So the Erindale people just huddle and decide?
O-102 /O: Yes.
O-103 /Qu: Are you one of the better players?
O-104 /O: I played for two years but most girls they have never played before.
O-105 /Qu: Okay, what makes a good innertube waterpolo player?
O-106 /O: One who can have possession of the ball quickly, strong arms
O-107 /   and legs; you have to be fit, people who are not are surprised at how hard it is.
O-108 /Qu: So you get out of breath quickly?
O-109 /O: Very quickly, it's a lot of energy exerted quickly.
O-110 /Qu: So is it a fast game?
O-111 /O: Very fast.
O-112 /Qu: Lot of yelling and screaming among the players?
O-113 /O: Yes, a lot of scratching too [laughter].
O-114 /Qu: Isn't that an infraction?
O-115 /O: Yes, but it can be done; referees can't see underwater.
O-116 /Qu: Right, so are there kicks, too?
O-117 /O: Yep, but I'm a goalie so I don't get that sort of thing.
O-118 /Qu: How did this game come out?
O-119 /O: We lost, 7–6. Tied right down to the end. A pretty exciting
O-120 /   game. We fretted right out, we were totally unprepared.
O-121 /Qu: You mean you didn't know they were going to be that good?
O-122 /O: Yes, and we didn't know they would play so dirty, all the scratching.
O-123 /Qu: Do you think the roughness is partially why they won?
O-124 /O: Yes, we made a formal complaint about them and so did the referees.
O-125 /Qu: So the Pharmacy girls were real rough?
O-126 /O: Yes, they were.

O-127/Qu: Okay, thank you very much.

Exhibit P: "P's Barbeque"

LINE#/SPEAKER: (QU = QUESTIONER; P = STUDENT P)

P-1   /Qu: I want to ask you today about a party you recently attended.
P-2   /P: Okay, it was two weeks ago, a barbeque party.
P-3   /Qu: And what made it a party?
P-4   /P: I guess the people gathering, alcohol.
P-5   /Qu: How was it announced to participants?
P-6   /P: I was invited by a friend. He asked whether I was free two
P-7   /   Sundays from then and whether I could come to a barbeque at his home.
P-8   /Qu: Was a specific time of day mentioned?
P-9   /P: No, I asked what time I should come, he said one o'clock.
P-10 /Qu: Did he say who else would be there?
P-11 /P: I asked will there be anybody there I know, he said probably not,
P-12 /   maybe one or two, but he wasn't sure how many would be there.
P-13 /   It was his brother's party so he didn't know how many his brother had invited.
P-14 /Qu: Did you ask him how to dress?
P-15 /P: Yes, and he said anything I want, so I assumed since it was a
P-16 /   barbeque, outside, naturally I would wear something like jeans, pants, informal.
P-17 /Qu: On that Sunday before you left home for the party, how did you dress?
P-18 /P: My clean jeans and brown silk shirt. It's old, I don't care for it much.
P-19 /Qu: Did you wear make-up?
P-20 /P: I always do, a little.
P-21 /Qu: Did you look in the mirror and decide you're all right for the party?
P-22 /P: Yeah! [laughter].
P-23 /Qu: And how did you go to the party?
P-24 /P: Well, this friend of mine picked me up in her car, I had invited
P-25 /   her to go with me. Oh yeah, I had asked the guy who invited
P-26 /   me if it was all right if I brought a friend, and he said sure, so we went together.

P-27 /Qu: Had you told her also to wear jeans?
P-28 /P: No, I didn't say, but she did wear jeans and a blouse and a blazer.
P-29 /Qu: When did you two arrive at the party?
P-30 /P: About twenty after two.
P-31 /Qu: Instead of one. Were the assembled guests mostly there by then?
P-32 /P: We were the first ones.
P-33 /Qu: So it was the two of you and the host and the brother who invited you?
P-34 /P: And the brother's girlfriend.
P-35 /Qu: So what happened?
P-36 /P: They were listening to music and drinking inside.
P-37 /Qu: Were they serving drinks amongst themselves?
P-38 /P: And to us.
P-39 /Qu: When you arrived, what was the first thing that happened?
P-40 /P: The dog attacked me, and my friend came out and brought the dog inside.
P-41 /Qu: So he hosted you in, and how did you introduce your girlfriend?
P-42 /P: I said, "This is my girlfriend, X, you remember"; he had already met her.
P-43 /Qu: So the two of you joined the three of them?
P-44 /P: In the living room, they offered drinks, and we sat around and talked.
P-45 /Qu: How long did this go on before anybody else arrived?
P-46 /P: An hour. Then another couple arrived, a man and woman, and
P-47 / the host introduced them, and gave them drinks, and they sat down and talked.
P-48 /Qu: Did the conversation change now that there were seven of you?
P-49 /P: Yes, mainly with the new couple.
P-50 /Qu: Um, how were they introduced?
P-51 /P: The brother's girlfriend said this is so and so, she knew them.
P-52 /Qu: Any indication of how they were a couple?
P-53 /P: Uh, well, later we found out that she just picked him up. It
P-54 / came out later in the conversation. So then me and my girlfriend,
P-55 / and the host and his brother, went to sit in the kitchen and make a few drinks.
P-56 /Qu: With the others in the living room, now there were two conversations?
P-57 /P: Right, and then the doorbell rang and another two girls came in.
P-58 /Qu: And where did they situate themselves?
P-59 /P: After they got drinks in the kitchen they joined the group in
P-60 / the living room; they knew them.
P-61 /Qu: Did the two girls come in on their own or were they hosted in?

P-62	/P:	They came in with bottles and put them in the refrigerator, so
P-63	/	I take it they were good friends. They said, "Hi," and that's about it.
P-64	/Qu:	How long did that setup remain?
P-65	/P:	An hour or two, meanwhile maybe seven more people arrived,
P-66	/	we were all talking, and the music was loud.
P-67	/Qu:	By six o'clock, fifteen people, in how many conversational groups?
P-68	/P:	Some were also outside, so I'd say three.
P-69	/Qu:	Had there been any barbequing going on up to now?
P-70	/P:	No.
P-71	/Qu:	Was there much wandering from one group to the other?
P-72	/P:	Some. Not me. Some girls came into the kitchen to get more
P-73	/	drinks, so some of the guys stayed in the kitchen, the girls left
P-74	/	for the living room and then they came back because there was more fun in the kitchen.
P-75	/Qu:	What kind of talk was going on?
P-76	/P:	Um, just about anything in general, working, um, cracking
P-77	/	jokes, people cutting up one another, best friends.
P-78	/Qu:	So what ended this gab session?
P-79	/P:	The brothers decided to start the barbeque, so me, my girlfriend
P-80	/	and a few people went outside with them, a couple of guys, and we played Frisbee.
P-81	/Qu:	And what was done when the food had been cooked?
P-82	/P:	The food was brought inside to the kitchen table, and some of
P-83	/	us sat down and the rest were standing because there weren't enough chairs.
P-84	/Qu:	And did the conversation continue as before?
P-81	/P:	Uh, it was more quiet, everyone was concentrating on eating.
P-86	/Qu:	When the eating was completed, did everyone stay in the kitchen?
P-87	/P:	Mostly, and more drinks were poured and the brother brought dessert.
P-88	/Qu:	And what happened after dessert?
P-89	/P:	Just more jokes, the girlfriends cutting one another up, until
P-90	/	about 11, and then we left, I had to work the next day, and so did my girlfriend.
P-91	/Qu:	Were you two the first to leave?
P-92	/P:	Yes. I just told the host and his brother I have to leave now.
P-93	/Qu:	Did somebody see you out?
P-94	/P:	Yes the host and his brother both walked us to the car.
P-95	/Qu:	What were your parting words?
P-96	/P:	"I really had a good time, thank you for inviting me," um, "we'll

P-97 /   see you again some time"; they said, "Thanks for coming, it was
P-98 /   good having you, drive carefully" and that's about it, and we drove home.
P-99 /Qu: Okay, thank you very much.

Exhibit Q: "Q's Pub Night"

LINE#/SPEAKER: (QU = QUESTIONER; Q = STUDENT Q)

Q-1 /Qu: I want to ask you about a time you went out to a pub recently.
Q-2 /Q: Well, my girlfriend called me up last Wednesday night and said,
Q-3 /   "Would you like to come down to the pub with us on Thursday?"
Q-4 /Qu: At that time did you know what she meant by "the pub"?
Q-5 /Q: I knew she wanted to go to the Ryerson Pub, she's always talking
Q-6 /   about it and she hasn't been yet so she wanted me to go with her and her friends.
Q-7 /Qu: Did you know what she meant by "us"?
Q-8 /Q: Well, she had several friends in mind, I knew two of them already
Q-9 /   but the others I didn't know.
Q-10 /Qu: So what did you say when she asked you to go?
Q-11 /Q: Sure, what time do you want to meet and where do you want
Q-12 /   to meet. And I asked if one girl, Robin, was going to be there and she said "yes."
Q-13 /Qu: What did she say about where and when?
Q-14 /Q: She said we're going to meet at 7 o'clock at Dundas and Yonge
Q-15 /   Streets. I asked her what she's wearing and she said she'll be wearing jeans.
Q-16 /Qu: So what did you do on Thursday night to prepare?
Q-17 /Q: Had dinner, washed up and I put on my clothes, and put some make-up on.
Q-18 /Qu: What all did you wear?
Q-19 /Q: I put on jeans, a shirt, and a jacket, casual wear.
Q-20 /Qu: When did you leave home, and how were you traveling?
Q-21 /Q: I left at six, went by bus and subway, got there a little late, at 7:10.
Q-22 /Qu: Were the others waiting for you there?
Q-23 /Q: Yes, it turned out to be a girl which I didn't know, her name
Q-24 /   was Martha, and Mary, my friend, the two of them.
Q-25 /Qu: What was the greeting when you saw them?
Q-26 /Q: She said, "Hi" and "Your hair looks good," and I said I didn't think so.
Q-27 /Qu: How did you get introduced to Martha?

Q-28 /Q: My friend Mary said "Mary, this is Martha; Martha, this is Mary."
Q-29 /Qu: Two Marys and a Martha, sounds like the Bible. What happened next?
Q-30 /Q: We went out of the subway stations and headed for the Ryerson Pub.
Q-31 /Qu: Did Mary tell you who else was going to be joining your group?
Q-32 /Q: Yes, she said Robin was going to be there which I already knew,
Q-33 / and somebody else, I can't remember her name.
Q-34 /Qu: So there's going to be five of you in a group?
Q-35 /Q: Right.
Q-36 /Qu: On the way, was there any talk about what the place was like?
Q-37 /Q: I asked her if it's like Okum House and she said no it's a little
Q-38 / bit different. Better music and the crowd is better, more rock and dancing.
Q-39 /Qu: Okay, now you got to the door, tell me exactly what happened.
Q-40 /Q: There was a long lineup and we were waiting there almost an
Q-41 / hour and we were really frustrated because we couldn't get in
Q-42 / so we decided to, um, kind of sneak in and we were successful at that.
Q-43 /Qu: How did you manage to sneak in?
Q-44 /Q: You need this stamp on your hand to get in and we forged it with ink.
Q-45 /Qu: What happened when you got inside?
Q-46 /Q: When you walk in you have to show your stamp, and then we
Q-47 / stood in line for tickets to buy drinks. We bought tickets, then
Q-48 / we went to get our drinks and went to a stand up place. There
Q-49 / was no room to sit down so we had to stand and put our drink on a shelf, then we drank and talked.
Q-50 /Qu: The three of you. Did the other two show up?
Q-51 /Q: The other two came later.
Q-52 /Qu: You drank and talked. Was there music playing? Did you dance?
Q-53 /Q: The band wasn't playing yet, it was the disc jockey. We had a
Q-54 / second drink and my two friends danced but I didn't.
Q-55 /Qu: How did it occur that they danced?
Q-56 /Q: Guys came over and asked.
Q-57 /Qu: Were there any turndowns?
Q-58 /Q: One, I did.
Q-59 /Qu: Did the other girls turn any down before they accepted somebody?
Q-60 /Q: No. They're really ... they like dancing so they dance with anyone.
Q-61 /Qu: All comers, eh? Did they dance with more than one partner?

Q-62	/Q:	Yes. Both.
Q-63	/Qu:	So when the other two arrived, did they also forge the stamps, or . . . ?
Q-64	/Q:	No, they got in legitimately, by waiting. By then we had gotten
Q-65	/	a table and we waved them over, we got our third drinks and brought them back.
Q-66	/Qu:	So now there are five of you sitting there, and what happened next?
Q-67	/Q:	One guy from another table had recognized my girlfriend and
Q-68	/	he came over to join us, she introduced him and we talked a
Q-69	/	little bit. Some of them were dancing, even me, somebody asked me to dance so I danced with him.
Q-70	/Qu:	And this was a more acceptable offer than previous ones?
Q-71	/Q:	Yes.
Q-72	/Qu:	So you danced, came back to the table, more conversation,
Q-73	/	listening to music. Was there a fourth drink?
Q-74	/Q:	Yes, I had a fourth drink and continued dancing.
Q-75	/Qu:	Until what time of night did this go on like that?
Q-76	/Q:	Well, I didn't know how long it went on because I had to leave
Q-77	/	at 11:30. I had classes Friday, I had to get up early so I didn't stay too late.
Q-78	/Qu:	Did anyone leave with you?
Q-79	/Q:	My friend offered to leave with me but I told her that she didn't
Q-80	/	have to. So she stayed.
Q-81	/Qu:	Then you went out, got on the subway and came home?
Q-82	/Q:	Yes. That's about it.
Q-83	/Qu:	Were any future arrangements made, with anyone you met that night?
Q-84	/Q:	Nothing specific, but one guy, I think we're probably going to
Q-85	/	meet again, probably by the same process, going to the same pub.
Q-86	/Qu:	When you see him again at a similar occasion you'll be acquaintances?
Q-87	/Q:	Right.
Q-88	/Qu:	Would you say the evening was a success from your point of view?
Q-89	/Q:	Yes.
Q-90	/Qu:	Was it enjoyable?
Q-91	/Q:	I had a lot of fun out of it. I talked to a lot of people.
Q-92	/Qu:	You spent your carfare and for four or five drinks, was it worthwhile?
Q-93	/Q:	Oh, yes, very much so.
Q-94	/Qu:	Okay, thank you very much.

Exhibit R: "R's Something"

LINE#/SPEAKER: (QU = QUESTIONER; R = STUDENT R)

R-1   /Qu: I wanted to talk with you today about a convivial occasion in which
R-2   /   you recently engaged. What can you tell us?
R-3   /R: This past Sunday evening a whole bunch of friends and myself
R-4   /   went over to my girlfriend's house, watched videos and had
         some drinks, to pass time.
R-5   /Qu: So, literally convivial. Now, when you say you and your girl-
         friend . . . ?
R-6   /R: Equally male and female, it was coupled off, everyone was with
R-7   /   their boyfriend or girlfriend.
R-8   /Qu: Did you call it a party?
R-9   /R: No, it's just something we do when there's nothing better to
         do.
R-10 /Qu: Okay. Who had the idea first?
R-11 /R: My boyfriend had called up. Usually one of the bunch calls, there
R-12 /   is about ten of us that do everything together. He called one of
R-13 /   my girlfriends, we can never get ahold of her boyfriend, and
R-14 /   from there everybody called each other so he called two and
         they called the rest.
R-15 /Qu: Were you there when he was calling?
R-16 /R: Yes, I was right beside him. He asked if they had anything
R-17 /   planned for he day and whether they would like to go and see
R-18 /   a movie. But everybody decided they didn't want to do any
R-19 /   thing in particular because they were low on cash so all decided
         to go to one girlfriend's house.
R-20 /Qu: How did that house get chosen?
R-21 /R: One couple was already there. Where the most people were, that
R-22 /   is where we ended up going.
R-23 /Qu: And where were you when your boyfriend was making the call?
R-24 /R: Sitting on the couch beside him, at my house.
R-25 /Qu: What time was this, on Sunday?
R-26 /R: Two p.m.
R-27 /Qu: And what time was the evening event scheduled?
R-28 /R: There wasn't really a time set, but my boyfriend and I were the
R-29 /   last ones there and we arrived at five-thirty p.m.
R-30 /Qu: And when you got there, what was the scene?
R-31 /R: Everybody was sprawled over the couch, the floor. It's a small
         room.
R-32 /Qu: Does it have a name?
R-33 /R: It's a "rec room."

R-34 /Qu: How many people were there when you arrived?
R-35 /R: Eight of us together, six before we arrived, so four couples.
R-36 /Qu: What was said when you arrived?
R-37 /R: "It's about time." We are always the last ones to get there.
R-38 /Qu: What were the others doing when you arrived?
R-39 /R: Watching a rented video, some movie.
R-40 /Qu: Was there food?
R-41 /R: Yes, just finger food, veggies with dip and chips.
R-42 /Qu: Who provided it?
R-43 /R: My girlfriend whose house it was.
R-44 /Qu: And did you bring anything?
R-45 /R: No.
R-46 /Qu: And what was to drink?
R-47 /R: Typical alcohol? Beer? I'm a gin drinker. We all drink separate
R-48 /   things. The guys tend to drink beer while the girls drink the mixed drinks.
R-49 /Qu: Who provided this drink?
R-50 /R: Sometimes the guys bring beer. Other times it depends on the
R-51 /   situation. Because this is like a regular occasion. If it's my house
R-52 /   I provide the alcohol. If it's at my girlfriend's house she does.
R-53 /Qu: You get your turn. Were people particularly interested in the movie?
R-54 /R: No. A lot were chatting about what was going on, the latest gossip.
R-55 /Qu: And what was the arrangement of the people in the room?
R-56 /R: More or less everybody was sitting beside their girlfriend or
R-57 /   boyfriend. Sort of sprawled out all over the place. Really comfortable.
R-58 /Qu: And the conversation was between couples? Across the room?
R-59 /R: Across the room, across conversations. When it comes to that
R-60 /   you usually end up screaming trying to get your words in.
R-61 /Qu: Was it mostly female to female or male to male?
R-62 /R: Mixed.
R-63 /Qu: And no little groups formed up separate from the others?
R-64 /R: We are a group. We do everything together. Close in personalities.
R-65 /Qu: Is this the totality of the group?
R-66 /R: No, there is another couple who weren't there because she was
R-67 /   tired and we couldn't get ahold of him.
R-68 /Qu: Was there any talk about them?
R-69 /R: No.
R-70 /Qu: You said there was gossip. Who was the gossip about?
R-71 /R: I belong to a Polish association so we have a tendency to talk

R-72	/	about all the other people that we really don't get along with.
R-73	/Qu:	Are all of these five couples members of the Polish association?
R-74	/R:	Yes, we all met through the ethnic group.
R-75	/Qu:	Are you all about the same age?
R-76	/R:	Twenty-two to twenty-six.
R-77	/Qu:	Some in college?
R-78	/R:	I'm the only one left in school, everyone else is out.
R-79	/Qu:	You're the kid?
R-80	/R:	Yes.
R-81	/Qu:	Are they all in occupations?
R-82	/R:	Yes.
R-83	/Qu:	Is that a subject matter in the conversation?
R-84	/R:	It is at times. I usually get, "When [are you] going to get a job?"
R-85	/Qu:	Are you considered lucky to be in school or unlucky not having a job?
R-86	/R:	A lot of them tell me they miss school but those that have great
R-87	/	jobs say it is really rewarding when placed in good positions.
R-88	/Qu:	Did you dress in any particular way to go to this gathering?
R-89	/R:	No, just casual attire, jeans.
R-90	/Qu:	What happened at the end of the movie?
R-91	/R:	Drinks were refreshed, the bottle sitting in the middle of the
R-92	/	floor. We tried to decide to stay or go somewhere else. Being a
R-93	/	Sunday everyone had a hard workload in the past week, we decided to watch videos.
R-94	/Qu:	So you watched another video, about the same pattern as before?
R-95	/R:	Yes.
R-96	/Qu:	And then what?
R-97	/R:	We stayed on talking, half the people left. More gossip and
R-98	/	drinking. My boyfriend and I left at about one thirty, he drove me home.
R-99	/Qu:	And thus ended your "something." Thank you very much.

3

Generic Agendas in Written, Spoken, and Tacit Formats: How Major Activity Modes Are Realized as Occasional Definitions of the Situation

Our working definition of "a live social occasion" may bear repeating: *A gathering inside spatial boundaries defined by them of two or more persons identified by each other as participants, over a period of time whose intervals, precedents, and antecedents they define, during which a named course of activity predominates, attached to which they display for attribution as normal and appropriate, explicit motives.*

We now have before us eighteen described instances which fit this definition. Our first crosscutting analysis of this data focuses on the "named course of activity" predominant upon each live occasion. This chapter develops the idea of generic modes of activity, first detailing how the eighteen exhibits presented above (and perhaps most of the billions of ordinary occasions of everybody's social life) are shaped and identified by participants as specific instances of more generalized but distinctive activity patterns, and second examining the transcript evidence for description of the procedures by which participants ordinarily reproduce, sustain, and operate within these activity patterns upon live occasions.*

Following up, in tandem with Berger and Luckmann (1967) and Maynard and Wilson (1980), the Marxian thesis that organized social reality is produced locally by the observable, concrete activity of ordinary people, which, contrary to Durkheim's sui generis domain of systematically constraining or causal social facts and forces, *can* be identified with "the observed patterns of interaction among actual people" (Maynard and Wilson, 1980: 290), we will here examine the collection of such patterned, indigenously produced activities described in the foregoing eighteen exhibits. We shall note empirically, as Maynard and Wilson argue theoretically, that participants display a tendency to *reify* the patterns they themselves create in interaction, that is, to treat them as things in themselves which govern their behavior.

Our explanation for the prevalence of such reification, derived from empirical analysis, is twofold: first, participants observably attempt to *reproduce* these activity patterns, fashioning the current occasion upon a standardized model, "the usual," so that each unique occasion becomes accepted among them as a reproduction of the previous occasions like it; this provides for the sense that the pattern itself exists in some sense outside of its replications. Routinization, or the intentional construction of ordinariness, thus promotes the reification of the pattern routinized. Second, these patterns are not the consequence of any individual's solo action, but of the joint activity or abstention from activity of all co-present participants. Authorship and agency become melded and blended in the joint construction and reproduction of these patterns, and thus they display for their makers an immediate supra-individual character which naturally gives rise to the interpretation that the patterns have origins and effects outside and beyond the control of any individual.

Their generation and reproduction among participants and their efficacy between participants is a complex matter to follow, but the local social production and the occasion-specific and even supra-occasional organizing force of these patterns once indigenously established is clear to see through our mode of analysis. Though not strictly ethnomethodological, our hybrid approach is designed to examine, as Maynard and Wilson recommend, "how reification is produced in actual social interaction" (296) and to develop the convergence between Marx and ethnomethodologists by which "both treat the apparently stable and concretely existing features of society as the accomplishment of ongoing practical activity by actual living people." We have found the most relevant theoretical guidance in this quest in the works of Simmel, Schutz, Garfinkel and Giddens, but the primary and ultimate principle followed has been faithful adherence to what the student respondents have attested to. Our abiding goal has been to understand the social occasion as it is seen by, contributed to, and lived with by natural participants.

Social events, the living cellular occasions in which we regularly participate, do not just happen on their own; we cannot take their occurrence for granted; we have to expend the conscious effort to make them happen. What kind of activity any occasion turns out to be is also in no sense automatic; it is daily and hourly up to us to define it, to shape it and craft it into a coherent social object, to realize it.

Focusing on our eighteen exhibits as descriptions from the inside of instances of activities defined, shaped and enacted by occasion participants, there appears among this small sample six different kinds or modes of activity, six different generic agendas of "do's and don'ts." We propose the possibility that much of the activity of all humans, a gigantic swathe of the billions of living occasions of everybody's social life, is in fact patterned after these six modes. Further analysis of cases will likely produce additional distinct activity patterns, but we argue that this initial list of six will in the end account for the lion's share.

We are claiming that among the most common, most ubiquitous things that humans regularly and ordinarily do together are these six: eating together, working together, audiencing together, conferring together, competing together, and being together for the fun of it. For convenience of analysis, we alliteratively call these activity modes commensality, collaboration, congregation, communication, competition, and conviviality.

These thematic wholes of activity, regenerated and adhered to during the live occasion, are in each case what Kendon (1990) calls the "working consensus" of the occasion according to which "only certain aspects of behavior count as action." The generic agendas are focused answers to the general question "What is to be done?," and during each separate live occasion, one of the six is defined in action by the participating group as their predominant or focal activity, the occasion's flagship mode for them, though most often one or more other activity patterns are also being enacted, like a "play within a play," or in some cases like a "three ring circus."

In some instances, which ring is defined as the center ring varies from one subgroup of participants to another, according to their particular focal involvement. For instance, at H's football game described above, the players were focally involved in a competitive activity, whereas H and the rest of the ten thousand fans were focally involved in a congregational activity, audiencing the game; and at C's dinner out the diners were engaged in commensality while, simultaneously and in the same place, the restaurant staff were engaged in collaborative activity.

The six modes we have been thus far able to differentiate are:

I. The commensal mode, whose generic agenda answers to the question "What is to be eaten?";
II. The collaborative mode, whose generic agenda answers to "What is to be produced?";
III. The congregational mode, answering to "What is to be audienced?";
IV. The communicative mode, with a generic agenda indicating "What is to be disclosed?" (our interview occasions themselves followed this pattern);
V. The competitive mode, answering to "What is to be contested?";
VI. The convivial mode, a generic agenda outlining "What is the manner in which the company is to be enjoyed?"

We shall try to understand the differences between these activity modes as found in the exhibits, and then to examine how participants normally go about implementing the generic agendas, how they realize these distinct activities as defining characteristics of live social occasions, and how they reify the activity patterns, giving them the appearance of self-standing features of a sui generis social structure.

I. Commensal Activity: The Reproduction of Meals

There are no more ordinary "routine dramas" than the daily meals we orchestrate and consume together in little groups of diners, but there is very little description of the ordinary meal, or "the context of the eating event" in Counihan's words (1992: 64) (to be distinguished from "special" occasions like feasts, dinner parties, prayer breakfasts, or luncheons), in the social science literature.[1] There are countless variations in the ways that humans eat together, yet there also appear to be profoundly generic commonalities, probably distinctive to our species. It would appear that humans generally prefer to eat at meals, because we take a great deal of time and trouble to organize and produce them, over and above what it would take to simply get nourished via the shortest, most efficient route.

In our analysis of the three meals described in Exhibits A, B, and C, and our attempts to project their commonalities to the generic features of the billions of meals humans construct and consume together each day, something extremely important about commensal occasions, mealtimes, as a constituent part of everybody's social life emerges: that commensality, the way humans eat together, above and beyond the "nourishing effects" (A-126), facilitates the reconstitution of a basic reciprocity of perspectives between diners, the rebuilding of multi-leveled bridges of apparent understanding, commonality and mutual concern between materially separate islands of consciousness.[2]

This direct, materially based form of intersubjectivity provides the essential foundation for the mutual construction of all the elaborate architecture of social structure. Eating together is everybody's way of manufacturing the connective tissue for social life's sandcastles. We may call this connective tissue empathic understanding, or in Weberian terminology, "Verstehen," call it reciprocity of perspectives after Schutz, or call it, as Garfinkel (1963) does, trust. Whatever its analytical name, we find in three instances present empirical evidence for its existence, its structure, and its means of creation and reproduction.

When our fellow diners are kin, as they most frequently are, and as those in our three instances are, then this trust manufactured during mealtimes serves first to cement our kinship bonds, to undergird the foundations of familial structure with pure, unadulterated, ingenuous trust. When, due to force of circumstance, our frequent meal companions are non-kin, then, as reported by boarding schools, military units, and prisons, a version of kinship feelings imbues the relationships of table mates, be they fellow students, soldiers, or inmates. In general, eating together in this uniquely human manner appears to express and help to produce "we feelings."

The activity of eating together is described as having occurred in Exhibit D during work breaks, in Exhibit H during half-time at the football stadium, in Exhibit P as part of the overall festivities of the barbeque party, and in Exhibit R as the "snacks" consumed throughout the convivial "something," but only in Exhibits A, B and C do participants describe themselves as having partaken of a *meal,* as the predominant and focal activity pattern of the occasion as a whole, from their perspective within it.

The fellow diners at the breakfast, the lunch and the dinner out as described composed their individual actions into a type of joint activity which appears to be highly ubiquitous among humans, the activity mode of commensality, which literally means "table sharing." The variations in human commensality are myriad, but our task is to reach for the humanly universal, from what is isomorphic among our three closely watched instances, through one's own memory banks of the thousand-per-year (plus or minus) meals one has shared with others, to what can be reasonably generalized about the commensality practiced globally by our species.

But there is so much variation, even between meals A, B, and C,[3] that we may at first despair of finding a concrete, not just abstracted, common theme. A's father doesn't eat anything, just drinks tea, yet A and father purport to share a meal. B, B's father and B's sister each eat distinctly different foods, yet the three of them eat "lunch" together. C and family sit around a table surrounded by other tablesful of diners, a "full house," eating food prepared and served by wage laborers and paid for by credit card, yet it is their only regular family meal. B's father doesn't even sit at the lunch table, but "stands watching over" his children while eating. From the memory banks one must include "ordinary" meals in which we the diners are served from common pots by a non-dining family member (who will eat later) onto freshly washed banana leaves spread out on an immaculate dining room floor where we sit cross-legged on the floor itself or on low stools for the feeble-kneed, ranged in a row around three sides of the small room, facing inward.

The cuisines (see Revel, 1982), the utensils, the furnishings, the critical question of who dines with whom, who prepares and serves the food for whom, who can speak during the meal about what, the etiquette of dining, or "table manners" (see Visser, 1991) the status-at-table of children, women, the elders, how the meal is begun, and ended, when and how to leave the "table," these and a thousand other components of the meal are almost infinitely variable among us. What could be the human mealtime constants?

Envision the concrete material facts in detail and as possible empirical generalizations (*not* the abstract possibilities, feasibilities and plausibilities as Simmel, Goffman, and others would have us do). At this very moment around the globe there are a billion (plus or minus) places set aside for dining, one or more in every human habitation and millions more as public eating places, restaurants. These locations (let us call them all "tables" to indicate their central and defining spatial characteristic—a surface upon which food is to be set, and around which diners are to assemble to eat it) have been constructed, furnished, provisioned, decorated and regularly cleaned by fellow humans whose intention (whatever their various motives) has universally been to make the space fit and proper for commensality. (An inordinate proportion of the foregoing has been traditionally defined and perjoratively degraded as "women's work.") The further material business of hunting, gathering, growing, harvesting, transporting, processing, packaging, marketing, retailing, purchasing, carrying, storing, cooking, portioning and serving of the food for those tables is also going on right now as always, a major portion of the work of the world dedicated to providing the material infrastructure for the repeated instances of this one occasional activity.

But also at this very moment, among each group of intending or now actualizing diners, there are some individuals who are physiologically perfectly ready to eat, just at the right phase of their biological cycle and circadian rhythm for the meal about to be served, and some who are not. Yet they will assemble at the common table at the appointed hour and together, and simultaneously, eat the meal. In this discrepancy between the singular degree of hunger or satiation, the differential readiness to eat of each individual human animal, and the humanly universal simultaneity of eating times among groups of diners, there is something, surely, that transcends biology. Part of the effort we all put into the construction of meals as social objects is the artificial control we each exert upon our own biologically induced desire to eat now in order to be ready and willing to eat properly, at table, with the others during mealtime. The human metabolism is thereby voluntarily "socialized," that is tamed and conquered for social purposes.

For who among us would willingly dine alone on a regular basis? The effort expended by A's father in "waiting for" A to join him for breakfast, by B's father and sister in "coming home" in the middle of a workday/schoolday to join lunch, and by all of C's relatives in pre-assembling at a coffee shop each Friday to join up for dinner out, attests to the voluntary desire of diners to be commensal. The worst part of solitary confinement must be for the prisoner to be forced to eat alone, meal after meal. To sleep alone, to contemplate alone, to read and write alone, even to labor alone, all the other solitary activities imposed upon the prisoner in solitary confinement have their desirable, satisfactory counterparts in the free world outside prison, things that people often *choose* to do alone. But to choose to dine in solitude?

The exception protrudes from the memory banks even as one tries to envision the general rule. The author's grandfather-in-law, now deceased, a banker, patriarch of a large extended family of which thirty-five members lived and ordinarily dined under his roof, himself was served, when he dined at home, in splendid isolation in a separate dining room in which no one ever ate but the man himself. When he lunched at his club at table with other bankers, industrialists, and government officials, that was another story. But at home, everyone in that household above the age of three understood full well that grandpa dined alone because, and to sustain the fact that, he recognized no equals in the house, so that his willful solitary dining was not so much an exception to the ordinary desire to be commensal, but *hyperordinary*, because ordinary commensality implies relative equality among tablemates, and this reasoning allows us to see the solitary dining of the prisoner to be *hypo-ordinary* because it defines him as *less than* equal to any potential fellow diner. Tablemates are relatively equal. To practice commensality is to express and acknowledge relative equality with one's tablemates. This we posit is a universal feature of human meal taking.

Of course there are degrees of inequality, of superordination and subordination, to use the Simmelian live-action terms for hierarchy, expressed and enacted by tablemates toward one another, something *between* the levels of absolute inequality expressed by my dining-in-splendid-isolation grandfather-in-law and our hypothetical dining-in-solitary-confinement prisoner. A's father deigning to "wait for" and "sit with" A while A eats could express the father's superordination over the child. B's father lunches in crude domination over his children, standing "watching over" them while eating. And C's elder brother not only patronizingly always pays the restaurant bill, but also enjoys the special privilege of choosing the fish dish for all to eat.

Every occasional activity is probably marked by some degree of subordination and superordination, and this is also probably characterized by the Simmelian limits: Every subordinate participates in the exchange to some degree willingly, expressing some degree of freedom by voluntarily superordinating the dominant partner; and every superordinate is constrained to some degree by the limits of participation, losing some freedom in exchange for the privilege of dominance over subordinates.[4] But in the case of commensality, this inequality is overshadowed by the *relative* equality of tablemates, compared to both the relative inequality expressed between those who *will not* or *may not* share the table, or ordinarily take meals together, and the relative inequality necessarily involved in most other modes of activity, as we shall see in the analysis below.

There are a number of good reasons why the regular sharing of a meal table should express and promote equality among diners, maximizing the freedom experienced by participants, which are to be found upon closer examination of the generic agenda of commensality, the relatively invariant features of the activity pattern engaged in by all humans when they share ordinary meals. We have noted that the biologically separate human animals, each with a unique degree of momentary hunger, yet club together in groups to start eating at socially determined mealtimes. The rest of the generic agenda, the single activity pattern common to our carefully observed instances and isomorphic with most of the meals we can recall, is as follows.[5] *Two or more people engage in something they define and label to be "a meal"; one or more of the participants eats, and all are in spatial position so as to be able to see the faces of the eaters, and they watch each others' eating; the meal continues through its one or more courses until the eating is officially done, and the diners may appropriately leave the table.*

As Kendon formulates it, this is one of various kinds of "formations" into which interactants enter in order to sustain a particular definition of the situation. In particular, it is an "F-formation" or facing-formation, in which participants "position themselves in such a way that their transactional segments overlap, thereby establishing a space between them to which they have equal access" (1990: 249). Such face-to-face positioning around food by diners appears to be the most commonplace meal arrangement amongst humans. Kendon finds it, in itself, "an excellent means by which interactional and therefore social and psychological 'withness' may be established" (ibid.). But we can go further. The specific mealtime version of the "F-formation" facilitates mutual alimentation monitoring, and this provides for a much deeper sense of sense of "withness." By watching each other eat, and displaying ourselves in the act of eating to the others, we are opening ourselves up to a deep level of interpersonal intimacy.[6] Even in the most intensive forms of conviviality, when we literally bare ourselves to each other for sexual intimacy, we can seldom convince ourselves that the other's passion is identical to, or even in any calculable sense similar to our own. But the generic agenda of the ordinary meal provides for just such intimate comparisons and identifications of bodily sensations.

Mutual alimentation monitoring is the basic behavioral feature of commensality, and it is more than a passive visual activity. Diners can be heard asking one another how it tastes, is it good, do you like it, are you full, or satisfied yet? They tell each other verbally or non-verbally (as in A and B's households where they don't talk about the food being eaten) whether it is hot enough or too hot or just right, too salty, too sweet, too spicy, too bland, or just right, or mmmmmm, I've never eaten anything as good as this! With the voice, in words, grunts, groans, of pleasure or displeasure, with the eyes, hands and shoulders, with smacking lips, lolling tongues, tooth-sucking and finger-licking, this hedonistic conversation goes on (or may be explicitly suppressed or stylized in obedience to "table manners," see Visser, 1992).

MEAL TALK

The centrality of this direct exchange of sensory data is underscored by the meal-specific limitations placed upon conversational topics. Talk at ordinary meals is background music to the intimate sensual exchange that nothing else should disturb. A and father converse "not very much" over breakfast (A-53) except for routine exchanges about errands to be done and "passing comments" (A-72) about the news heard on the radio, and specifically not about A's health or studies (A-61–A-64). B's father confines the lunch talk to sports by asking his two grown children questions about "football, hockey, or baseball" (B-54) but about school, dates, how your life is going, "No, I think he's scared to ask. We keep it general." And at C's dinner out "we just usually talked about family things" (C-28).

When the talk is at the foreground, the occasion's activity mode probably isn't predominantly commensal, an ordinary meal, but either collaborative, with talk as work, and some food and eating as secondary background, as at a business lunch, or communicative, with talk as disclosure, coincidentally over food, or conviviality, with talk as fun, with food thrown in, as in the barbeque party described in Exhibit P.

The distinct character of meal talk in contrast to talk in various other activity mode contexts confirms our agreement with Mchoul (1978) that "basic conversational mechanisms" vary with institutional settings (or as in our instances with institutionalized modes of occasional activity) and our disagreement with Maynard and Wilson, and other conversational analysts who argue that these mechanisms are "the same across institutional contexts" (1980: 316, note 28).

It would appear from the evidence that everybody's social life consists in large part of ordinary occasions recognizable as "meals," whose agenda corresponds closely to the pattern we can see in common among our three instances and thousands of others.

If this is the case, we may ask, why do humans eat this way? What is it about assembling more or less face-to-face while consuming food and monitoring each other's mastication that would explain everybody taking the trouble to do it day after day? We could just as well graze, or eat alone whenever hungry, or turn our backs on each other to eat the way the chimpanzees at the zoo do. Does commensality serve extra-nutritional functions that would justify the time and trouble it takes to eat in this characteristically human fashion? Three possibilities arise: Our first potential gain from repeated participation in the mutual sensuous display of commensality is to be reminded, in a totally mythologized world (whether by the magical myths of pre-industrial life or the mechanical, technical, myths of our own) that we are in plain material fact, animals. It brings us down to earth and back into our bodies, into that portion of our experience that cannot be socially pre-defined. The great man is reduced to the slobberer he is over his food, the wizened schoolmarm melts and heats up the room with her little cries over the pate.

The materiality of our eating together brings home the truth of the materiality of our social being together. And the ordering of this corner of the material world by the mealtime routine provides a degree of ontological security to diners.

The second gain, based upon the physicality of the first, is to be reminded again every mealtime that we and our fellow diners and potentially all such human diners, are one, that we are together in the fundamental physical equality of species unity. The sensing of the temperature, the consistency, the spice and the taste of the food, the mastication of it into a paste mixed with digestive juices flowing in the mouth, the swallowing, the progressive sense of fullness, satiety—this is intensely personal, interiorized experience, but because it is biologically based, physico-chemical experience, we know and are reminded we are all made of the same basic material stuff, and that makes the experience of eating believably, globally shareable as everybody's, with instantly recognizable analogies to all other kinds of human experiences.

Each of our fellow diners has idiosyncrasies with regard to this eating we are doing "together." Some like it hot, some like it fast, some hunger for quantity ("gourmands") while others insist on quality ("gourmets"); there are foods some cannot eat and foods some must have. But we place more faith in our actual bio-chemical similarities than in these differences, so that for all intents and purposes we come to believe that the "same" things happen in your experience as happen in mine when you chew and taste the "same" food that I chew and taste. When you eat and I watch you, I am enabled to believe that I share experience directly and immediately with you, and when I eat, and you watch me, you may come to believe my experience is directly accessible to you.

Based on the return to animality, based on the realization of biological species unity, this is our third and greatest gain from participation in commensal activity. It temporarily solves, or seems to solve (which may be all the solution we need) "the problem of intersubjectivity," which if left problematic makes social life impossible.

We begin and sustain our social engagements based on the firm belief that we share a world in common with the other participants, even while knowing for certain that literally, we cannot. The construction and enactment of commensal occasions confirms and reconfirms that belief, or suspension of disbelief, and thus makes the rest of our social lives doable, by enabling us to achieve and regularly reconstitute an apparently literal reciprocity of perspectives.

But still it must be asked, why do we do it? Even if our analysis is correct, and the practice of commensal ritual has as its major social effect the re-establishment between diners of a reciprocity of perspectives, and this in turn underwrites the sense of trust, or intersubjective suspension of disbelief, that makes all social life possible, why isn't it done once we've done it? Why do we practice this ritual tens of thousands of times in each lifetime? If this is "socialization," why doesn't it "take"; if social learning, have we forgotten by lunchtime everything we learned over breakfast?

Like sandcastles, the structural features of social life have a tendency to dissolve back into relatively formless stuff. No one can constitute social structure, or any feature of it, "once and for all." We don't take any of it for granted because we cannot. Reciprocity of perspectives, which underlies the trust that is the foundation for all social structures and arrangements, is never established once and for all, but re-established, even among the closest of social intimates, once, twice, thrice a day if we can manage it, at mealtimes.

The reciprocity of perspectives built and reproduced amongst fellow diners at mealtimes through mutual alimentation monitoring is even more than the vital *cognitive* structure theorized by Schutz and others. It is not just presumed *knowing* of the other's interior state and its momentary changes, it is an expressly reciprocal *caring* about the basic well being and material satisfaction of the other. Thus it is a repeated life-lesson in altruism, which is also foundational for collective social life.

As the observational studies of infant/caretaker interaction by Bullowa (1975) and others document, every human's first life lessons in social interaction are as a partner in "feeding events" in which *both* parties learn to communicate to the other which actions will be most appropriate as the next actions in the sequence that becomes standardized between each mother or caretaker and infant. From the start of everybody's social life it is clearly observable that alimentation monitoring is not just watching each other eat but seeing to it, through interactive communication, that the other is adequately and satisfactorily fed. Thus a reciprocity of perspectives girded round by purposeful mutual concern is repeatedly reconstituted at mealtimes.

This is the glue that holds together our relationships, that cements the blocks of institutions and the other sandcastles into shape, at least for now, at least until we have to pile them up and cement them together again. And even the glue needs no deus ex machina to explain its existence. Ordinary humans, doing the most ordinary thing we do together, regularly perform the miracle of creating the substance which is the substratum of social life. We manufacture this wonderful glue together by watching each other eat, like symbiotic, symbolic silkworms. The universal human ritual of commensality performs the social life giving function of confirmation of the possibility and the reality of intersubjective trust.

IMPLEMENTING THE COMMENSAL AGENDA: THE REALIZATION OF AN ACTIVITY PATTERN

In a discourse of words and gestures (including movements of the whole body from one location to another) the participants realized[7] the activity patterns of breakfast, lunch, and dinner out, turned them into implemented facts, real events in the empirical world, through their utilization and invocation of tacit, spoken and written versions of the generic agenda of commensality. These are three media through which individual actions are transformed into melded socially interactive activities, actions without perceptible or claimable individual authorship, but which only have meaning in the light of the established-in-action fact that *we* are doing this.

To initiate occasions A, B, and C, participants enacted the beginning of a tacit agenda, based on learning acquired at repeated earlier run-throughs of the "same" meal. (The "same" obviously only by definition, since it must be a materially different event from any other occurring prior to it.)

When A comes "down from upstairs" (A-40) to find the father "already waiting" at the kitchen table (A-34), he "usually asks me if I've got up" (A-54), verbally asserting and establishing their standard morning co-presence, and breakfast begins. It is the word "usually" that is the tip-off to the presence and use of a tacit agenda at this occasion, what Cicourel would call "an emergent (constructed) action scheme" (1972). A is telling us that what occurs *this* time is what usually occurs, what is standard operating procedure for breakfast.

B waits at home until father gets home from work and sister gets home from school and then, after "we all make our own food" (B-68) and bring it to the table, "my father never sits down to eat, he stands and watches over us" (B-25). Here it is the word "never" that describes the tacit agenda at work.

C's residentially and occupationally scattered family members "meet at a coffee shop first" which is located near the restaurant they go to "every week" (C-12, C-6). Then they proceed as a group to the restaurant and are shown to a table and seated by staff. "Every week" announces a tacit agenda.

The first phase of the commensal agenda is thereby realized: Participants have assembled themselves around a food-bearing surface with the explicit intention to partake together of an ordinary meal.

Clearly this activity pattern, though repeated "every weekday" by A and B, and "every Friday" in the case of C, is anything but automatic, habitual, or taken-for-granted. A's father need not wait, B's father and sister need not come home for lunch, and C's relatives need not show up at the coffee shop. The fact that they all do, with regularity, indicates the active, intentional and voluntary establishment of routine, not its absent-minded occurrence by default. By their initiatory actions the participants demonstrate that they *know how* to form up the activity pattern of breakfast, lunch, or dinner. (Which establishes in concrete form the abstract idea of "knowledgeability" proposed by Giddens [op. cit., ch. 1].)

This first phase being realized then makes possible (though not at all necessary or inevitable) the ensuing enactment of an "ordinary meal." The defining agenda of the meal, the menu of what is to be eaten and the background rules about what is and what is not to be discussed, is realized tacitly in Exhibit A, tacitly and verbally in Exhibit B, and tacitly, verbally, and in writing in Exhibit C.

The menu for A's breakfast is standard fare: the father "usually drinks tea" (A-10) and for A it is "just toast, an egg or cheese" (A-93); whereas at B's lunch it is more exotic and personalized: "My father is Polish and he likes his Polish food. My little sister has a normal sandwich and I'm a vegetarian so I usually have salad" (B-12, 13). In common between A and B's menus is that they are tacit but "as usual," contain different foods for each diner, and the foods are prepared and served by the diners themselves. Exhibit B adds a second medium for realizing the agenda: B's father prompts the conversation, even controls and directs it, by asking questions only about "football, hockey or baseball" (B-54).

In contrast to all of these points is C's menu. It is offered in printed form to the diners, who must verbally enunciate their choices of dishes from it, so that "what is to be eaten" becomes both a written and spoken matter. Further, the foods are prepared by unseen cooks in the kitchen, and served to table by waiters, none of whom are fellow diners.[8]

These contrasts among only three instances, plus the burgeoning variety of menu features our recollection of meals eaten evokes, suggests a likely possibility: that the only generalized answer to the question posed by the generic agenda of commensality, "What is to be eaten?," that would be empirically true to all of these myriad instances is, "the meal itself, as a live social object, breakfast together, lunch together, or dinner out together." For all of its materiality, its display of animality, its sensuous interchange, discussed above, commensality is still, at base, a symbol-laden ritual of social engagement. Meals are not scheduled to suit the biological rhythms of hunger and digestion of each diner or the average diner, they are made to occur at breakfast time, lunch time, or dinner time. The size of the table shared and the number of diners is not determined by the size of the animal killed in the hunt or the size of the corn harvest, but by the size of the group considering itself intimate and equal enough to dine regularly together. The foods are not biologically appropriate or determined morning foods, afternoon foods, or evening foods (though many cultural groups hold theories that this is the case—what the British and the Chinese will ordinarily eat for breakfast is appalling and stomach-turning each to the other) but culturally traditional breakfast foods, lunch foods and dinner foods. Commensality is a symbolic ritual *about* animality, *about* sensuous display, *about* the interchangeability of standpoints.

And the meal that is eaten, partaken of, shared by the assembled diners in each instance is not reducible to the sum of the food consumed by each individual participant. The generic agenda of commensality, the expanded menu, is greater than the sum of its parts because it includes the voluntary participation, the caring about the physical and emotional well-being of the others, the import of mutual alimentation monitoring by all participants together, and is thus more potent than its material substance, a symbolic social object which performs the extra-nutritional function of the reproduction of socially foundational trust.

Further, the breakfast, the lunch, or the dinner out that is shared, produced and consumed materially and symbolically by the designated diners is constituted as a larger, more significant entity than any one of its occasional instances. This is how Giddens' idea of the extension across time and space of occasion-generated meanings is substantiated, in the case of commensality. As they "repeat" the meal, every weekday or every Friday, to be among those who "have lunch together" comes to mean participation "as usual" in the entire chain of weekday lunches considered as a collective unity. The definition by participants of each discrete occasion as a replication therefore has the powerful consequence of stabilizing the "fleeting reality" of the living occasion over extended time spans. The greater significance to social life of *ordinary* occasions over unusual, special ones inheres in this stabilization.

C's dinner out contains an additional written agenda segment of a type which further stabilizes the apparent objectivity and facticity of the occasion over time. The restaurant bill, paid by the elder brother "as usual" documents the meal that was eaten and paid for and becomes part of the records kept by the business, for a variety of purposes. We shall find that many different kinds of occasions include in their standard activity agendas the generation and preservation of such a *commemorative* device (commemoration being the commitment to common memory of some selected features of a passing live social event). Sometimes, as Zimmerman demonstrates, the commemorative reality of records kept overshadows the living reality of the occasion itself, becoming the end all and be all of the occasioned activity, the *only* fact that counts as fact (1969: ff.). At the wedding (Exhibit I), the commemorative picture-taking took a longer time than the ceremony itself.

The dinner out is also our first look at an instance of a "multiple agenda" occasion, in which more than one activity mode is operational during the same "routine drama" in the manner of a "play within the play." (Which of these is seen and defined as the "outer" play and which the "inner" play, which activity foreground and which background, depends on the participant's mode of involvement.) For the restaurant staff, the occasion is not commensal at all, but part of an evening's work shift, a collaboration, which activity mode we shall address next. Our reporter C, however, did not participate in this work but was only a recipient of the service produced, so we see collaboration in Exhibit C only from the outside looking in. (Exhibits D, E, and F, to be discussed next below, are insiders' views of collaboration.)

But how did the commensal participants become insiders, how did they merge and coordinate their individual actions to become component parts of the activity pattern that was the shape of the living social occasion? A and father entered into a silent interactional contract to reproduce "breakfast" together, he by waiting, A by coming down to the kitchen at the appropriate time. All the details of the standard agenda are tacitly encapsulated for them within the name they give to the occasion itself and to the string of its reiterations, "breakfast," by which they mean specifically weekday breakfasts shared exclusively by A and father. "Weekend breakfasts" are something else, when "the whole family is there" (A-106). B and family also relied on the standard agenda items they had learned through prior practice to associate with the occasion-name "lunch" but they were in addition prompted and cued in to appropriate lunch behavior by the verbal agenda spoken by the father, directing lunchtime conversation by asking sports questions. C's tableful of diners performed the tacit elements of "dinner out" as well, but in addition were presented with a written agenda, the restaurant's printed menu, from which they spoke their "orders" to the waiter. Verbal direction beyond this was limited to the bill-paying elder brother's privilege of choosing the "fresh fish dish." By these tacit, spoken, and written means, the participants were enabled to "tune in" to the joint activity and dovetail and integrate their personal actions into it.

II. COLLABORATIVE ACTIVITY: THE REPRODUCTION OF TEAMWORK

Collaboration as a mode of activity may be seen to occur in almost all eighteen of our ordinary occasions. Whenever two or more participants blend their effortful actions into an activity designed, monitored and judged to result in a joint material outcome or output, we shall call it collaboration, whatever may be the variation in what motivates each individual participant.

We see it in Exhibit B among the diners preparing and bringing to table the foods that will materially constitute their lunch; in Exhibit C among the restaurant staff as they welcome and comfort guests, cook and serve food, and collect and record payment; in Exhibit G among the chairman, the pastor, the organist, the ushers and the choir as they organize and present to the congregation the "performance" side of the Sunday service; in Exhibit H among the ushers and ticket takers, the stadium police, the food, drink and souvenir vendors, the scorekeepers and timekeepers, the umpires and referees, the coaches and trainers, the professional football players and even the "little marching band," all of whom collaborate to present the football game as a dramatic show to the paying audience of fans; in Exhibit I between the priest, the ushers and the photographer, all functionaries in the collaborative production of the wedding before its transformed audience; in Exhibit J between the doctor and his nurse receptionist to co-produce the service offered to J at the appointment; *not* in Exhibits K and L where the professor and the priest work, but as solo practitioners, not collaborators; in Exhibit M where the manufacture of the display of "justice" is a collaboration between the judge, court officials, attorneys, police officers, and functionaries like the stenographers; in Exhibit N where the social mechanism for democratic decision making is reproduced via collaboration between polling officials and functionaries; in Exhibit O between referees and scorekeepers to produce the material conditions for "fair play," in Exhibit P between the party-host brothers to construct the necessary infrastructure for a successful barbeque party; and in Exhibit Q between the doorman-bouncers, the bartenders, the disc-jockey and the musicians to present as a service to the customers the opportunity to have fun together in the pub.

But only in Exhibits E, F and G is collaboration the core agenda of the occasion as a whole, the activity mode that is the major focus of participants' attention and effort. At the midnight, at the practice, at the move, the participants were there, if they were there at all, to work together, to bend their individual efforts collaboratively toward the achievement of a collective output.

Collaboration as occasion is the multi-party work task. The end product of collaborative occasions comprises all the work that gets done in the world, producing everything that is distributed and consumed, including goods, services, artifacts, information, knowledge, truth, beauty and justice,[9] *minus* only the product of work performed by individuals in solitude.

COLLABORATION COMPARED TO COMMENSALITY

On the empirical base of the three instances here plus all sessions of group work we can each recall, we can begin to outline the morphology of collaboration insofar as it displays a distinct form compared to commensality.

Working versus Eating Together

The core activity of collaborative occasions is the direct material production of things (including symbolic objects, like "pieces of music" which are nevertheless materially produced) or their re-arrangement, making a sharp contrast to commensal occasions, where things worked up into edible food are consumed. The central agenda question for every collaborative occasion is "What is to be accomplished by us on this occasion?," whereas for commensal occasions it is "What is to be eaten by us on this occasion?"

What is the generic agenda for collaboration? In each of our three cases, the agenda is dominated by a goal that participants envision at the start of the occasion, the intended state of affairs at the end, what Garfinkel calls "the potter's object."[10] With different degrees of imperative determination, the achievement of the goal defines the appropriate activity of all participants. (This is how the "humanistic" Marx differentiates human work from that of other species. The spider, he points out, has no conception of the design of the web, what it will look like when completed, in her mind's eye before she starts to spin.)

D's night crew worked toward producing restocked shelves ready for the morning shoppers; E's choir worked toward producing sounds acceptable to the ear of the conductress, and F's movers worked toward producing a set of household goods relocated in the "new" residence. Actions that "count" upon collaborative occasions are relevant to this collective goal, and other actions would then be seen as "sideline" activity, or diversions. The activity described by our respondents is either directly goal-oriented teamwork or sideline activity whose purpose or function appears to be the sustaining of "team spirit," like the singing, and screaming across the aisles by D's night crew or the dressing up, looking good, and smelling right of E's choir. F's move is the exception that proves the rule: No team spirit sustaining sideline actions, a breakdown in work team communication, and a failure of teamwork to get the job done.

Whereas diners appear to consume food together so as to concentrate on each other, co-workers appear to promote solidarity amongst teammates so as to bring their united concentration to bear on completion of the task at hand. In the commensal case the promotion of solidarity is an end, in collaboration a means. The "fellowship of work" that we find here to be such a critical element, sociologically, is not visible from Marxist, Weberian, nor Durkheimian perspectives on labor. For Marx, the closest phenomenon would be the "consciousness" of commonality that workers should develop over time as they are all cast into the same exploitative situation by the development of capitalism, but this concept is an abstraction at the system level of Marx's analysis, not the living reality experienced by workers engaged in teamwork. Weber's idea of a work ethic applies only to typical individuals, and in *The Protestant Ethic and the Spirit of Capitalism* to individual entrepreneurs, the capitalists who are most significant to large scale economic analysis, but not to the ordinary workers who actually do the work in teams. And for Durkheim, the modern organization of work in "organic solidarity," the division of labor and the allocation of reward in functional terms are the subjects of interest, not the quality of immediate interaction between workers and its consequences for them and for the work. The insights we are able to gain about the social reality of work in this research are products of our chosen level of analysis, the lived reality of social life.

We have before us in Exhibits D, E, and F instances of three kinds of collaborative work:

a.) D and the crew collaborate typically for employees doing hourly wage labor, whether the work is labeled "blue collar" or "white collar." Offices, factories, and other proprietary establishments are locales for work stints isomorphic in format to D's midnight. They have names for their shifts, they characterize the personalities of their direct supervisors, they socialize convivially during their breaks, and they evaluate the importance of each other's performance of assigned tasks to the completion of the overall project. The material progress of the work done, and the appropriate contribution to it by each worker, is monitored by the co-present supervisor, who thereby imposes "quality control." The concerted work of the crew manipulates and transforms physical objects into marketable commodities.

b.) E and the choir engage in the work of practice, the laborious perfection of skills and capabilities to perform as a harmonious collectivity upon future occasions. Here it is neither physical objects and materials, nor symbolic organization of information (as in "paperwork") that the workers manipulate, but themselves. This is work typical to performing arts troupes, sports teams, military units, fire-fighting brigades, and hunting parties. They monitor themselves, or are closely monitored by a supervisor like the conductress, whose specific expertise is the ability to recognize and prompt quality of performance. Because it is the participants' behavior itself that is being worked on, everything they do during practice counts, so there will be little or no side-chatting, or "yelling and screaming across the aisles" as was perfectly all right during D's midnight.

c.) F and family, with a little help from their friends, engage in another kind of work that is familiar in format to all of us. A task needs to be done, and a crew of relatives and friends needs to be recruited, ad hoc, to do it. Without standardized routine, without a clearly articulated agenda, without predetermined task IDs and without a clear line of supervision and authority, these pieces of work very often get done, if at all, like F's move—in fits and starts, with collateral damage, and followed by arguments. The positive effect of routinization upon collaborative outcomes is here displayed in the negative.

This leads us into a further comparison between commensality and collaboration, "the point" of each activity, the underlying generic purpose for which participants organize commensal as compared to collaborative occasions. If as postulated the point of commensality is the socialization of gastronomic pleasure, the building of inter-subjective trust and alignment, then, the sociological point of collaboration, the extra "payoff" we get from working together other than the intrinsic reward of completing the task plus extrinsic rewards like wages or gratitude, is *the socialization of the pain of physical effort*. The expenditure of effort to complete a task is, I think, always and everywhere a pain, of sorts. (A "workaholic" like the crew chief is someone who deviates from this principle by treating work as a pleasure, instead, perhaps even an addiction.) Anyone who has experienced productive teamwork, no matter how hard the job, knows that the expenditure of effort can be made pleasurable, or at least less painful, by doing it together.

D is valued and cherished by the rest of "the guys" because "What I'm doing" (the "fiddly" work of price-changing) "is a favor for them . . . all the stuff that they don't want to do" (D-123–D-133). Despite the fact that this work is considered to be tedious by the others, D says "I enjoy doing it." The money is good, but "it's not just the money," "the time goes by quickly" (D-141, 143, 145, 167). As D understands the term, this work is not "alienating" (D-197). Why not? We cannot understand D's alleged enjoyment of this tedious work, the sense of being "at home" in the store, feeling that "I'm going in there and coming right out again," without consideration of the pleasurable interaction D experiences with the night crew.

This is a clear case wherein the inherent "pain" of labor is made into something experienced as enjoyable through the socialization of effort, turning the sub-task assigned to an individual into a valued component of the whole task of the team and the individual worker into an emotionally treasured and stroked member of the team. To redefine required labor as the welcome contribution of a valued member transforms expenditure into gain, pain into pleasure, through the fellowship of teamwork.

The other two instances fit well in this regard into the pattern outlined for D's midnight. E doesn't particularly enjoy the singing in itself, the songs themselves, as much as other features of practice. What makes E go out these weekday evenings, dress up and gargle up, make the right sounds, and work at it with the others as long as it takes, is the desire to be accepted as a Wesnivka, to be "one of" these upper-middle-class Ukrainian/Canadians (E-204–E-217).

F tells the other side of the story, when collaboration fails to get the job done. How could the brother and brother-in-law have done this?, F remonstrates after the fact. Members of the family are simply expected to help out when help is needed and asked for. In two cases, the burden of work was lightened by the socializing that accompanied it. In the one exception it was the acknowledged failure of social ties to motivate workers that prevented task completion.

Of the billions of collaborative occasions upon which the work of the world gets done every day, how many would fit this motivational pattern? How common, how ubiquitous is it among human participants to motivate and stimulate one another to work harder and suffer less the pain of labor, by making each participant feel valued by the others, and as a team, through enjoyment of the pleasure of each other's company, turning hard work into a good time?

Work Talk

Whereas talk at meals appeared to consist of "light" background conversation plus gestural/verbal expressions of diners' eating experience, the talk described in our three work examples is either instrumental communication facilitating the task ("sing that again" or "please stay and watch the truck") or sideline chat, fragmentary conversation "across the aisles" or "between the songs." The dining conventions established among each group of diners appeared to rule out certain conversational topics as not appropriate for the mealtime, whereas the contingencies of the work task appeared to limit the length of attention focused on casual conversation between co-workers. In both activity modes there is a type of talk structured specifically to facilitate the activity, eating talk or working talk. Much of the work talk in D was done non-verbally through the crew chief's exemplary leadership setting the pace, and the workers answered back in negotiations with their chief over break length and working hard; in E, instructions and judgments came both verbally and non-verbally from the conductress, but there was really no talking back, no opportunity for conversational turn taking by subordinate workers.

Subordination of Workers

The question of equality/inequality expressed and established among participants, of subordinating and superordinating interactions, will be our final comparison between commensality and collaboration. Whereas dining together appeared to be inherently a relatively egalitarian activity, expressing and promoting a sense of equality between tablemates, working together appears to entail a high degree of inequality, of order giving and instruction taking, of command and control, if the team's work goal is to be efficiently achieved.

D changes the prices the management's written instructions ordered changed, achieving some small degree of Simmelian "freedom of the subordinate" by whimsically altering the order of the list through the night "so it doesn't get too monotonous" (D-156). The crew chief controls the pace of work by leading through example rather than giving orders, and through negotiation, as when the workers promise to "work extra hard" in exchange for their extended coffee breaks (D-48). At choir practice the conductress is the taskmaster in complete control of the others, and her word is law as to when one may leave the practice and whether one may remain in the choir. Her authority is absolute and unchallenged, and this degree of superordination appears to be minimally necessary for the achievement of an aesthetically pleasing outcome for the entire group's work. The counter-example is F, where no one is clearly in charge, and the equality among friends and kin posing as a work team leads to failure in the work task.

IMPLEMENTATION OF THE COLLABORATIVE AGENDA

Participants use tacit, spoken and written agenda segments to realize and integrate themselves into the activity pattern of collaborative occasions.

First, by naming the occasion, participants invoke the tacit agenda, their unspoken intentions to act appropriately for the occasion at hand. For instance, the names given to our three collaborative occasions by their participants characterize the kind of work each was intended to be. D and the crew call their shift of work "a midnight." The use of a time frame as a name highlights two distinctive features of the work to be done: that it occurs at night, when most other workers are asleep, and that it is wage labor, the workers being paid for the hours they put in. E and the choir exert themselves in what they call "a practice." This name describes another widespread form of work, in which the object of the workers' effortful manipulation is themselves, and the work accomplished is measured by differences in workers' performance before and after practice. F, kin, and friends participated in what they called "a move." This designation cites only the task to be accomplished, indexing a third kind of work: ad hoc, without a routinized agenda, without established task IDs, established lines of authority and supervision, clear benchmarks, nor a predetermined reward structure.

The process of realization in these instances is advanced considerably by the acts of naming done by participants. Realization of a symbolic entity which can nonetheless be materially "shared," as we saw in our three meals, in the case of collaboration is accomplished through a sense of jointly "doing" the task that is pre-defined by its name. We have assembled as a crew to work a midnight; we have gathered as the choir to practice, and we all, more or less, are here to make a move. Naming the occasion begins to make it real, brings it into incipient being, by focusing the participants' attention and intention on the agenda. The name of the occasion inherently defines it as a group activity, beyond the purview of the actions of any one individual, and as one of a series or type of activities, making detailed articulation of its full agenda ordinarily unnecessary, a tacit understanding. Nevertheless, there is considerable spoken and written direction in the two work sessions that achieved their objective, and none in the one that failed. At F's almost aborted move, the existence and efficacy of an adequate tacit agenda was taken for granted, despite the fact that for these participants this was a one-time- only occasion, and this proved to be the collaborative sticking point, as F complains later about the delinquent brother: "Who did he think was going to move it in? (F-90, 91).

In contrast, D's portion of the crew's midnight task is not only verbally and gesturally acknowledged and appreciated by the rest of the crew, it is spelled out in writing on the "papers" left for D by the daytime managers. In addition, the crew chief supervises the activity, making sure each part gets done, and gesturally directs the pace of activity through his ceaseless "workaholic" efforts. Nothing taken for granted here. D's self-announced occupational label is "price changer"; which prices are to be changed and by how much is a written agenda for the night, and other crew members behave gratefully, D perceives, for the "fiddly work" D does and they don't have to do. As lubricant to this directed, supervised goal oriented activity, the crew members chat and joke, sing and laugh, and yell and scream across the aisles while working, helping each other to get through the night in a pattern of activity auxiliary to collaboration that has been noted in another work setting by Roy (1960).

The agenda devices used at E's choir practice are even more redundant and meticulous, reflecting the more complex, precise, and demanding nature of the teamwork in this case. The production of harmonized choral sound is a task that may define the extreme limits of "teamwork." If any individual voice stands out, as either a "worse" or a "better" rendition of the smallest part of a choral song, the entire output of the assembled group of singers is spoilt. All participants must pull together with precision in the exertion of their voices, in articulation, in tone, and above all in exquisite synchronization.

The goal is to make the individual voices of singing choir members blend to sound to the audiencing ear like one multi-hued voice. But the work task of choir practice is much more than this. It is the making tacit of many written, spoken, and gesturally communicated agenda items by committing them to participants' memories, so that next time, or at the performance following a long series of "practices," the harmonized choral sound in all its refinement can be reproduced from the memories of the participants, as part of their learned "know how," their *repertoire*, with only minimal prompting necessary from the task leader.

Written agendas spell out the words and notes to be sung by each participant, in the form of the "sheet music" distributed to the choristers. Each singer knows the job assigned by the "section" of the choir she belongs to, first or second alto, first or second soprano, and the sheet music spells out the line of music to be sung by each voice. Then there is the pianist, audibly prompting both the notes to be sung and the timing of beginning, continuing, and stopping singing. But above all there is the "conductress," speaking, singing, and mouthing what is to be sung by each section, cueing in the timing of each word and each breath, and saying imperatively with each twitch of her shoulders, arms, hands and fingers, "now, and now, and now." At the same time the conductress is judging the singing, in whole and in parts, and determining through her judgments what needs to be sung again, and how, and by whom. Even the length of the practice is determined for each section of singers by the conductress' judgment of whether they have sung well enough. E says, "If she wouldn't like the way you sang, she'd say, 'Okay, we have to do it till we do it right,' keep them for an extra hour" (E-183, 184). Individual singers are also judged by the conductress, and in E's case, the jury is still out, "I don't know if I'll be able to sing in the choir" (E-161), that is, whether the conductress will judge her voice to be good enough.

In both cases where the subordination of workers to the rule of a taskmaster led to achievement of the intended collaborative outcomes—the store was readied as a market by the end of the midnight; the choir's music making was defined as "better" by the end of the practice—their submission appeared to be relatively voluntary rather than coerced. The crew chief's benign supervision was legitimated by his ceaseless work at the task himself, and acceptance of flexibility in the work time of the crew. The conductress' authority was legitimated by her presumed and demonstrated superior aesthetic judgment—when the choir sang it *her* way, it sounded better.

Such "ordinary" domination of workers is a long way indeed from the relation of slavery, which even still, according to Simmel, contains some elements of freedom for the subordinate slave, and some restrictions for the master.[11] We would probably have to go to the extreme of an Auschwitz to find subordinated workers with zero freedom, zero power of reciprocity vis-à-vis their task masters, an exception to Simmel's law. But then Simmel did not live to see the Holocaust, and we unfortunately did. We cannot discuss the relationship between work and freedom without awareness of the sickening shadow of the grotesque sign over the death camp entrance: "ARBEIT MACHT FREI."

Distasteful as that may make it, discussion of this relationship is nevertheless still a core necessity for any comprehensive sociology, as it was for Marx, Weber, and Durkheim. In grain-of-sand perspective, we have before us clear and unyieldingly authentic instances of three degrees of command and control over workers, on the one hand, and degrees of worker autonomy, on the other, and some comparable indication of the productive consequences of each arrangement.

E's choir practice was as imperiously dominated by the conductress as any work situation short of slavery is likely to be, though a lot of schoolwork is like this too. The most minuscule expression of effort of each chorister— a breath, a whisper, a moment of inattention—was prompted, judged, corrected and punished by imposition of longer work hours. The conductress was a complete dictator with absolute authority, her decisions all final. Paid laborers treated this way today, even some military troops, would revolt, desert, walk off the job. Spouses experiencing this degree of domination are likely to file for divorce. Only in the performing arts and in team sports (ironically the supreme symbolic expressions of freedom in action) will we accept and freely submit ourselves to this degree of authoritarian control over our labors, as willing puppets. (In professional sports, athletes even allow themselves to be bought and sold, symbolic slaves but material millionaires.)

In the case of choir practice, it was authoritarianism from the bottom up. Because they accepted the superiority of the conductress' aesthetic judgment, the choristers superordinated her without question, even to the point of waiting in the hallway to allow her to enter the practice hall first. And because they understood the precise coordination and blending of their actions necessary to produce harmonious choral sound, they subordinated themselves absolutely to her every command, even if delivered only by the changing nuance of her facial expression.

The authority of D's night crew chief was less overtly expressed, the actions of his subordinates less close-coupled with his vaguer commands. His command and control over the work of the crew consisted of benignly flexible supervision of the worker's entry times, casting a blind eye on the eating of company groceries at break times, negotiating with the crew about the duration of breaks and the intensity of work stints, and finally, leadership through example by working continuously to earn the label "workaholic" from the crew. D exerted autonomy by altering the order of price changing tasks at will, and claims to *feel* more autonomous on this job than on the day shift as a cashier, working under the watchful eyes of management and customers. Compared to the conductress, who commands compliance through her unquestioned aesthetic superordination, the night crew chief downplays his authority, working alongside the crew and persuading them to comply with the work demands.

F is the rule-enhancing exception in this regard as well. There is no one in this team of "movers" with recognized authority over the others, no one gives commands, suggestions, or leadership, and some workers express maximum autonomy by leaving the task in mid-stream as and when they feel like it. As a result, the work simply doesn't get done, to anyone's satisfaction.

These three cases point toward some possible generalizations, still to be substantiated by study of large numbers of cases:

Teamwork requires leadership, and leadership is based on worker-acknowledged authority, or legitimation.

At the other end of the equation, worker autonomy has inherent limits which, if exceeded, will make teamwork impossible, collaboration unproductive.

On another level, workers will tolerate voluntarily a large degree of authoritarian control if they share the goal of articulated output, and if they acknowledge the expertise of the leader in producing and judging that articulation.

Realization of Collaboration

In similarity to the pattern we discerned in commensality, collaborators in the two successful cases realized the occasion, the teamwork, and their work teams, and thus reified them as components of longer term stable social structure. It was not only the rearrangement of groceries that the night crew accomplished, but also the construction of another midnight, the continuation of their lives as night workers, and the further solidification of their coherence as a group, the night crew; it was not only the improved singing of certain songs that the choir achieved, but also the artful orchestration of another practice, the improvement of their concerted ability to learn and perform new songs, and their cohesion as an ethnic-group choir; it was not only the furniture left in the driveway that F's friends and relatives argued about, but also the breakdown of the intended move as an occasion and the failure of the participants to act as and become a cohesive work group.

D says "I work two midnights a week" (D-40), naming the occasion as a recognized entity which occurs repeatedly each night. The midnight is a something to participants, something which appears to them to have an effect on their lives. D participates "on a part time basis" (D-94), which D thinks makes D immune to these effects compared to the full timers whose "social life is limited" by the job. "They socialize mainly with themselves because they are off during the day when everyone else is working" (D-189–D-191). But D socializes with them, has become "good friends" with several, "we've become very close" (D-210, 211). A succession of midnights has thus influenced the non-work lives of participants, estranging them in some ways from non- participants, and promoting solidarity as friends among the work team.

E's practice was work intentionally designed to realize and reify structure. E claims participation is a way to "continue being Ukrainian" (E-220). The choir practices with the anticipated goal of excellence in future public performance in mind, and each practice makes that goal more of an experiencable reality. The choir as an entity, as an organized group of ethnically, economically, and musically united participants, is also hammered into a firmer, more tangible-seeming social object on the anvil of practice. As they progressively learn to sing with one voice, they also strengthen the sense of being organic parts of one living being, the choir.

Production versus Reproduction

As in our three examples, ordinary collaboration is mostly a matter of reproduction of a material outcome, rather than original or primary production, which is most often the result of extraordinary, or at least non-ordinary activity.

D self-proclaimedly does "price changing," but it is not D who changes the prices at which goods will be sold. The actual making of the changes in prices, as economic decision making in the light of market conditions, is done by the grocery store chain managers, who leave their "lists" for D and the "price changers" at the other stores in the chain. D merely reproduces these changed prices as labels peeled from, and replaced upon, the items themselves. The work of the night crew as a team, provisioning the shelves of the store, is similarly a realization of the plan envisaged by managers as to how the groceries in all of the chain's stores should be displayed for sale.

The work of E's choir, while it is certainly a work of art, the production of aesthetically pleasing sound, is nevertheless reproductive rather than original or creative. Musicians, whether folk artists or more modern professional composers, produced the songs and their musical arrangements which appear on the choir's sheet music. The choir's efforts are dedicated toward faithful reproduction of the artists' primary musical productions.

And F's move is familiar to us as a project because of its mundane character as a task. To furnish or decorate an apartment might be a creative, productive task, perhaps even meeting artistic standards, but the mere moving of a set of furnishings and decorations from building A to building B is clearly reproductive. At its best, it produces no changes in the objects from one end to the other, except for relocation, but one of F's move's many failures was that prized things got broken.

Commemoration of Collaboration

The transitory live action of occasions of work, like commensality's dirty dishes, full stomachs and sometimes a restaurant receipt, also produces characteristic "leavings," commemorative records that extend the facticity of the occasion beyond the time span of its living events, tangible traces that often serve to reify the intangibles of collaborative social interaction.

After occasions of wage labor like D's midnight, material products of the team's work remain, often to be taken up as the raw materials of the next shift of workers to come on the job. The morning staff of the grocery store can make use of the night crew's work in their task of retailing to consumers the unpacked, priced and attractively displayed groceries. The crew chief's records, however recorded and kept, also indicate who it is that has earned a full night's pay, the accumulation of which will be commemorated and transacted on the worker's weekly or monthly paychecks. D, like others in the crew, will also have compiled a "record of employment" which can be presented to a future prospective employer, a bank officer, or a police official. E's work at the practice is commemorated by the improved singing that can be displayed at a future practice or public performance. Tangible evidence of the work done accumulates in the ability of the choir to sing well, perhaps in the "memory traces" in the brains of the choristers. In a military unit, this accumulated product of drill would be its "fighting readiness." And F's fractured move was commemorated in family feuding that probably only began to run its course with the "related arguments" immediately afterwards.

III. CONGREGATIONAL ACTIVITY: THE REPRODUCTION OF MASS AUDIENCING

Three meals, three work sessions, and then we consider G's Sunday service, H's football game, and I's wedding. As joint concerted activities, these three stand out from the rest of our collection of eighteen first with regard to the gross number of participants in simultaneous engagement. Simmel makes much of the significance of numbers in interaction (1950: 87–180 ff.) based on his analytic speculation and interpretation of historical examples, but our collection of three dyads (A's breakfast, L's confession, and J's appointment), a triad (B's lunch), and eleven "small group" activities ranging from five to thirty-five participants, displays little of strictly numerical significance except for the striking difference between all of these taken together, on the one hand, and the Sunday service with 150 worshippers, the football game with over 10,000 fans, and the wedding with more than 100 guests. The latter are our only possible instances of *mass* activity.

The single activity that the mass of participants engages in upon each of these occasions is to constitute themselves as an audience for some kind of performance, and to act and react as a single, massified participant vis-à-vis the performance considered as an acting unit. This pattern of action and interaction we shall call congregation, and occasions whose activity is dominated by this mode, congregational occasions.

Simmel hints at how reification normally occurs in such massified assemblies of individual participants: "They are the embodiment of the group forces and thus have a super-personal and objective character with which they confront the individual. . . . For, it is this large number which paralyzes the individual element and which causes the general element to emerge at such a distance from it that it seems as if it could exist by itself, without any individuals" (1950: 96).

But it is Durkheim who lays this out most clearly, using the religious ceremonies of "primitive" peoples as his concrete examples. (*The Elementary Forms of the Religious Life* is a major exception to the rule of social causality promulgated in the rest of Durkheim's work. Here he sees social order as something participants actively impose upon themselves, and the idea of a sui generis social structure as an *idea,* a concept arising in the minds of participants naturally because of their voluntary and conscious participation in a course of action—"assembling." No invisible normative order, no society reified by the sociologist.)

Durkheim, like Simmel, speculated that a major effect of ritual activity which entails mass assembly is to impress upon individuals the size, power and tangible existence as an entity of the collectivity. This impression reinforces individual and sub-group loyalty to society at large, according to Durkheim, even when participants are tempted by anti-social, selfish opportunities. "Society is able to revivify the sentiment it has of itself only by assembling" (1912: 391).

Durkheim made this point directly about *other* people, "primitives," and only indirectly about all of us. He nevertheless identified a mode of activity which appears to be ubiquitous among us. The assembling of numerous participants into an audience for a performance or spectacle,[12] is not only characteristic of the religious practices of primitives. Everybody participates in occasions of congregation, an activity mode independent of the occasion's institutional relationship IDs; participants can be observed to congregate religiously, but also politically, economically, or under the institutional aegis of kinship, friendship, learning, art, sport, and various combinations. Our three instances are combinations, respectively, of religious/ethnic congregation, economic/sports congregation, and kinship/religious/friendship congregation.

There is some congregational audiencing going on at M's hearing in the "spectators" section of the courtroom, among the three-person audience to O's waterpolo finals, in the small crowd at the pub when the band played, and among R's bunch of revelers when they watch videotapes, but in these cases congregation is a background activity, with something else (respectively, competition, competition, conviviality, and conviviality) strongly in the foreground. Only in G, H, and I were the mass of participants including our student reporter predominantly engaged in congregation.

To begin a fresh understanding of the significance of this ubiquitous human activity as part of *everybody's* social life, let us look rigorously at "G's Sunday Service," "H's Football Game," and "I's Wedding." They appear to strongly confirm and elaborate the Durkheimian idea that whatever else we participants are doing when we congregate, we are also knowingly celebrating and intensifying the direct, immediate reality of social solidarity of the kind Durkheim called "mechanical." This celebration of mass identification also has elements of catharsis built into it, perhaps as a means to socially unifying ends, perhaps to achieve a desirable therapeutic effect on individuals, and likely both.

G says the occasion was "the Sunday service" (G-10) rather than an "evangelistic meeting" (G-44). "Before the service starts" (G-16), comes "singspiration" (G-14), a "warm-up" routine. Then there is "a prayer" (G-70); "some gospel songs" (G-97); "the choir will present a song" (G-123); the Pastor "will give out the message" (G-37); "we have an offering" (G-16); "the announcement" (G-156); "the last hymn" (G-161); and finally, "the blessing" (G-159) and exeunt.

The order of these events and the titles and page-numbers of the hymns to be sung appear in the "mimeographed bulletin, just a paper," "the program" that is given out by ushers at the door (G-18). It is consulted by participants on what is to happen next, and as a written agenda, is similar to C's restaurant menu and D's "lists" of prices to be changed. In addition, there is the hymnody which informs the singers of the words and notes to be sung, a secondary written agenda similar to E's "sheet music."

But compared to the other written agendas examined (the menu in C, the list of price changes in D, the sheet music in E), the church service program is more comprehensive, less flexible, and more completely outside the control of ordinary participants. The menu offers choices of what to eat, whereas the church program declares what everyone will do next. D's list describes D's tasks only, and D varies the order at whim, whereas the program is for everyone in the church, the order of events predetermined. Which songs will be sung, which parts of the sheet music repeated, and how much time devoted to any song or part of a song, is decided on the spot by the conductress, whereas the church program's songs are not variable. In all of these respects the written agenda of the church service was designed to make it more ritualized (in Turner's sense, 1974) than the other occasions.

Though the singing is in different languages, tonally it is "in unison" (G-114). Together, the congregation sings and prays, as one entity rises for the hymn, each one's monetary contribution is subsumed into "the offering," and everything they do from beginning to end of "the service" can be summed up as one action, worship.

Directors of the action included the organist, the chairman, the ushers and the pastor. When the choir finishes its song the chairman redoubles the written agenda by stating, "give the time to the pastor" (G-131). The ushers prompt the donations when they "pass around the red velvet bags" (G-164).

The mass participation of the congregation as audience to the performances of the chairman, pastor, choir and organist categorizes the occasion's mode of activity as congregational. In this instance the agenda for congregation, telling everyone what to do all at once, is exceedingly redundant, in written, spoken, and tacit formats. Perhaps a redundantly iterated agenda is what it takes to orchestrate a congregational occasion, to guide all participants in precisely going through the motions, repeating without variation a long and complex chain of actions from beginning to end, in total unison.

Exhibit H is categorized as predominantly congregational because most of the occasion's participants, "over ten thousand" (H-50), remained assembled over its temporal course as an audience witnessing a performance. H names the occasion "a football game" (H-4), as the father had named it when he presented H with the tickets (H-10), but this does not label the activity in which H and the ten thousand others participated; it cites the performance they gathered together to watch.

There were two major modes of activity enacted in the stadium; a contest, an occasion of competition such as those to be discussed below, was going on down on the field among a tiny minority of the participants present; in the stands, the ten-thousand-plus-strong mass of participants were engaged in the same generic agenda of activity as were the congregants at G's Sunday service.

Whereas G's fellow congregants worshipped, H's fellow congregants rooted. And whereas the chairman, the Pastor, and the choir presented a "service" as the performance to be witnessed in Exhibit G, the teams, the referees, and the "little high school band" presented a "football game" in Exhibit H.

H tells us that the football game itself is not altogether the point of H's, or the crowd's participation. H has watched games before on TV, and "there's no comparison" (H-110). The "real thrill" is "being in that crowd" (H-143).

Here we find a new written agenda format, the "tickets" to the game with which H's dad "confronted" H (H-9), which indicated which teams were to play against each other, at which stadium, and also, "what the time was, what the date was, where we sat and where we entered" (H-20, 21). H first used the tickets to inform friend Ken about these details. At the stadium they served as an entry "map": "All the gates are numbered and it says on your ticket which one to go" (H-42, 43), and inside "we found our section and our seats which were all numbered and on your ticket" (H-45, 46). At the game there were other written agendas available, such as the scoreboard and the game program.

The actions of the players also serve in themselves as spoken agenda fragments or prompts. How you respond to each play is a tacit agenda for initiates, and there are spoken sets of instructions for novices like the "quite a few wives that go probably because their husbands have tickets and don't understand what's going on and just sit there . . . it's 'What did he do? Oh, good. Clap'" (H-99, 100,102).

But the "fan participation" (H-110) that most participants get "into" (H-103) also has its limits, its tacit "don'ts." These were made explicit by the two incidents of arrest or ejection by stadium police that H describes. One fan appeared too inebriated ("wasted" was H's term, H-86) and perhaps displayed his bottle, so he was grabbed by "five policemen" and hauled off. (H-83) A second, "drunk too," was a "sort of heckler," "commenting on every single play." This behavior aggravated surrounding fans because "it's just so jerky, you just don't do that" (H-89, 90, 91, 93). When asked "What do you do?" (H-94), H stated the rule broken, and thereby enunciated by, the deviant heckler: "you can cheer and everything, and some people do heckle, but not constantly, you don't comment on every single play" (H-95, 96). Thus do publicly displayed sanctions of deviants everywhere serve as "examples to the others," delineating in the negative what is, on a specified occasion, "good behavior." The generalized behavioral directive for congregation, which the "deviants" evidently violated is: mimic. If you behave like the others in the mass, you generally can't go wrong.

The congregational agenda was interdependent with the contest agenda being enacted on the field, spelled out by the articulation of fan outbursts with particular "plays" on the field, and the significance of those plays in the developing agenda of the game, plus H's emergent belief that the reactions of the fans are felt by the players, spurring them on (H-117,118).

For I, who wore the same flower as at a previous wedding, Exhibit I was an ordinary congregational occasion. But was it that for everyone there?

A major difficulty in categorizing occasions as to activity mode is that each witness has a unique perspective based on the degree and nature of their involvement. In the case at hand, probably everyone involved would agree on the correct name for the occasion, "a wedding," just as everyone at H's occasion would call it "a football game."

But for the priest this is one more wedding he is officiating, one of the duties of his occupation, as the game is for the umpire, an ordinary occasion, though neither priest nor umpire are congregants. And for the marrying couple and at least their closest relatives this is an extraordinary occasion, a high point in their lives. So is it an occasion of ordinary collaboration managed by the priest and resulting in the manufacture of a new nuclear family, or is it an extraordinary occasion of ceremonial conference moderated by the priest and productive of new knowledge in the minds of informed participants, or is it a predominantly congregational occasion which includes the other two as secondary modes?

The simplest criterion for deciding this is sheer numbers. Most of the participants are gathered to witness the performance of the wedding ceremony so on this rough scale the occasion merits the predominantly congregational category.

But there is also a deeper measure in terms of the major, determinative point of the activity. The pastor and chairman at G's church worked to orchestrate the involvement of the entire congregation in mass worship. The football teams, officials and stadium workers tried to give the fans their money's worth of entertainment by involving them in simultaneous mass enthusiasm. The marriage could have been legally accomplished in the privacy of a government office, if getting married was all the couple intended to do. But the wedding as occasion did much more. Symbolized by the two "sides" of the church that ushers guided guests to sit in, relatives and friends of the bride or relatives and friends of the groom (I-51–I-54) the wedding joined two communities of participants in an intentionally permanent relationship, a mass simultaneous joining. That's what makes it predominantly, intentionally congregational. Just as in the religious service and in the football game, the audiencing participants transformed themselves into a mass, a unity, a congregation.

There is a written agenda in the printed invitations, which informs the invitee not only of where and when, but whose daughter is about to be wedded to whose son, advance notice of the community joining to be done. The spoken agenda includes the instructions given by the ushers as to which side of the church to sit on, and the priest's admonition, adding an unusual "don't" to this agenda, "please, no throwing of confetti" (I-83). I implies that the rest of the agenda was tacit, based on prior attendance at weddings and rehearsals by the wedding party.

MORPHOLOGY OF CONGREGATION

Among the most ubiquitous, most universal, most frequent things that we humans do together are: eat together, work together, and gather as an audience together. Recent contingencies of modern life are an assault upon social life in all three of these activity modes. Many of us are forced to eat often in isolation, or at best sitting side by side at a counter next to strangers; more and more of our work involves socially isolated interaction with written records, a computer or some other machine; and most antisocial of all, more and more of our audiencing occurs in isolation before a bloodless television set, which cannot even acknowledge our applause, so we don't clap. These trends reduce the quality as well as the quantity of our social lives, with long-term consequences we cannot predict, but will inevitably suffer.

At the same time there are counter-trends, at least in the case of our third great activity mode. Never before in human history have so many of us, nor such a large percentage of us, congregated in classrooms for elementary instruction, secondary training, and higher learning. In spite of increased TV watching (maybe even because of it) regular church attendance, theater attendance, live music concerts, public lecture audiencing, and fans at sporting events, are all on the increase worldwide.[13]

Only movie audiences have dwindled in certain locations, and that may not be much of a loss in terms of social life, because movie audiencing prevents any interaction between audience and performance, and in the darkness, little or none between spectators as a mass—maybe cinema is only "quasi-social" congregation to begin with.

The core difference between congregational occasions and commensal and collaborative ones (whose point is the socialization of physical pleasure and the socialization of physical effort, respectively) is that the central theme and purpose of congregation is massification toward the production of cathartic solidarity, the emotional/cognitive blending of individual and subgroup actions into the experience of a single mass action, mass being, mass movement, mass weight, and mass purpose, the production of what Durkheim called "mechanical solidarity."

An agenda-invoking device commonly used (among literate, printing equipped collectivities) to realize the activity patterns of congregational occasions is the prefabricated written program put into the hands of all intending participants, adding to the name of the occasion a vast array of information about what is to be done by those present, en masse. The efficacy of this device is seen in our trio of congregational occasions, in which all who go to G's service are first given printed programs, all who go to H's football game are carrying informative tickets, and all who go to I's wedding have first received printed invitations.

Beyond following this written agenda, all that congregational participants need do to realize the activity mode of the occasion is to mimic the rest of the crowd, and audience together. The imitative behavior of crowds was noted a century ago by French sociologists Gustav LeBon and Gabriel Tarde. The programming of group activity does not of course automatically or mechanistically cause it to be realized. It provides a device by means of which participants can successfully coordinate themselves with each other massively, if appropriate, and if they so wish. The unison lockstep of the whole is completely dependent upon the voluntary compliance with the program by each participant singly, and just as in choir practice, a sour note can ruin things for everybody as the "jerky" fan did. Mass ritual is a flawless performance of effortful homogeneity, not a robotic or habitual knee-jerk reaction. Ask the Rockettes!

This fact of social life is the bane of educators who, as McLaren describes in detail (1986) are assigned the Herculean task of prompting free spirited youth into mass voluntary compliance (you can't *force* anyone to learn in response to a teacher's performance) with the world's most elaborate program, the school curriculum, boiled down to occasion-scale and served up as today's lesson plan.

The congregational agenda approximates Aristotle's delineation of tragedy (Aristotle, 1952), Durkheim's description of "the positive rite" (Durkheim, 1912), Scheff's analysis of catharsis (Scheff, 1979), and McLaren's outline of classroom ritual (McLaren, 1986).

Its surface agenda (the play, the football game, the religious ritual, the curriculum, the marriage ceremony) contains the meanings to be portrayed as performance, at a distance from the audience but within their collective sight and hearing, but the deeper objective of these performances is what happens among and to the audience.

The events making up the deep agenda of congregation are interactions within the audience and between audience and performance. Some occasions of congregation "work" better than others to produce the desired ends, but all have the following intended outcome in common:

From Aristotle we learn that the performance must "be an imitation of an action that is complete and entire . . . which has a beginning, a middle, and an end" (Aristotle, 1952: 232). Exhibits G, H, and I clearly fill this bill. It must be, as McLaren finds sessions of classroom schooling (1986), a complete ritual performance, which includes the audience as essential performers.

Aristotle also tells us the generic functional purpose of such performances: "effecting through pity and terror the correction and refinement of such passions" in the audience (1952: 230). Scheff (1979), though emphasizing individual rather than social life, insists that such cathartic experiences, purging us of accumulated sorrows and fears (pity and terror), are therapeutic for all humans and necessary to relieve us of incapacitating emotional burdens. McLaren makes it clear that in the high school classroom, the agenda organized as "rituals of instruction" uses such "correction and refinement of passions" to transform the congregation of young people "from the streetcorner state to the student state" in session after session of schooling.

But it is Durkheim who makes the most telling statement about the difference between collaborative (hunting and fishing in "little groups") and congregational occasions, the mass catharsis of ritual drama, and the transfer of individual burdens of pity and terror to the collective representation with the power to "correct and refine" such passions: society. I think printing the following excerpt from *The Elementary Forms* in full is warranted:

> Howsoever little importance the religious ceremonies may have, they put the group into action; the groups assemble to celebrate them. So their first effect is to bring individuals together, to multiply the relations between them and to make then more intimate with one another. By this very fact, the contents of their consciousnesses is changed. . . . When the Australians, scattered in little groups, spend their time in hunting and fishing, they lose sight of what concerns their clan or tribe. . . . On feast days, on the contrary, . . . their thoughts are centered upon their common beliefs, their common traditions, the memory of their great ancestors, the collective ideal of which they are the incarnation; in a word, upon social things. . . . So it is society that is in the foreground of every consciousness; it dominates and directs all conduct; this is equivalent to saying that it is more living and active, and consequently more real. . . . So men do not deceive themselves when they feel at this time that there is something outside of them which is born again, that there are forces which are reanimated and a life which reawakens. This renewal is in no way imaginary and the individuals themselves profit from it. For the spark of a social being which each bears within him necessarily participates in this collective renovation. (1912: 389ff.)

With regard to our three examples, we may look past their topical content (Protestant worship, a football contest, the sacrament of marriage) as Durkheim looked past the "little" (sociological) "importance the religious ceremonies may have," and focus on how congregational occasions "put the group into action." The primary item on any congregational agenda is to assemble, to gather, to become massively co-present. G's one hundred fifty Chinese Canadian Protestants fill the church and sing "very loud," H's ten thousand Argos fans are "tightly packed," and I's friend's friends' wedding attracted "all the friends and relatives" of the bride and the groom, in two crowds on either side of the aisle.

The major action contributed to the occasion by most participating individuals is simply to attend, which means to show up, to position oneself so that attentiveness is facilitated, and to remain so situated for the appropriate duration. This may be done voluntarily, as in our three instances, or by various degrees of coercion, as in McLaren's required schoolroom attendances or in Aristotle's Athens, where theater attendance was mandatory for citizens, but in all cases it is the participants who form the gathered collectivity by their actions, so the "effects" if any, are also direct results of the actions of participants, and not of any "deus ex machina," such as Durkheim's vaunted, but mistaken "society sui generis."

By showing up and remaining attentive, participants expose themselves to two simultaneous but distinct meaningful displays: the performance at the lectern, at the altar, or in the arena, and the action of the audience as a crowd of which they are parts. But the dramatic action which provokes and refines terror and pity, which unifies and revivifies the collectivity, takes place in the third ring of this generic activity circus: all present are involved in and impressed by the action and reaction which takes place between the performance and the audience acting as a mass unit.

The degree of intensity of this interaction varies from very mild to very powerful, and this determines the potency of the mass catharsis produced, but occasions whose predominant mode of activity is congregational will always point and move in this direction. This unified activity of the audience in direct response to the activity "on stage" is the second feature of congregational agendas to which we now turn.

The programmatic written agenda utilized at G's Sunday service (as at many thousands of ordinary church services) is particularly significant in this regard. Participants at the service are all "regular members," who, like G, "go every week," and the order of events in the service is the same every week, yet the ushers make it their business to get a printed copy of this week's program into the hands of every participant upon arrival. And, G tells us, everyone consults the program for what is to happen next. This is so that everyone will rise at once, hymnal in hand opened to the right page, and sing "very loudly" in unison, the one hundred fifty voices making a great noise unto the Lord, and then be seated and immediately pay attention to the pastor or the chairman. When the ushers come around with the red velvet bags the envelopes full of money will be ready to hand, the bags will pass swiftly down the aisles, and in a moment, in a single gesture by one hundred fifty individuals, "the offering" will be accumulated and served up to the deity. The action by the congregation in response to the performance onstage, their acting as one, in unison, unifies them and creates the experience of a unity called "the congregation," merges individuals into the mass entity.

It is the same for the football fans and the members of the wedding. When the fans "get into it," "up on their seats, and cheering" or "throwing toilet paper and waving little banners, and horns" in response to an exciting play, H thinks the players "feel it a lot. I never used to think it made much difference but you hear them comment how important fans are" (H-117, 118). For H, "It's a real thrill, being in that crowd" (H-143). The wedding interaction is more sedate, but tears are common, and the priest in this case had to restrain the fan-enthusiasm of the wedding guests by imploring, "please, no throwing of confetti" (I-83). The ceremony had a direct and powerful effect on the assembled guests, legally and religiously joining them into one family and *its* circle of friends. For congregational occasions the most sociologically significant action is the action of the audience, seen, heard, felt by the audience itself as its own spectator.

Our analysis confirms not only Simmel's and Durkheim's, but also Aristotle's, which claimed that tragedy audiencing made Greeks better citizens through catharsis. That is what is so quintessentially social about congregational occasions: Whatever may be the topicality of the spectacle, they are designed to submerge the individual and the parochial into the whole. One of the great anti-social forces contributing to the perpetual dissolution of our sandcastle social structures is the tendency toward individuation, selfishness, involvement of more and more of one's life in smaller and smaller groups of others, until only one's own nuclear family, or individual self has value, can stimulate effort, commands respect. Through cathartic consummation and submersion of individuals in massed collectivities, congregational occasions produce and reproduce the "critical mass" of social life's vital dynamic: solidarity.[14] If our cases can be projected to the billions which regularly occur, a universal human rite of congregation is practiced whose intentional consequence is enhanced unity, in feeling and in fact, among large collectivities.

The commemorative "leavings" of our congregational occasions are different than the dirty dishes and restaurant bills of commensality, or the material product changes and work/reward records of collaboration. The church service leaves behind an "offering" of monies donated by individuals but adding up to a total to be calculated later on. The football game similarly precipitates the "gate," or total amount of ticket prices collected, but also there is the official record of scores and points scored, all of the complex sports statistics. The wedding's commemoration included not only the signed certificates but the hour and a half of photography which will eventuate in "albums" as records and keepsakes of the event. But more significant and lasting than any of these, we must speculate, would be the "memory traces" of intense unity left in the congregational participants, the cathartic gains in social solidarity that have been made by them.

Freedom of Assembly

If the core activity of commensal occasions is mutual alimentation monitoring, and of collaborative occasions purposeful teaming, then the core activity of congregational occasions appears to be *voluntary self-massification*. Participants strive to look the same (the team sweaters and pennants of H's fans; the already used "wedding flower" in I's hair), sound the same (the loud unison singing of G's trilingual congregation; the roar of H's crowd, but the suppression of "jerky" heckling on every play), move the same, momentarily be the same as everyone else in the mass, jointly creating an undifferentiated whole by willful individual self-abnegation.

Rather than determined, driven, or manipulated behavior, the massified, united activity of at least these ordinary congregations (which we argue represent the vast majority of all such events, if not all of the "ordinary" ones) looks more like, as the title of McPhail's book on the social organization of crowds catches it, *Acting Together* (1994). None of the congregational participants in Exhibits G, H, and I attended unwillingly, in fact the football game's 10,000 plus fans were there on the basis of ticket purchases and the wedding's crowd of guests were privileged to receive invitations. So their initial assembly was by their free choice to participate in this and not some other social occasion. And all were free to leave at any time (nonconforming fans were *ejected* from the football stadium) so that their sustained presence as a massed audience was also voluntary.

The church service program, the football game tickets, the wedding invitations, the organs in the churches and the seating-viewing arrangements in the stadium stands were all *enabling* devices, facilitating the desire of participants to act as one with the assembled mass if they so chose. The only efforts at "crowd control" observed, the priest's admonition to wedding guests not to throw confetti and the ejection of obstreperous or drunken fans by stadium police, were attempts to prevent or halt behavior defined as "over the line," *beyond* acceptable crowd conformity.

So whatever social effects may result from such massive assembling, such as catharsis and/or social solidarity, a realization of the strength and solidarity of "the social," our evidence indicates these effects are *sought* and *intentionally produced* by participants. In life, they are as far as could be from unintended/unanticipated consequences.

IV. COMMUNICATIVE ACTIVITY:
THE REPRODUCTION OF CONFERENCES

Direct face-to-face communication, the back-and-forth flow of information transmitted verbally and non-verbally between human interactants, is a vital and ubiquitous activity essential to all social occasions, the lifeblood of all social life. It is a common means toward the end of accomplishing the reproduction of social reality, live, in all generic modes of activity, the via media for the animation of all possible agendas. Diners, workers, audiences, contestants, and revelers can all be said to be "in" communication with each other in the specific manner of their current activity mode, but upon certain occasions, communication among participants is not only the means, but also the end in view. The occasions whose predominant activity goal is the achievement of a certain level of communication, which are designed to facilitate this communication and whose situational definitions define "communication" in its most complete social form, we shall call communicative occasions, or conferences.

The generic agenda of a conference provides for the constitution of a complete, and closed, communication loop. Participants comport themselves so as to mutually and exclusively share specific information, and to closely monitor that mutuality and exclusivity of information sharing. This is what distinguishes the activity pattern of occasions J, K, and L from all of the others, even though all social occasions are equally reliant upon communication among participants for their life and structure as social events.

J's appointment, K's French class, and L's confession are organized by their participants so that the specified topical information may be maximally communicated in a back-and-forth flow among them; so that the appropriate level of transfer of this information, its transmission, receipt and understanding, may be mutually monitored and acknowledged, and so that the proper boundaries to this information flow, its exclusivity among participants authorized to know it, can be maintained.

A football team's between-plays "huddle" on the field is a good diagrammatic example of what the generic conference "looks like." The players on one team gather in a tight circle facing in, their arms around each other to make sure *everything* about the next planned play is heard and acknowledged by *every* player on the team, and that *nothing* is heard by *any* member of the opposing team.

Our live instances provide more detailed evidence about this activity mode in practice. Exhibit J is a conference between doctor and patient, an ordinary medical "appointment" in J's words, what is often called a "consultation" in other researches.[15] Exhibit K is a conference between a professor of French and her small class of "supposedly advanced"[16] students

(K's words), an ordinary university seminar. And Exhibit L is a conference between a penitent, a priest, and, some believe, the deity, an ordinary Catholic confession.

Nowhere is our method of ingenuous reporting about authentic observation more of a minimal necessity to get at the truth about social life than it is in dedicatedly communicative occasions such as these. Any third-party observer, any spy, any peephole, camera or tape recorder is utterly destructive of the confidentiality that is the *sine qua non* of the situational definition of conferences, one of their major definitional characteristics. Communication upon communicative occasions is intentionally and by definition exclusive, a closed loop meant to divide those who know from those who do not and should not. To pry it open by intrusive methods (even surreptitious ones) is to destroy its authentic informational value. All that we can legitimately and authentically know about other people's conferences is what they are willing to tell non-participant "outsiders" after the fact.

The generic agenda of a communicative occasion, or conference, answers to the question, "What is to be disclosed?"

In what J calls "an appointment" (J-3), "to take an examination" (J-43) in which J's doctor "did the complete physical" (J-57), what is disclosed to both participants, and *only* to them, is J's state of health. This agenda is realized via tacit, spoken, and written media.

The written agenda includes "a little doctor's card" telling J when and where to attend (J-5), the nurse's appointment book where "she had it written down that I was to be there at 2:15" (J-22, 23) and most extensive and important, "my file," which the doctor took out from his desk drawer, read from and wrote in (J-36, 62). The interaction here runs significantly "through" this written file. It is consulted before and after the physical examination, which is the key act of information disclosure at the heart of this communicative occasion. Before, the file indicates what needs to be examined, reminding doctor and patient in detail of the physical conditions whose state is to be updated by the new examination. After, the disclosures produced by the examination are recorded, providing guidance for the next examination six months hence. Cumulatively, the file is the official record of J's treatment and condition, a legally confidential document commemorating but also privatizing the events of this occasion.

The examination is verbally and gesturally accomplished first by the doctor asking J "how I had been" and J answering, "no problems" (J-37, 39). The doctor then prompted and cued J through the examination. He "pointed to the chair" in which J should sit (J-34), "said I could go behind the curtain and undress" (J-43), and later "said I could get dressed" (J-57). During the examination the doctor asked J a series of close-order questions, such as, "Does this hurt?" and gave detailed instructions, such as "breathe" (J-51, 52, 53) reminding us of the minute commands given the Wesnivkas by the conductress.[17]

Everything else on the agenda is a standard feature of "an appointment," a routine J performs "every six months" (J-3), and for the doctor, the daily replication of the appointment routine constitutes a medical "practice," thus for both participants, a tacit, learned agenda.[18]

Exhibit K is a communicative occasion, a conference, because unlike large lecture classes, which are congregational, this class is constituted in the smaller "seminar" mode, with facilitation for back and forth simultaneous communication. There is not as much emphasis in this case as in Exhibit J on the privacy of the information exchanged, but the relatively small size of the seminar and the purportedly "advanced" level of the subject matter lends it the sense of "exclusive" participation. What is to be disclosed is, on the students' part, what they have learned thus far about French literature through their presentations and questions, and on the professor's part, new insights into French plays being read and analyzed by the class, through her lecture. The occasion is designed as a mechanism for these disclosures.

K names the occasion and its component parts: "French 423," "the class," "two presentations," "the lecture," and "roll call." Each of these participant-defined action segments has its own written agenda. "French 423" has its course description in the university's annual "Calendar," and K tells us that it is "supposedly" an "advanced" course (K-7, 8). For this class session K brought along "the appropriate books . . . and papers," "the text," and "my notebook" (K-28, 29). For her presentation Kim "pulled out her papers," and the others "took notes when appropriate" (K-55, 60). During her lecture, the professor "refers to . . . essays or books" scattered on the table and "we tried to" take notes (K-80, 83, 84). Finally the roll call relies upon names being read out "from index cards" (K-94).

The first "official word" spoken by the professor, "Bonjour," reminds participants that the official verbal activity will be in the French language (K-38, 39, 40, 41). This particular salutation has many of the formal features, and apparently performs many of the functions of salutations in general as outlined by Kendon (1990: 258): "They serve to acknowledge a social relationship, and the form of the salutation itself also makes reference to the nature of the social relationship . . . the formality of the occasion." The "conventionalization" of salutations, Kendon argues, reduces "the degree of uncertainty of the participants about what may ensue at the moment of salutation."

The professor then continues verbalization of the agenda by saying, in French, "we're supposed to have two presentations today. Kim, would you like to start?" (K-47, 48). K calls this a polite command, because "The

French language is supposedly more polite" (K-53, 54). After each presentation, "the professor asked if there were any questions" (K-62). During her lecture she indicates what students should write down in their notes when she "repeats everything word for word ten times over" (K-82). For roll call the professor "shouts out the names" (K-94) and at the appropriate time says "stop for a break now" (K-96). Finally she "tells us what we'll be doing the following week" (K-96).

Everything else about what to do, such as precisely "when" it is "appropriate" to take notes on student presentations, participants have learned before, and carry with them now as memory traces to be cued into action, the tacit agenda.

The ordinary Catholic confession L describes is an exquisite instantiation of the conference activity mode. No one but the person confessing, the priest, and presumably the deity through the priest-as-medium is privy to the communication. As L answers when asked whether L's brother revealed what he would or did confess to, "No, it's private" (L-39).

The agenda for "what is to be confessed, and what is to be done about it," is mostly tacit, but partly spoken by the priest when he says, "Go on, tell me what you did" (L-55, 56), "Is that everything?" (L-62), "Say a little prayer to confess your sins" (L-65, 66), and "how many 'Hail Marys' and 'Our Fathers' to say" (L-68).

We may infer the origin and development of the tacit agenda from L's twice-a-year attendance and the priest's every-five-minutes repetition of the event. L knows "how to say it in Croatian" (L-77), what to "tell him." L claims to have the freedom to choose which of the "Ten Commandments" have been broken, and how frequently, since L's last confession, and reports on these violations in a general, vague way. "You don't say how many times or exactly what you did," but indicate, for instance, that you've broken the commandment to "Honor thy father and thy mother," by saying, "I made my parents mad often, once . . . " (L-58, 59). And the priest's tacit agenda relates the sins confessed to a matching checklist of expiatory prayers to be prescribed as penance.

CONFERENCE AND CONFIDENTIALITY

As it is embodied in the team "huddle," the mode of assembly of participants in an intentionally communicative occasion is designed to facilitate both internal openness for the flow of transmission and reception simultaneously back and forth, and the closing of the loop against external input or outflow, "leaks." The tension between openness and closedness is thus the underlying dynamic characterizing this activity mode.

The disclosive medical examination is conducted inside an inner room within the doctor's office, itself a suite of rooms within a building, and the doctor interviews the patient even while both participants consult the patient's file and body. The information thus disclosed is sealed off from outsiders' knowledge by professional and legal regulations as well as by locked drawers and doors. The seminar is confined within a small classroom, all participants seated face-to-face around a table, in contrast with the row upon row of forward-facing seats in the standard lecture-hall classroom at the university campus. The entire campus is a restricted area, where those with no particular standing at the university have no entitlement to be. Inside the seminar room, a glance tells K that "everyone" is there, and only advanced students of French were entitled to become part of this exclusive circle through enrollment. Everything disclosive about knowledge of French literature is mandatorily spoken in French, among a population whose everyday language is English. The professor is in the business of awarding distinction to those participants who demonstrate competence as exclusive possessors of the "advanced" knowledge disclosed.

The confession maximizes both the open and closed aspects of communication in the conference mode. Situated within a tiny cubicle, "the size of a bathroom" according to L, itself within the inner sanctum of a church, the penitent kneels and speaks directly into the ear of the priest who is seated facing sideways to the penitent's face, only inches away. They both could whisper and be heard as clearly as lovers hear each other's "pillow talk." But this apparent intimacy of physical closeness is negated by "the little screen" that masks the participants from each others' sight or touch, and thus depersonalizes the conversation. As in a telephone conversation, the conversants remain anonymous to each other except for the signature of the voice. This anonymity is designed to open up the communication even as it clamps maximum seals on the loop. It is believed that apparent anonymity frees the penitent to disclose the worst without fear of repercussion, and thus clear the conscience. At the same time it eases the priest's religiously and legally imposed burden of confidentiality—even if he did hear horrible crimes confessed, he could not legally identify the confessor by sight.

There is a sense in which every communicative occasion establishes a small, transient "secret society" whose members are sworn to secrecy and are at the same time privileged possessors of knowledge which could be translated into power. (See Simmel, again, for larger implications of more extraordinary secret societies, 1950: 307–376 ff.) Participants in conferences become possessors of secret knowledge, things that are intended to remain mysteries to non-participants, defined by the occasion as "outsiders." Those who share the mysteries exclusively communicated in conferences are thereby indoctrinated into an exclusive membership bounded by the possession of the mysterious knowledge, and bound by an obligation not to disclose these mysteries to outsiders.

The confidences between journalists and "sources," lawyers and clients, doctors and patients, priests and penitents, cannot be legally pried from them by the profane power of the state. Secrets exchanged between best friends can have value transcendent over kinship, economics, or politics, and even in the less rule-bound confines of the university seminar room, it is a special privilege, hedged round with propriety and rules of decorum, to sit in on a class as a non-member with the designated situational ID "auditor." The universal rite of communication confers knowledge and exclusivity upon participants, such that members know intensively the secrets of belonging. This rite assures the relationship in any society between the possession of secret knowledge and special status, the nexus of power of magicians and other professionals.

PROFESSIONAL SUBORDINATION/SUPERORDINATION

The exclusive possession and privileged application of specialized knowledge is the hallmark of the professions, so it should come as no surprise that our three conferences are also client/professional interactions, nor that much of the billable work of professionals in general consists of such "consultations," occasions in the communicative mode.

Not all communicative disclosure is done under professional auspices, of course. Conferences can just as well be held among informational equals, or with an "amateur" officially in charge of knowledge dispensation. But given the luck of the draw with regard to our concrete instances of the genre, we shall try to confine our generalizations to professional/client interaction in conference.

The doctor, the professor, and the priest, as professional possessors of exclusive knowledge, are clearly the superiors in these interactions, and the patient, the students and the penitent clearly the subordinate clients. In their actions and demeanor (the patient waiting patiently for attention in the waiting room and then obediently following "doctor's orders"; the students behaving themselves in proper French and following the professor's instructions; the penitent kneeling before the seated priest and seeking his guidance), the clients overtly superordinated their professional "masters."[19]

Yet the conference could not be a mere dispensation of information from professional to client. For the disclosure to occur, and even for the efficacy of the professional to be demonstrated and confirmed, the voluntary collaboration in communication and knowledge production by the client, the putative subordinate, was absolutely essential. Both parties would have to be equally responsible for the production of the disclosed information, elevating the situational importance of the subordinate and modifying the eminence of the superior.

The patient had to show up voluntarily at the office, answer questions about "feelings" accessible only to the patient, undress and position the body to be examined, in order for the doctor to co-produce the disclosure sought as the objective of the occasion. At the seminar, the core answer to "what is to be disclosed" concerns how knowledgeable the students have up to now become about French literature, and while it is the professional expertise of the professor which lays the groundwork and sets the scene for this, only the students, through their presentations, their questions and comments and finally their examination performances, can disclose this knowledgeability. It was completely up to the penitent to decide what to confess and what to believe about the efficacy of the assigned penance.

Professionals' power over their clients is thus limited to *prompting*, as did our doctor, our professor, and our priest. Professional prompters can only "lead the horse to water." The patient who will not voluntarily follow "doctor's orders" will not benefit from treatment. The student who *will not* learn, will not learn. And clearly, genuine repentance cannot be coerced. Professionals in general suffer from this disconnect between the application of their professional knowledge and skills and the beneficial effects on their clients—the client has the choice to participate fully or not in the interaction. Of course this also gives the professional a loophole when treatment fails.

V. Competitive Activity: The Reproduction of Contests

A fifth major generic mode of social activity characterizing billions of ordinary social occasions is competition. Occasions of competition, the struggle to identify winners and losers, are "contests," to differentiate them from meals, tasks, gatherings, and conferences. We find overlap in most live instances of these analytically distinct categories: the congregational occasion attended by H "contained" a contest on the field as a "play within a play"; there is grade competition in university courses like K's.

"M's Hearing," Exhibit M, is mainly a contest, contradictory testimony before a court being the etymological origin of the word "contest," but there are also spectator galleries fulfilling the common law's congregational task: for justice to be done it must be publicly seen to be done. And M is collaborating with a partner, the attorneys, the policemen, and the judge to get the job of producing "justice" done. In addition there occurred "a bit of a conference between the two lawyers and the judge" (M-105).

The action at "N's Vote," Exhibit N, is dedicated to the identification of winning and losing candidates, a clear and unambiguous case of competitive activity. Yet the election officials are collaborating to do their job, and "this guy" confers with N to demonstrate and disclose a new voting technique.

Finally "O's Waterpolo Finals," Exhibit O, is so ferociously competitive, as O describes it, that "the pool turns pink" with the blood of contestants. Yet some of the reason O "loves it" is convivial, to have fun with and "meet all the colleges from downtown" (O-31).

So there is competition mixed in with many predominantly non-competitive activities, and other activity modes mixed in with what are predominantly contests. Participants do not appear to be confused by this mixture, though sociological analysts might. Apparently they are better at building complex sandcastles than we are at understanding them but this has always been the difference between artists, no matter how bad at it, and critics, no matter how good at it.

The major dynamic of competition is to settle what has been made uncertain at the outset, but will be definite at the conclusion: who shall wear the laurels of victory, and who the sackcloth and ashes of defeat? Contests include battles in war, spelling bees, boxing bouts, card games, horse races, and beauty pageants, as well as the court cases, elections, and team sports instantiated here. The search for humanly universal features of competitive activity is accompanied by examination of the ways and means by which participants reproduce competitive activity patterns, and use them in the reproduction of larger scale meaning structures. What kinds of sandcastles do we build up and tear down when we compete?

M and a fellow store detective have "gone to court" (M-4) for a "hearing" on "our case" (M-12, 15, 45). What is to be heard is testimony pro and con, hence "contest." The intended outcome is the official finding of guilt or innocence for each defendant charged. This hearing did not develop into a "trial" with definitive outcomes, though three of the defendants did "plead" their guilt or innocence before the judge, and "a decision was reached" (M- 105) to hold the case over for a later date. Whereas the activity structure of this single occasion, the answer to "what is being done" is the court hearing as contest arena, its conceptual structure, answering "what is it about" is the case, also structurally a contest, but one subsuming many hearings. (For analysis of courtroom interaction based on first-hand evidence, see also Atkinson and Drew, 1979; Beach, 1985; Bennett and Feldman, 1981; Brannigan and Lynch, 1987; Lynch, 1982; Maynard, 1982; Nofsinger, 1983; O'Barr, 1982; Pollner, 1979.)

The contest agenda was enunciated in writing, speech and gesture, and inferably via tacit knowledge. Verbally the agenda was twice prefabricated, once when "it was rumored throughout the department" that "Simpsons likes us to get dressed up" for court (M-18, 20), and again when the "sergeant from 52 Division phones in" information (M-38). Spoken prompts surfaced when "the policeman . . . said come along" into the courtroom (M-69), the bailiff "announced the judge was coming in, please stand" (M-80, 81), "the judge asked [the defendants] to come forward and . . . plead," and the crown attorney explained the investigators' options to them (M-106–M-109).

The written agenda was prefabricated, first as "dope sheets" kept by M and partner in the Simpsons security office, notes on "what happened" and "who was involved" that they had "written down" at the time of the theft and arrests. The partners re-read the dope sheets before the hearing, then brought them to the courtroom for reference (M-11,12). Then there was the "great big calendar" "marked down with the names of the investigators, the date, the police officers and the courtroom" (M-38, 39, 40). Also there were the judge's "papers" that he was "riffling through" at the bench (M-88).

Another portion of the written agenda was being compiled by the "two court stenographers" transcribing everything officially said and done at the hearing. These writings served the immediate purpose of structuring action at the scene and the more integrative purpose of structuring "the case" into a social object, spanning discrete times and places. The court case is not only the state's case and the defendants' case (the documents are filed under the title "Ontario versus Smith, Jones, et al.") it is M and partner's case as documented in their notes from which they might be called upon to publicly testify, and it is Simpsons' case against certain alleged shoplifters, plus it is one of the judge's docket of cases, part of his workload, one of 52 Division's police cases, one of the prosecuting crown attorney's cases for which he is "trying to get things organized" (M-38), and one of the defense attorney's cases, part of his "practice."

The hearing is dramatically public in contrast, for example, to the exaggerated privacy of J's medical examination, which clarifies one of the major differences between contests and conferences: a conference is not a true conference unless it is officially private, and a contest is not a true contest unless it is officially public.

N describes participation in an occasion of voting. N is the central participant, the voter, as the judge was in the Exhibit M, for N has the decision-making power over who shall win and who shall lose. Parallel to the way in which the legal case in Exhibit M was composed of several discrete hearings, of which M described only one, N's vote is but one of the thousands of decision-making occasions which in the aggregate will decide the outcome of the municipal election, the contest at issue.

N's own words give the clearest picture of what N well knew N was doing: "I voted in the Mississauga municipal election" (N-2). There is no need to theorize an invisible hand guiding N's actions because observed evidence of concrete instructions in writing, in speech, and in specified recall of past learning obviates abstract or invisible explanations for the organized, socially meaningful and effective character of N's conduct.

In writing the agenda is prefabricated a week in advance by "a little card in the mail" that "tells you where your polling station is, and what time it's open" (N-4, 5). At the poll N confronts an official who consults "a list of names and addresses of voters" (N-34). To commemorate the fact of N's voting, "she just crosses out my name," and to facilitate the action, "she gave me my ballot" (N-43), another written agenda, as well as a commemorative record, "like a computer card" displaying the names of the candidates, in which N "punched a hole opposite the candidate you are voting for" (N-45, 46). Finally the vote is made secret and inviolable, an official government document: "there's a little cover for it, you slip it in and hand it back to the lady," who locks it in a box (N-54).

In speech and gesture, the spoken agenda, "there's this guy" "demonstrating a new technique for voting," "he would show you how to use it"" (N-36, 37, 38). Then, "he asked me . . . what street I lived on, and he told me which table with the lists to go to, and I told the lady my name and she asked me what street I live on . . . and she gave me my ballot" (N-41, 42, 43). The election contest results came to N in a verbal postscript: "my dad told me," "one of the neighbors phoned and told him" (N-61, 66).

N also carried tacit knowledge of how to behave. In the city council election, N "knew who I wanted" to win (N-52) because "she lives in our area and I know her daughter" (N-13). As to N's previous balloting experience, it was "just with a pencil, you mark it" (N-39), so N required instruction on the "new technique."

The intensity of the competition in Exhibit O is the fiercest of our three contests. The courtroom decorum of Exhibit M and the almost casual ballot casting in Exhibit N literally pale to insignificance when compared to the bloody underwater gouging "where the referees can't see" (O-79) between contestants in the waterpolo finals, until (O-82) "the pool turns pink." But all that is at stake in the waterpolo game is an intramural championship in a not-yet-popular sport before a three-person audience, whereas the election determined several employments and unemployments and urban and educational policies for years to come, and the court case would decide the freedom or incarceration of five women. This inverse relationship between the weightiness of the outcome and the ferocity of competitive activity raises interesting questions.

The core agenda for any competitive occasion is what is to be done and not done in the contest, "the rules of the game." In "women's innertube waterpolo," as O names it (O-2), O first claims there are only two rules (O-6) and then goes on to name five more, with exceptions. The list:

1. Don't physically touch an opponent's body (O-6).
2. Don't hold the ball for more than ten seconds (O-7).
3. Do have six and only six people on a side (O-5).

4. Do try to score by throwing the ball into the net (O-7, 10).
5. Don't touch ball if not in your tube, except goalies (O-84).
6. Do release ball if you are "dunked out" (O-84, 85).
7. Do grab opponent's tube to dunk her out (O-78).

When we look more closely at this or any other ordinary social occasion, there are thousands more "rules," things to be done and not to be done because it is *this* designated occasion. The two rules that O ingenuously recites as the only rules of innertube waterpolo are the primary "fouls" which, if detected, will lead a referee to blow the whistle and award possession of the ball to the other team. With regard to rule 2, holding the ball for more than ten seconds (O-87), "the referee is counting." The no touching rule is more difficult to enforce, because (O-115) "referees can't see underwater." "The Pharmacy girls," according to O, violated this rule so vigorously through underwater fingernail gouging that not only did the pool turn pink, but such "dirty play" determined the margin of victory, and afterwards "we made a formal complaint about them and so did the referees" (O-124).

We have evidence that there was some agenda writing, a bit of instructional talk, and a great deal of tacit recall going on about how to participate in an innertube waterpolo game. The referees "keep score on clipboards" (O-68) and because it's a championship game there is "one more girl who is seated at a table who writes it down" (O-69), providing the written commemoration of the occasion's events.

The other teams had official coaches to instruct them on strategy, whereas O's team relied on strategic advice from an "experienced player" (evidently O). Even O's experience was inadequate to forewarn the team about the degree to which the Pharmacy girls would engage in "dirty play" (O-122). O's tacit agenda, in other words, did not include the possibility of this much scratching, but O knew which activity mode was predominant: "It is very competitive" (O-33).

Competitive struggle appears to be deeply embedded in everybody's social life, both as a secondary mode of activity in a wide range of social occasions that are predominantly something else, and as the predominant activity mode in a specific subset of ordinary occasions. The proposition submitted here, thus far substantiated by only three rigorously observed instances, is that competition as a process, and contests as specific types of occasions, are human universals.

Contest is a unique mode of activity in that it builds in conflict between participants and uncertainty of outcomes as positive, appropriate features of the occasion, not as deviance or breakdown. In this sense competition serves to demonstrate to us all, in a regularly recurring manner, that certain of the chaotic or chaos-producing elements always confronting and eroding the normalcy of social order, such as conflict and uncertainty, can be embraced and "tamed" in structured interaction. Competition is risky business, which is probably why it is hedged in with more conspicuous, more exacting rule enforcement and boundary maintenance than are found in other activity modes. It is a vehicle for flirting with danger, an adventure into the void of dissolution and meaninglessness, but with plenty of safety harness, a full supply of Ariadne's thread to lead us back out of the labyrinth. In a contest we provoke unpredictable change, and willingly unleash the forces that tear relationships apart. There is wisdom in reproducing our peril with manageable parameters as practice in crisis management. Why else put our hard-won certainties of normalcy and permanence at unnecessary risk? ("Unnecessary" because, using the old Hobbesian standbys of force and fraud, winners could just as well stay winners, as in "president for life" or "slave owner.")

If, as speculated earlier, meals serve to socialize the isolation of personal organic gratification, and collaborative work serves to socialize the required expenditure of painful effort, the condition of existence socialized and made more humanly bearable by contests is the uncertainty generated by conflict. This condition is so universally confronted that we should expect ubiquity of competitive occasions among all human groupings, and within any collectivity, as one of the recurrent activity modes enacted under the regime of every major institutional relationship ID. The Human Relations Area Files confirm the first point, documenting games, mock battles, trials and prize awarding contests in the repertoire of every known human group. The second question we can only begin to answer here.

The function of organized competition in social life is to legitimate ranking, inequality, social power. Contests habituate us to the idea that the winners, the holders of more power and privilege than the rest of us, have been differentiated from the losers by a rule-bound process of competitive performance and officially "fair" judging, and therefore somehow we deserve our relative fates. Critics who claim that the poor never had a chance, or that elections are a choice between Tweedle-dum and Tweedle-dee, can be dismissed in such a competition-besotted society as ours as "poor sports." Always and everywhere amongst humans, we speculate, the rite of competition functions to reorganize hierarchies, to re-identify winners and losers, and thus provide a legitimate channel for social change, or at least for the hope- sustaining belief that change is possible. This belief is most illusory when the contest format resembles that of a lottery.

VI. CONVIVIAL ACTIVITY: THE REPRODUCTION OF FUN

The conceptual crafting of the previous five activity modes was a search of many years through descriptions and memories of ordinary occasions to identify and differentiate all of the activities that human social life consists of, to develop an exhaustive set of action categories that would both aid in analysis and possibly reflect humanly universal definitions of situations. However there remains a recurrent, commonplace form of interaction, a type of social activity whose generic agenda is itself residual, whose defining characteristic, to the analyst as well as to participants, is that it is "none of the above," once we have considered meals, tasks, gatherings, conferences and contests. The focus, the purpose, the generic activity mode of such residual occasions for their participants is nothing but, or at least nothing predominant over, the enjoyment of the pleasure of each other's company. It is proposed that we identify these as a separate activity category, convivial occasions, good times, where the life of social life itself is celebrated and consummated. Simmel called them occasions of sociability (1892).

Occasions of consensual sex are included in this category, except for those defined by the participants as in conformance with Papal decree, and therefore strictly for the purpose of producing offspring, and therefore at least predominantly, if not exclusively, collaborative, not convivial. Sex is a prime example of this mode of activity, for what else is there to experience and enjoy in sex but the pleasure of the other's intimate company?

One can see via the sexual example that admixture of other activity modes within a convivial occasion diminishes its conviviality. Whereas sex might be comfortably preceded by a meal, to intertwine the two is a problem, or at least no longer an *ordinary* sexual occasion. If one sex partner is working at it for a living, the full possibilities of sexual enjoyment, like enjoying the enjoyment of one's partner, are limited. Sex before or among a large audience may be difficult to fully enjoy. If the information being confided between bedmates takes priority over the sex, problems of performance might arise. And the sex contest, in which one partner wins and the other loses, is probably generically close to everybody's definition of rape. Other convivial occasions may be less intense and less intimate than sexual encounters, but their content is nevertheless the enjoyment of the mere presence of the other participants, the focal activity being the pleasuring of each other. This chapter presents and analyzes participants' descriptions of three actually occurring instances of conviviality, Exhibit P, "P's Barbeque," Exhibit Q, "Q's Pub Night," and Exhibit R, "R's Something."

For many people, including many students I have asked about it, convivial occasions make up the sum total of what they consider to be their "social life." Studenthood is the time in one's life when being sociable, engaging in social intercourse, socializing, is the prime activity on the agenda, the conscious intention of every participant, whether that agenda is printed like an invitation to a ball, spoken, as "let the good times roll!" or tacit as when a friend is considered to be "a real party animal." Let us note that even if the convivial agenda is residual and loosely structured, and even though participation in convivial occasions is "just for the fun of it," every participant has to learn "how to have a good time," and every convivial group has its own particular "rules of engagement" so that it is just as easy and frequent for someone to be a "party deviant" ("wet blanket," "party pooper") as any other kind of deviant.

As prefabrication for P's attendance at "a barbeque" a verbal agenda was negotiated in the form of an "invitation" (P-6–P-16) The invitation contained a truncated version which then was spelled out in more detail through questions and answers. The "what" was "a barbeque," the "who" the "friend of mine" plus unspecified others, the "when" a Sunday, the "where" "at his home," and the "why" implied by the festive implication of "barbeque" (P-6, 7) and the host's asking if P would be "free" to participate. P asked him further, "What time?" and he answered, "One o'clock." Then P asked who else would be there and got a vague answer, indicating there would "probably not" be anyone else there that P knows, because "it was his brother's party" (F-11, 12, 13). Finally P asked how to dress, but the host only answered "anything I want," which was not specific enough for P, "so I assumed since it was a barbeque, outside, naturally I would wear something like jeans, pants, informal" (P-14, 15, 16). (Here P relied upon a tacit repertoire, that "a barbeque" implies a party where food is cooked out of doors, so "naturally" outdoor clothes would be appropriate.)

P posits the generic agenda for a "party": "people gathering, alcohol" (P-4). What actually occurred was mostly that "they were listening to music and drinking" (P-36); "they offered us drinks, and we sat around" (P-44); "the host introduced them, and gave them drinks" (P-46,47); "me and my girlfriend, the host and his brother went to sit in the kitchen and make a few drinks" (P-55); "they got drinks in the kitchen" (P-59); "girls came into the kitchen to get more drinks" (P-72); and "more drinks were poured" (P-87). The action also consisted heavily of conversation: "we sat around and talked" (P-44); "they sat down and talked" (P-47); "later in the conversation" (P-53-54); "we were all talking" (P-65); "about anything, working, um, cracking jokes, people cutting up one another" (P-76, 77).

A minor portion of the activity fit the billing of a "barbeque": "The brothers decided to start the barbeque, so me and my girlfriend and a few other people went outside with them . . . and we played Frisbee" (P-79, 80). The food was brought inside and for a while "it was more quiet, everyone was concentrating on eating" (P-85). So there was some shred of a contest in the "Frisbee," something like a meal, and some conferencing, but none of these prevailed. The actual, positive agenda for this occasion and generically for all successfully convivial occasions is stated by P in parting words to the host, "I really had a good time" (P-96).

Exhibit Q is the first ordinary occasion not named by the witness. It is labeled "Q's pub night" by the analyst. This further illustrates how ill-defined the "what" dimension of a convivial occasion is. Until line Q-38, "dancing," we get no description of what's on the agenda. Q and friends "stood in line to get tickets to buy drinks" (Q-46, 47); "we drank and talked" (Q-49); "we had a second drink" (Q-53); "my two friends danced but I didn't" (Q-54); "we got our third drinks" (Q-65); "one of the guys from the other table came over to join us and we talked" (Q-67, 68); "some of them were dancing, even me" (Q-69); "I had a fourth drink and continued dancing," and that was that.

Q considered the occasion a success, worth the cost and effort, because "I had a lot of fun out of it. I talked to a lot of people." The convivial agenda continues to appear comparatively amorphous, "free style," residual. In addition to the predominant conviviality, there was also collaboration among bartenders, bouncers, disk jockey and the band; congregation when the band came on to play and the merrymakers acted like an audience; communication between pairs of talkers in fragmentary conferences; and even some competition between suitors contesting for Q's agreement to dance. However, except for the addition of dancing, what we have here is the basic convivial agenda enunciated by P: "people gathering, alcohol." And again as in P's account, the reason Q had to leave early was to meet school work commitments the next morning: conviviality as the activity mode residual to all other modes. Convivial talk then, is both an instrument used to give life to important parts of our social lives, and it is a desirable consequence of participating in social life. In this one circumstance, at least, we can truly eat our cake and have it, too.

Exhibit R is our third look at a convivial occasion, and a more residual agenda would be hard to find. R tells us it was "a drinking occasion, to pass time" (R-4); "just something we do on a Sunday night when there's nothing better to do" (R-9); an occasion arranged when "everybody decided they didn't want to do anything in particular" (R-17, 18). "This is like a regular occasion" (R-51), wherein the activities include "watching a video" "sprawled over the couch, the floor" (R-39, 31), "eating finger food, veggies with dip and chips" (R-41), drinking, "The guys tend to drink beer while the girls drink the mixed drinks" (R-47, 48), and predominantly, recreational talk: "chatting," "the latest gossip" (R-54), "across the room, across conversations," "you usually end up screaming trying to get your words in," sometimes about jobs and each other, but mostly gossip "about all the other people that we don't get along with" (R-71, 72).

There is a small amount of congregation in the video-watching, a bit of commensality in the "finger foods," and some degree of conferencing in the group-wide talk about outsiders. This is hardly noticeable at the occasion itself. The relative lack of specific content is best summed up by R's three words: "something we do." I recognize this amorphous generic agenda as an important component of my social life, as do my students, colleagues and friends. Perhaps it is universal among humans, and if so, it must serve a significant purpose in everybody's social life.

The paradox of conviviality is that while it is the activity mode least burdened with actions required of participants, the residual activity that is "time out" from other interactive demands, it is at the same time the most intensely, most fully social kind of activity to perform, because there is nothing to it, really, but the reality of each other's co-presence. Conviviality is what we do together when there's nothing to do, but for good friends it's everything we do together, and "we do everything together," as R told us.

The major contrast between conviviality and competition as predominant activity modes is that whereas contests are ID transforming, putting the relationship between contestants into question and then resolving it as winners and losers, good times are ID confirming, enhancing and strengthening the intimacy of the cohesive relationship between all participants, who enter a convivial occasion as equals, and leave it even more equal, and unified, than before. If competitive occasions provide practice in crisis management by tightening up the rules while risking uncertain outcomes, convivial occasions invert this. The outcome of conviviality is not in doubt: Participants are here together to give and take enjoyment, and so the rules can be thrown right out the window to allow us to find the most direct path to "fun."

The sense of free choice is probably the icing on the cake, the extra exhilaration of the experience of conviviality among friends. But it is also another source of subversion, after egalitarianism, with regard to other activities and other institutions. Your relatives, your employees and employers, your co-religionists, your classmates, your countrymen, cannot be so freely chosen or changed as your friends, and the enjoyment of friendship chafes against the contrasting restraints of these other relationship IDs.

Participation in meals, work, audiences, conferences and contests is also less free than participation in the minimum, loose rule set of conviviality. But conviviality has its costs as well as its benefits in everybody's social life. We all seek and seem to need the freedom, equality and uninhibited enjoyment of each other that conviviality offers. The cohesion of friendship groups is also cemented by this potent glue, the critical group being the couple, whose growing and deepening erotic love for one another may be foundational for social cohesion in general. But the cost of too much conviviality may be to make all other social demands appear unreasonable, and threaten cohesion in other institutional areas and activity participations.

Conviviality probably does not complete an exhaustive list of activity modes, however it is proposed that this form is universal, and is universally defined and experienced as rewarding in itself, just for participation's sake. The purest distillation of social interaction is the enjoyment it brings, the pleasure of each other's company, and this pleasure is our greatest motivation to participate in social life at all. (This analysis of empirical evidence substantiates many of Simmel's speculations about "sociability" [1892].)

Like meals, convivial occasions are designed to bring their participants closer together as persons and as members of the dining or partying group. But commensality relies upon the materiality of the food and the table, and their utilization in mutual alimentation monitoring, to work its solidarity producing magic. Conviviality dispenses with material props and pretexts and goes directly for the participants' mutual objective—intimacy. In this sense Simmel's ideas about sociability don't suit the facts of conviviality as we observe it. Conviviality, at least in its ordinary versions, is not artificial, non-consequential, and indirect like the sociability outlined by Simmel, but instead ingenuous, direct, and maximally efficient in the production and maintenance of deep and perceivably genuine social bonds.

All it takes for a party, according to P is "people, alcohol." For R's bunch, conviviality needs no name, it is just "something we do."

It is an irony of conviviality that whereas the material elements of interaction are reduced to a minimum, it is precisely the material, sensual, physical pleasures of the mere *presence* of the others that is most thoroughly enjoyed in this activity mode. And, contrary to the artificiality of Simmel's sociability, ordinary conviviality allows participants to come to "know" each other in the most genuine, unvarnished manner possible in social interaction.

NOTES

* The study of the nature and types of socially interactive *activity*, per se, has been sadly neglected by sociologists since Homans (1950: 336) laid it out as a basic "analytical concept for the study of social groups." The focus should be, Homans said, "things that people do," "movements of the muscles," the importance of some of which "like talk and ceremonies, depends on their symbolic meaning." Anthropologists have been better at describing activities, though their focus has been almost exclusively on the feasts and festivals of "others" rather than the ordinary meals and gatherings of people like us.

1. Some exceptions include Counihan, 1992; Douglas, 1972 and 1974; Farb and Armelagos, 1980; Goode and Theophano, 1984; Gross, 1984; Roy, 1960; and

Visser, 1991. But in none of these is the focus directly on the social organization of meal-taking. Counihan, for example, reports students' declared food preferences, but leaves for future research "questions about how they actually relate to eating while doing it" (1992: 64). In my opinion the ignoring of commensality as a basic and important form of social interaction is an expression and a symptom of the underlying sexism of sociological research and analysis, practiced without exception by sociologists of both genders until recently, because most often the organization of meals is defined perjoratively as "women's work."

2. Harre (1979: 61) following Douglas (1972) notes that "the mere orderliness of a meal, the standardization of its sequencing, allows the accompanying social interaction to proceed unimpeded by doubts, fears of digestive upsets, or by social uncertainty, as dish follows dish in accordance with some recognized cuisine."
3. Note that these are not drawn from the even more varied collection of festive, ceremonial and special occasion meals that are the stock in trade of Anthropologists, but are described by participating informants as ordinary replications of regular, routine meals.
4. "What is called 'authority' presupposes, in much higher degree than is usually recognized, a freedom on the part of the person subjected to authority. . . . He [the subordinate element] participates in a sociological event which requires his spontaneous participation. . . . All leaders are also led; in innumerable cases, the master is the slave of his slaves" (Simmel, 1950: 183, 184, 185).
5. A generic agenda, to remain clear, is a list of "do's" and "don'ts," one of the devices participants use to sustain the "stability of social routine," which Garfinkel correctly argues "is a condition which enables persons in the course of their everyday affairs to recognize each other's actions . . . as reasonable, normal, legitimate, understandable and realistic" (1974: 73).
6. "Phenomenological" sociologist Alfred Schutz calls this simulated overlap of internally experienced reality "the reciprocity of perspectives," by which we are enabled to believe that we share the same world of things and events with other humans, even while knowing that this is not logically possible. Schutz reasons that "Commonsense thinking overcomes the differences in individual perspectives . . . by two basic idealizations:

i) The idealization of the interchangeability of standpoints: I take it for granted—and assume my fellow-man does the same—that if I change places with him so that his 'here' becomes mine, I shall be at the same distance from things and see them with the same typicality as he actually does; moreover, the same things would be in my reach which are actually in his. (The reverse is also true.)

ii) The idealization of the congruency of the system of relevances: Until counterevidence I take it for granted and assume my fellow-man does the same—that the differences in perspectives originating in our unique biographical situations are irrelevant for the purpose at hand of either of us and that he and I, that 'We' assume that both of us have selected and interpreted the actually or potentially common objects and their features in an identical manner or at least an 'empirically identical' manner, i.e., one sufficient for all practical purposes" (Schutz, 1963: 311).

We find the blind spot in Schutz's argument to be his assumption that "we take it for granted." Instead, this research demonstrates how "we make it appear" that "these "idealizations" are achieved and ustained by conscious, intentional effort.

7. "Realized" simultaneously in all three of its dictionary meanings: "1. to make real; to bring into being; to achieve. 2. to make appear real. 3. to understand fully; to apprehend."
8. The mix of tacit, spoken, and written aspects of the occasioned agenda is displayed in all its variety in the subsequent occasions to be examined below.
9. This is not to imply it is "faked" justice; the manufacture and display of it is as real as it gets.
10. Garfinkel calls all such sought-after situational definitions, social structure in the making, "the potter's object" (1988). It is precisely this that distinguishes, for the "humanistic Marx," the human weaver from the spider. Remove the end-in-view from the mind's eye of the worker, Marx argued, and you have reduced the human being to a preprogrammed animal or insect, one major component of alienation.
11. See Simmel (1950: 268-300 ff.).
12. I had thought to call the foci of attention during congregational occasions "spectacles," meaning, neutrally, "that which is audienced." But MacAloon (1984) and others make the valuable point that "spectacle" is a judgment-laden term meaning "mere spectacle," or implying distantiation from an audience. To avoid such judgments, and to emphasize our focus on the actions of the assembled audience, "performance" has mainly been used instead, and the occasions of audiencing called "gatherings," or "congregations." "Spectacle" then would refer to one specific "genre" of cultural performance, in MacAloon's terms.
13. MacAloon (1984) makes the point that the vast increase in TV viewing of the Olympic Games has been accompanied by large increases in the live audiences for the games as well, and that no one assumes the former to be a substitute for the latter.
14. This is not MacAloon's focus, but he notes in passing the Olympic Games' stated purpose of producing universal human solidarity.
15. This economic relationship between a service provider and a client is a special one; the doctor/patient relationship is a well studied one in sociology, though I think it would be better studied as a type of professional/client relationship (cf. Atkinson and Heath, 1981; Heath 1984, 1986).
16. K's "supposedly" implies that in this case, as is true in many others, course descriptions contain elements of "false advertising." It is also a word that may apply in some degree to all written agendas: they list what is "supposedly" to be done, not necessarily what is actually done or intended.
17. This phenomenon, "the coordination of verbal and nonverbal behavior between the doctor and the patient," is in itself the subject of Heath's fascinating paper (1984).
18. It is my contention that the empirically observable basis for a "socialization process" as a major organizing factor in social life is precisely the series of previous run-throughs of such routines which serve as "life lessons." Everyone experiences a "first" medical appointment, and after that, the rest is practice.
19. If we combine Simmel's ideas about secrecy and Hughes' ideas about professionalization with reference to these three communicative conferences, the following speculations are reasonable: To the extent that "knowledge is power" in social life, it is the *withholding* of knowledge from the subordinate, and the subordinate's superordination of those with exclusive possession of knowledge, that makes the proposition true. The hallmark and the foundational feature

of professionalism is the possession and application of arcane, that is narrowly distributed knowledge, or *lore*. Professionals therefore wield in social life in proportion to the critical importance their exclusive knowledge is believed to have for the lives of others, and to the difficulty of its attainment by anyone and everyone. In our three examples, the patient could attain knowledge of the patient's own state of health only *through* the doctor; the student could achieve mastery of French literature only *through* the professor, and the penitent could find the straightest path from guilt to forgiveness only *through* the priest. The power of the doctor increases as the public becomes more concerned with the importance and value of good health, and decreases as medical knowledge (how to use nutrition and exercise to enhance good health) becomes more widely distributed in the populace. The power of the professor rises and falls with the changing public perceptions of the value of various subject matters (how does French literature *matter?*) and with the ease or difficulty in achieving a Ph. D. The power of the priest varies with public perceptions of the value of divine intercession in private life, and with the perceived holiness and thus specialness and efficacy of the priesthood.

4

The Display and Acquisition of Social ID during Live Social Occasions

Looking from a different analytical angle at the collection of eighteen descriptions of ordinary social occasions presented above, we can see that they exhibit not only the establishment and enactment by participants of a variety of patterns of activity, but also the interactive reproduction of *social IDs*, which are the live material building blocks of symbolically realized structural entities such as status hierarchies, relationships, institutions, and organizations.

Each participant described by our student informants is given one or more appellations indicating who the informant recognized that participant *to be* during the live course of the occasion, and often who the other participants recognized the specified participant to be. (For instance, A claimed to have routine weekday breakfasts with "my father.") The appellations, social IDs, name the "badges" or "labels" symbolically worn during interaction, like devices on medieval shields, which identify the players to one another. Through analysis of our transcript data, we are enabled to lay out a range of types of social ID and modes of social identification, the products and the procedures of the *process* of social identification. In some cases, we can actually observe the creation of new IDs intended to last beyond the occasion into the future. Who we are to each other and who we are becoming is thus explicated as a dynamically reproduced social reality.

Social ID versus Personal Identity, Labels, and Roles

We wish to sharply distinguish here, between all versions of the term "identity" which refer to who individuals think they are, or the self as perceived by the self, on the one hand, and on the other hand "social ID," or just "ID" for short, which refers exclusively to who others define and declare individuals and collectivities to be, social participants identified by other social participants. (A participant can of course self-describe who it is that other participants identify that self to be. E can say "I am a price changer" only because that is the task that has been assigned to E by grocery store managers.) ID is strictly an overt, external, objective matter (though it may be highly symbolic or abstract in content) as compared to the covert, internal, subjective nature of "identity."

The concept of social ID and the identification process is similar in many ways to the idea of label and labeling process which challenged standard notions of "identity and "role" in social science literature in the seventies and eighties, but the differences are deep and critical. "Labeling" helpfully focuses attention on the *process* of identification in social life, opening up the realization that stigmatizations like "deviant," "crazy," "stupid," or "evil" cannot be about anything which inheres in the stigmatized, but exist entirely and only in the eye, the mouth and the meaning-constituting actions of the beholder. A label is also an exteriorized social phenomenon, applied from the outside by others, rather than an interior, psychological concept like identity. But the idea of labeling casts too narrow a beam of light on the identification process ubiquitous in social life, emphasizing pejorative labels, the "names" people "call" one another, and the superficiality of labels, which by analogy with stationery items, can be "stuck on" and "peeled off" like the grocery prices E changes (see also Pollner, 1978).

"Role" is a concept so overused in recent social science that its core of meaning is worn out, like a machine bearing. So many different phenomena, at so many different levels of analysis, have been referred to as "roles" that the term no longer has any clear referent. Most of the meanings of "role" reify the concept, conjuring up images of sui generis pre-existing molds of identity and activity into which active, live persons fit themselves, to become merely the role's incumbents. This idea is off course by 180 degrees in light of our data, so we simply avoid the term as contaminated with incorrigible error. We also reject analyst-generated categorizations of types of persons as so much superficial labeling, without foundation in any actual process of social identification (see also Pfohl, 1975).

"ID" encompasses all of the descriptive nouns and adjectives applied to single and multiple participants by other social participants, "epithets" in the Homeric sense, some of which are positively or negatively judgmental, and some of which are value neutral, strictly descriptive. The process of identification in which IDs are applied is not only ubiquitous throughout social life, it is also the serious business of constructing the bone-deep reality of who we are to each other, and who we treat each other "as," the most rock-solid features of the otherwise shifting sandcastle structures of character, status, organizations and institutions.

Multiple IDs

Perhaps the most significant difference between "ID" as used here and "identity" as generally meant in the human sciences is that the latter term emphasizes singularity and a unified inner core of "the real self," as in "who am I, *really*?," whereas with every look we take at the living process of mutual social identification it becomes more evident that each of us bears a large and growing number of incompatible and discontinuous social IDs, none of which can be said to be more or less "real" than any other, and all of which are subject to change, renewal, re-negotiation and momentary termination.

An ID is a "guise" in which a participant appears to other participants on occasion, a characterization of the self for the purposes at hand. The existence of permanent, hyper-real selves, is a question beyond the scope of our empirical analysis, which simply provides a look at the many types of social ID bestowed upon participants in our eighteen exemplary occasions by other participants, all of which could become part and parcel of the kitbag of IDs carried and lived by in the social life of any one of us. We can also examine some of the standard procedures of ID bestowal, the routine practices making up the identification process, as they are carried out by the participants in our exhibits, and by all of us.

Mechanically speaking, the analysis presented below began with the excerpting from the transcripts of all references in words and phrases to persons acting as participants in the occasions, and sorting the references into categories. Special attention was then given to the contexts of interaction within which, during the live occasions, these references were explicitly utilized, negotiated, changed or newly minted.

Task ID and Link ID

In the eighteen occasions under consideration, participants can be observed to present themselves to each other or to be recognized by the others in two major forms of ID-guise, which I call task ID and link ID. Task ID identifies participants, singly and in groups, according to what they do upon the occasion, whereas link ID identifies them, again singly and in groups, according to whom they are related among the other participants, how they are related, and what is the nature of the relationship or membership. Task ID is shaped in relation to and in co-determination of the activity mode of the immediate occasion, whereas link ID reflects and gives substance to longer- term and larger scale meaning structures, such as relationships, organizations and institutions.

Some examples of task ID: our table of diners; the night crew; the crowd of fans; the class; the prosecution; the waiter; the conductress; the chairman; the doctor; the goalie, the host. Some examples of link ID: my sister, the rest of the family; my best friend, our gang; my co-religionists, this church; my classmates, the university; my teammates, intercollegiate waterpolo; my section, the altos, Ukrainian choral music; my doctor, his practice; my polling district of registered voters, the municipal government.

These two forms of ID serve as building blocks for the construction of two different sets of structured entities which are reified through the repeated enactment of the relevant occasioned IDs. Repeated enactment of task IDs yields the apparent reality of individual and group *character*, based on judgmental evaluations of how well or ill individuals or groups perform the activity task at hand. (For instance, the sister who lunches on "normal foods'" the "workaholic" crew chief, the "jerky" football fan, the waterpolo team that "plays dirty.") In addition, task IDs cumulate into apparently real and substantial structures of *status ranking*, hierarchies formed by the extrinsic judgmental ranking of tasks relative to each other, which directly ranks the *doers* of these tasks, and by the inherent superordination/subordination built into various modes of activity, which we began to examine in chapter 3, above.

Repeated enactment of link IDs yields the apparent long-term existence of *relationships*, whose qualities differentiate them into various institutional realms of meaning (kinship, friendship, religion, learning, sport, art, the economy, the polity). Institutionally defined relationships, in turn, are linked up in clusters as *organizational memberships* (in families, cliques, churches, schools, leagues, publics, businesses, governments, and the like). The living social reality of institutions and organizations we can thus demonstrate, inheres in these live relationship and membership enactments upon occasion.

A status quo analysis of the social IDs displayed to each other and enacted by the participants in our eighteen occasional instances precipitates a tremendous variety of guises in which participants ordinarily appear, documenting the claim that "multiple IDs" are standard in social life, and it allows for the analytically valuable task/link distinction just introduced; but the most surprising and illuminating result is the serendipitous finding that in only five of the eighteen cases is ID of whatever form and variety an apparently static, stable, continuous matter. In the other thirteen cases, significant participant ID undergoes change, in varying degree, right before our eyes, as it were, and literally in the sight and hearing of fellow participants. This is surprising because we expected to find routine replication of the essential features of such *ordinary* occasions, with the dynamics of change a relatively rare phenomenon. Instead we find the negotiation and transformation of IDs to be a widely commonplace event, and are led to wonder whether the cases of apparent ID constancy may not be the extraordinary exceptions requiring further explanation.

So we present our ID analysis in terms of degree and type of change versus stability during the occasion, or, what happens to participant IDs over the course of ordinary social occasions?

1. FIVE CASES WHERE ID IS CONFIRMED AND SUSTAINED

What Exhibits A, B, C, D, and R have in common with regard to the dynamics of ID is that no change of IDs visibly occurred during these occasions. On the contrary, participants acted consistently to confirm and sustain their own and each others' singular and collective IDs, reproducing them as constants in their mutual social lives.

The task IDs indicated in Exhibit A are all pre-established, and routinely confirmed by repetition on this live occasion. Once again, as usual, it is A who comes downstairs to enter the kitchen, and the father who waits there, confirming and reestablishing their collective task ID as "the diners" at breakfast (even though the father doesn't eat anything, but characteristically "drinks his tea"). It is A who prepares and eats toast and eggs, and the father who asks "have you got up?," passes messages and assignments to A from the mother, asks A to walk the dog, offers to drive A to school later, and so it goes.

Exhibit A's link IDs are similarly confirmed as pre-existent as described by A at the center of the chain of linkages. "My father" and "my mother" are appellations indicating the lifelong existence of paternal and maternal relationships with A, indexing the structure of the kinship institution. When the rest of the family is referred to as "everyone" (A-47), the organizational reality of this embodiment of kinship, the family of which A is a member, is brought into play. The pre-existing link IDs of relationship and membership, confirmed by reenactment on this occasion, thus invoke both the structural realities of kinship in general and of this particular family.

The general point, illustrated in the first instance here in A but to be found the case in all subsequently analyzed occasions, is that the nature and existence of any institution or organization depends upon, respectively, how relationships are defined in action and how memberships are enacted and evaluated.

The reproduction through repetition at successive breakfasts of their kinship relationships and family memberships confirms and sustains, for exhibit A's participants, the structural reality of the kinship institution and the family organization.

In Exhibit B also the usual diners assemble themselves, though with much more effort and coordination required to reassert their task IDs. B, who waits, the sister, who comes home from school, and the father, who comes home from work, further characterize themselves as diners of a particular sort: B self-identifies as "a vegetarian," "so I usually have a salad," and "My father is Polish and [so] he likes his Polish food," and "My little sister has a normal sandwich" (B-12, 13). Each diner prepares and serves his own food, and two more task IDs have been assigned to non-participants: the mother, who shops for the food, and provisions the refrigerator for lunch, and the "Cinderella sister" who comes home later and washes everybody else's dishes. In clear assertion of his dominion over lunch, the father subordinates his children by "standing watching over them" while he eats, and tries to control the conversation by asking questions about sports. (He regularly fails, "My father just opens up the conversation, then my sister and I start talking and forget him" B-61, 62.) All of these task IDs are repeated in action as usual, every lunchtime, and thereby confirmed as features of the participants' normality.

B's link IDs are also modally the same as in A. "My father," "my little sister," and B on-stage at lunch, and "my mother" and "my other sister" behind the scenes, name the kinship relationships in play for B at lunch. B tells us that these lunches are an important contribution to the solidarity of this family as an organization because "it's about the only time I ever talk to my father" (B-91).

The kinship interaction over lunch is neatly contrasted with two other institutional domains within which the lunchers have other, sometimes competing relationships and memberships—the economy, embodied as the paid "work" the father comes home from and returns to after lunch, and the institution of learning, concretized in the school little sister leaves and returns to for lunch, and the university B is bound for after lunch. As members of those other organizations, the kin at lunch take on new IDs as worker, employee, student, classmate.

Exhibit C brings us into a scene of live interaction involving many more participants with a much larger variety of task IDs and link IDs in play, but all are still being reproduced and enacted "as usual," confirming the ID structures as preexistent and continuing, constant factors.

The task IDs making up Exhibit C's "cast of characters" include the manager who greets customers at the door, the waiters who show them to their tables, take their orders and serve them food, the cooks who work backstage, their presence evident only in the cooked food presented at table, and the cashier who accepts payment. All of the above act as a team to superordinate the other task-constituted group present, the "full house" (C-94) of tablesful of diners. C's tableful dines there regularly, so that all of the task IDs are reenacted "as usual," including the elder brother's choosing of the fish dish and paying the bill by credit card.

C's relatives reproduce their link IDs as kin on this occasion also. It is the only time they can spend together in their otherwise fragmented life as a family, time to talk "about family, all family talk" (C-56). And the elder brother takes on his traditional kinship responsibility by paying the bill on behalf of the others, "as always." Their relationships as kin are thus expressed and reinforced over the course of these dinners out.

What was the institutional relationship between C's party and the others present in the restaurant? The answer comes at the end of the occasion, when elder brother pays the bill, adding a "ten percent" tip for the waiters. C and family have been paying customers to the "boss" of the restaurant; the manager, waiters, cooks and cashier are the boss's paid employees, and the other diners are fellow customers, the restaurant's clientele. The tip makes the economic relationship between service personnel and the served at least ten percent direct.

Thus two institutions, kinship and the economy, are in simultaneous operation at the scene, erected as contextual settings by the link ID enactments of various participants. This duality of institutional settings is not confusing for participants (as we shall see below, many occasions are overarched with meaning by multiple institutional settings) and even for outsider-analysts, the hinge of contact between the institutions is clear. C's elder brother enacts a dual membership, as the responsible elder of C's family organization, and as a member of the economic group, "paying customers" who transact with the third organizational entity, "the Jade Garden restaurant as a business."

The kinship IDs, we must assume, were acquired through birth or marriage, and the economic relationships established at some occasion of hiring or investing or first customer-contact in the past, but all we can see before us in the present life of Exhibit C is an occasion of confirmation of these IDs, and thus of continuation and stabilization of the institutional frameworks and organizational entities they constitute.

All eight of the participants in exhibit D were engaged in an occasion of concerted work as were the members of the server team in C. Their collective task ID, D tells us, was "the night crew." Singly, D says, "I do price changing" (D-3); there is the "only one guy" who "brings it all out in front" (D-83); "the boys" (D-92) who stock the shelves and label items with their initial prices; and finally, there is the night crew chief, who works right on through the others' breaks because "he is a workaholic" (D-112). This is not only an allegation of deviant ID, but also a description of the chief's leadership style, his manner of exerting domination over his subordinate workers. He leads by example rather than subordination, and controls the pace of work via negotiation.

Institutionally, the link IDs displayed and enacted on this occasion indicate that the economy and friendship are active and interactive as institutional definitions.

Economically speaking, the night crew as an organization of paid employees has three categories of membership: hourly wage part timers, like D, hourly wage full timers, and the salaried chief, naming their salient institutional relationship to each other and to "management," which is straightforwardly economic.

But another type of relationship is enacted also. When they share coffee and food during breaks, and when they chat, yell and sing across the aisles during their labors, the participants relate to each other as friends. D has become "good friends" with some, socializes outside of working hours with several, and has kept up friendships with former coworkers. The friendships help keep the workplace livable (see Fine, 1986), the friendly banter helping get the workers through the night, but there is potential conflict between friendly and economic relations as expressed in the chief's avoidance of sharing the work breaks. To do so, he would have to collude in the theft of the store's food, rather than just condone it with a wink, and he would lose his reputation as a "workaholic" to be emulated. He is in the classic "straw boss" bind due to the leveling implications of conviviality among friends.

We see all of these IDs, task and link, in the process of being reproduced on this occasion, as constantly and unchangingly as can be effected. The ranking system of chief, full timers, part timers is kept in place and in force, and the relationships among friends and among coworkers are kept in balance and in stasis, just as the material objects along the aisles of the store have achieved appropriate reorganization and placement by the end of the midnight. However these IDs were originally acquired and established as social realities, it must have been upon prior occasions of interaction, because we see none of that happening here.

R is the last exhibit in which IDs are displayed, assumed, enacted, but not in any way intentionally changed over the course of the live occasion, not challenged or contested, not re-negotiated, transformed, or newly minted, but only confirmed and sustained as components of continuous normalcy.

By doing nothing "in particular," "something," and "everything" together, the eight participants in R plus the "missing" couple keep up a floating conversation of opinions, expressions of feeling, ideas, and gossip, and it is this talk, enjoyable in itself, that constructs the sense that they are "close in personalities" (R-64). This sense of closeness, in turn, generates further convivial interaction. They even develop IDs as couples with distinct personalities, as when R and boyfriend are chided as the couple that is "always the last ones to get there" (R-37). The creation, the evaluation and judgment, and the expression of "personalities" is the natural product of conviviality as mode of interaction.

The convivial space (the "rec room") and the conversational sounds that fill it are designed to tighten bonds and also to strengthen barriers, to draw friends closer to each other in terms of personal knowledge and intimacy, and at the same time to sharpen the distinctions and widen the distance between "us" and "not us." The casualness of dress and deportment makes the visual statement of participants being their true, unvarnished selves, and their arrangement in the small room "sprawled out all over the place" gives tangible shape to the sandcastle structure of "close friends." The members of the "bunch" engaged in "more gossip and drinking," "sprawled" over the rec room staying "really comfortable" while "screaming trying to get your words in," appear as the embodiment of consummatory social interaction, displaying this motive to the exclusion of all others continuously to each other.

Their task IDs as those who enjoy each others' company is thus solidified and confirmed by this occasion's convivial interaction.

R's "whole bunch of friends" who "do everything together" all "belong to a Polish association" and "all met through the ethnic group" (R-3, 12, 71, 74). They differentiate themselves as a subgroup from the rest of the association, "all the other people that we really don't get along with" (R-72), by gossiping about them, but not about each other. Everybody but R, who is at university, has a job, and school and work are also topics of their recreational conversation during their "something," at which they also watch videotaped films.

The above paragraph cites evidence that five different institutional relationship IDs were enacted during the life course of this single occasion: between the audience and the creators of certain films, something happened in the institution of art; between a university student and a number of graduates and non-students, something happened in the institution of learning; between several employees of different employers, and one as yet unemployed person, something happened in the institution of the economy; between members of a self-labeled ethnic group, something happened in the institution of kinship; and finally, and clearly predominantly, between eight participants in the scene, the two who didn't show up, and between the partners of each "couple," a great deal happened in the institution of friendship.

Each of these institutions receives its substance from the multiple enactments of relationship IDs in its institutional bailiwick, but for all that happened here, no new IDs were formed, and none were substantially changed beyond their reconfirmation in repeated enactment.

2. THREE CASES WHERE ID IS CONFIRMED BY MOMENTARY TRANSFORMATION

Looking at the social IDs of the participants in G, the church service, H, the football game (*except* for the tiny minority of participants comprising the two opposing teams) and J, the medical appointment, *before* they entered the occasion's locale and *after* they left it, one would have to say that these three cases belong in our first category because no noticeable change has taken place in the occasion-relevant IDs. If anything, a before-and-after comparison would reveal confirmation and strengthening of the initial IDs as religious denominational adherents, sports fans, and doctor/patient, professional/client. Nevertheless, *during* each of these occasions a remarkable and dramatic transformation of ID takes place, a momentary transformation whose ID changing effects are then reversed and dissipated by the occasion's end. In each of these three cases the dynamic process of social identification appears to contradict itself—a dramatic intentional transformation of ID momentarily during the occasion has the effect (intended and anticipated, mind you) of confirming and sustaining preexisting task and link IDs over the long run.

The congregants at G's Sunday service arrive at the church in family groupings, in groups of friends like G's, or singly, converging on this officially designated sacred place from their essentially secular and scattered world of everyday life. Handed a printed program at the door, they are led by it and by ushers, choir, organist, chairman and pastor (all task ID's assumed essentially "for" the service occasion), beginning with a meditative two-minute preparation for each new arrival called "singspiration," into an ever more massified unity of action and experience.

The high point of this mass identification, the sense that only the congregation as a unit is acting and that more individuated, fragmentary IDs have been canceled and erased, may be when all 150 individuals, any one of whose everyday speech could be in English, or Mandarin, or Cantonese, are singing the same well-known hymn in all three languages simultaneously, what would be a cacophony if it were not tonally in unison, and "very loud" (G-117), so that the sound filling the church is of one voice despite the internal differentiation of the singers.

The congregation manages to *become* one three-hundred-legged religious creature which worships, sings, and makes *a* monetary offering to the deity. Then, at the end of the occasion it literally disintegrates. At the door of the church, now "the exit," the pastor shakes hands and "says good-bye" (G-172) to each individual congregant, the official dispersal. G and friends proceed to shopping and lunch at a restaurant, back to individual and small group economic and friendship IDs. But G's task ID as congregant and religious/ethnic membership ID in this church organization are confirmed and sustained through this transformation for the moment. I go every week "because I go every week," G says (G-178).

An even larger beast of temporarily unified ID is created and then dissipated at the football stadium, venue for exhibit H. The audiencing crowd assembles on the basis of the most tenuous of economic relationships—as fellow ticket buyers, a purchase entitling each participant to possession of a marked hip-wide space in the stands for a few hours of carefully monitored viewing time. They also, by their sweaters, pennants and demeanor, assert a fleeting but intense relationship as fellow sports fans. Entering the stadium like H and friend in couples, in family groupings, singly or as bunches of friends, from anywhere and everywhere in and around the city, the participants merge over the course of the game into one gigantic ten-thousand-mouthed sports fan, screaming and gesticulating in articulated response to the dramatic performance on the playing field. The thrill for each of them, like it is for H, is "being in that crowd." Catharsis accomplished, individuated concerns and ID skins having been shed for a few hours ("purged of pity and terror") the fans disperse with their initial IDs intact, perhaps made more livable via the therapeutic effects of mass hysteria.

Perhaps our most vivid instance of the phenomenon of momentary ID transformation with only temporary ID-changing effects is described in Exhibit J, the medical appointment. In G and H, the individual congregation participants merged their IDs to become a single mass being, then broke up again into their fragmented separate IDs. In J, the two conference participants, acting as self-determined subjects, over the course of the occasion create a third participant, a passive object of their joint scrutiny who is then erased, and the same two participants leave the inner sanctum of the doctor's office who went in, their IDs virtually unchanged.

J begins the occasion in full possession of personhood, a full-fledged participant telling the new secretary "my name and that I was there for my appointment" (J-22). It was also established that J's own insurance coverage would pay the doctor's fee, that J would no longer seek medical treatment as a dependent child (J-78, 79). J's economic relationship ID was thus confirmed as a purchaser of medical services.

But J's subordination into the standardized "patient" ID (a specific variant of the more generic "master/tyro" relationship which is definitional for the learning institution) began immediately upon being directed into the "waiting room" where other patients waited, and to which the doctor came to identify and fetch "the next patient." This defined the ID situation clearly in two ways: that J, as "one of the patients waiting," would be treated as one of a category of persons rather than as unique and incomparable; and that the doctor's time is far more valuable than the time of any patient, who must wait for him. J is then ushered into the doctor's consulting rooms and directed where to sit.

At this point, however, the descent of J's relative status is slowed if not reversed. The doctor and patient together consult the file of J's medical history, which J has the status at this point to call "my file" (J-36), and the doctor asks J to describe any changes in medical condition over the past few months, an exchange, as between one medical expert and another, that inherently respects the intelligence and personhood of the patient on a plane of relative equality with the doctor. (As some teachers sometimes respect some students as "fellow learners.")

The next step creates a third participant, one without subjective status, a participant with a task ID as purely an *object* of the knowledge disclosure which is the heart of the conference agenda. The doctor "was ready to do an examination. He said I could go behind the curtain and undress into the white gown. So I did . . ." (J-42, 43, 44).

The doctor, dressed in "white medical garb over a suit" (J-48), proceeded to touch and probe J's naked body, which threatened or embarrassed J "not at all" (J-55). He also asked J questions in addition to extracting information directly from J's body, so J the subjective patient was active and present along with J the objectified body. I conclude from this that *both* J and the doctor objectified J's undressed body, which became the third participant, the object of J's and the doctor's joint inquiries.

J was transformed into a dual, separated ID by this series of ritual procedures, and then, "he said I could get dressed" (J-57), and J and the doctor once again sat at the doctor's desk and consulted and updated J's file. The doctor "announced he was pleased" with the findings (J-64), "that everything had gotten better" (J-59), told J "what he wanted me to do next" (J-66), walked J out to the waiting room to greet the "next patient," and the nurse/secretary arranged "another appointment for January, and that was it, and I went back to my car" (J-82, 83). The objectified ID as a body had evaporated, and all IDs as a person reestablished just as before.

3. SEVEN CASES WHERE ID IS RE-NEGOTIATED BUT INCOMPLETELY TRANSFORMED, WITH LONG-TERM OUTCOMES UNCERTAIN

Sometimes, the re-negotiation of ID is clearly evident during an occasion, long-standing ID transformation appears imminent, yet the process of ID change cannot be completed here and now, so the occasion ends without preexisting IDs having been terminated or brand new IDs having been created and established, but instead it ends in uncertainty, with IDs left suspended in doubt. It happens that this changeful but inconclusive pattern is to be found in a plurality of our cases, the seven exhibits marked E, F, K,

L, M, P, and Q, which describe a choir practice, a move, a seminar, a confession, a court hearing, a barbecue party, and a pub night.

In F and L, ID change is almost as ephemeral as in the three cases above, but there are unresolved questions left over at the end of the occasion.

F's botched move is a mild case in terms of serious ID change. A group of relatives and a friend of the family were asked by F's sister to take on the temporary task ID of "movers," a job which the "three guys" involved "didn't finish" (F-46). An additional friend "who works for a moving company" (F-56, 57) (a "real" mover) had to be called in to finish the job. F and his sister wound up mad and angry that "a hand made stained glass mirror got broken" (F-91) and "that my brother would leave the truck in the driveway. . . . Who did he think was going to move it in?" (F-88, 89, 90).

All of this put strains on the kinship and friendship relationships involved, seen as violations of the institutional rule stated by F: "The way it is in our family is if you need a favor I'll do it" (F-80). Whether the arguments and the anger over the move will change kinship and friendship relationship IDs in the long run remains to be seen, but "my brother the mover" is not a label F or his sister are likely to use in a positive sense for a long time to come.

L's religious ID is also only mildly brought into question at the confession. In conformance with kinship relationships (L's membership in a family—"my parents made me go" [L-4, 91]—which belongs as a group to a particular Catholic church), L obeyed the summons that "we have to go to confession" (L-5). Upon entering the tiny cubicle, L achieves personal anonymity at the same moment that intimate personal secrets are to be disclosed. The priest, his face veiled by a mesh screen, stares ahead in profile in relation to L's face. The ID-changing negotiation of confession, then, is defined as a performance of self by L in the eyes of the deity, with the priest acting as coach. It is left for God to judge whether L shall be identified as "saved," a mystery to be revealed only after death.

Exhibits P and Q describe occasions designed as incubators for the hatching of new friendships.

When invited by "a friend" to a barbeque party at his home, P asked, "Will there be anybody there I know?" and the answer was, "Probably not" (P-11). P brought along another already established friend, and at the party, the friend with the task ID "host" introduced new arrivals to P. From that point on, the interaction consisted of talk and play directed toward getting to "know" each other better. The next time they meet or plan to meet, all of the guests will be "somebody I know" to each of the others, in various degrees of acquaintanceship, so some manner of ID change has definitely occurred. Whether new friendship relationships began, or already established ones grew deeper and stronger, remains unknown as yet by the end of the occasion, but the exchange of personal information and gossip at the party provided the infrastructure for the development of such nascent IDs. (In fact, "P" visited my office as an alumna several years after Exhibit P was produced in class, and informed me that "the host" at that barbeque party had recently married one of the guests he had met then and there.)

Q's night at the pub was full of such opportunities and possibilities also, especially for Q's table companions who "dance with anyone" who asks (Q-60). Q turned down all requests for a dance save "one guy," who also conversed with Q and companions at their table, and this *might* have been the start of a longer-term friendship, though we can't be sure as yet. "I think we're probably going to meet again," Q opines, "probably by the same process, going to the same pub" (Q-84, 85). Such are the uncertainties of the friendship formation process, but each of us who has acquired a long-term friendship ID as "significant other" to someone can look back to some such beginning of one of our most important, stable, and life-sustaining ID acquisitions.

In Exhibits K and E we see negotiated attempts to acquire IDs in the institutional frameworks of learning and art, respectively, but though judgments are made, and the process of ID transformation progresses, the final decision in each of these cases is postponed to a future occasion.

In K the professor dominates the communicative activity as her task ID requires, and the subordinate students take notes, ask and answer questions, and make their "presentations." A major objective of all participants in this occasion as in the series of seminar classes like it making up the semester, is to negotiate new learning institution IDs to be certified for and displayed by the student participants in future. The students perform, the professor judges the performances, and at the end the successful students are certified to have become "knowledgeable" in advanced French literature, for whatever that institutional ID is worth in further interaction.

In E the conductress most imperiously dominates the collaborative activity of choir practice, and ID negotiation is at the heart of the matter for the choir as a whole and even more so for E in particular. The difference sought in the choir as a whole, from start to finish of the practice, is more artful singing, to be judged exclusively by the aesthetic expertise of the conductress. But the long range goal is "artful enough" to qualify for an international performance tour, and that institutionally defined ID cannot be achieved in one occasion, but will take an unknown number of practice sessions before the conductress' standards are satisfied, and the desired artistic ID can be bestowed upon the choir.

For E's ID quest the judgment of the conductress is more immediately critical. Is E's voice good enough to win the cherished ID "Wesnivka" (choir member)? Will E's task ID be "first alto," "second alto," or nonsinger? Will E be able to identify as one of these "upper-middle to upper-class" young ladies of Toronto, the desired economic ID? Will E achieve the goal of "becoming more Ukrainian," the preferred kinship ID? All of these intended ID transformations depend on the conductress' judgment of E's performance, and even after tonight's practice, the decision has not yet been made. Maybe next week.

But our most dramatic ID cliffhanger has to be Exhibit M, the court hearing, where a changed ID could have the most serious negative social consequences. M refers to the participants whose IDs are to be contested in this competitive occasion as "some shoplifters" (M-3) (violating, in this appellation, the presumption of innocence until proven guilty), the "five charged" (M-31) (though what they are to be charged with is still subject to negotiation), "the girls" (M-42, 111, 124), and "the defendants" (M-51, 77, 127). What was to be decided by the judge, based on the comparative performances before him of the defense team (the defendants and their lawyer) versus the prosecution team (the crown attorney, the policemen, and M and partner, store detectives) was the critical future political/legal ID of the defendants as presumed-to-be innocent free citizens, persons guilty of a misdemeanor who must pay a fine but will not be certified as criminals via a "criminal record," or in the worst case, convicted felons subject to incarceration and branded for life with a permanent criminal record.

During the occasion at hand, there is negotiation between the crown attorney and the store M works for about the economic value of the goods "lifted." If the deviant shoppers failed to pay for goods whose value is deemed less than two hundred dollars, the charge is a misdemeanor, easier to negotiate in court, saving the state time and money. But apparently the store's management is adamant, "it was still over" (M-121), so a felony charge must be pressed. Also being negotiated at the scene was the continuity of identification of "the defendants." Were the "girls" present in court the same persons as those "stopped" at the store? M found it hard to tell, because those in court were "all dressed up, not like we had seen them before" (M- 124). And perhaps this was a defense ruse, to put identification in doubt, because their court attire was almost a costume, "Two of the girls had the same dress on" (M-124, 125). It would be M's task to identify them before the judge, an identification that would be legally necessary to define them officially as the culprits, to create a new criminal ID.

The decision made this day was to put off a trial hearing, and the judge's ultimate decision about changing IDs, for two months, at which time, M says, "we're going back," and until which time, at least, the five girls can sustain their political/legal IDs as unconvicted free citizens.

4. FOUR CASES OF METAMORPHOSIS: NEW IDS ARE PERMANENTLY CREATED[1]

Exhibits H, O, N, and I describe re-negotiations of ID that were completed within the time frame of the single occasion observed, cases whose IDs were truly different at the end from what they had been at the beginning, where a complete process of metamorphosis has taken place, a process generated and controlled by the concerted intentional actions of the participants. New social IDs, new relationships, new components of organizational and institutional reality have been brought into being, and permanent change has been made in everybody's social life. Of course the weight and seriousness of the consequences of these new IDs, these changes, these new creations, varies, and they are valued differently from different points of view. But the facticity and substantiality of change cannot be denied in these instances, which indicate that real intentional change on many levels is ubiquitous in our social life, a common built-in feature of our ongoing reality side by side with the depredations of unwanted and unexpected change in the form of breakdown and dissolution toward chaos which we are ceaselessly working to stabilize and rebuild.

We have already examined H's football game as an instance of the transitory, ephemeral ID change that occurs when a large number of spectators congregates, merges into a unified mass, and then disintegrates back into its component sub-groupings and individuals. But a separate stream of ID re-negotiation occurred on the playing field itself as the contending teams battled out the question at issue in all contests: Who shall be the winner, who the loser, who shall wear the laurels of victory, and who the sackcloth and ashes of defeat?

Players' team performances (enactments of their organizational membership IDs) were judged by sports officials (acting in their institutional relationship IDs) to be in conformance with game rules and as "counting" toward the score or not. The cumulative score at the end of the game defined the Toronto Argonauts as the winning team, an ID ("winner of that game") permanently certified in the sports' record books and the press, but to be proudly worn as a living ID by the victors only until the outcome of next week's game.

The ID change wrought during O's waterpolo finals was comparatively much more long-lasting and significant. This competitive occasion was designed and implemented as an instrument to determine which of two teams would be league champion in the sport for an entire year. O's team, in fact, carried into this game the ID of league champion for the past three years running, seeking to make it four years in a row.

Once again we see in the institutional framework of sport, as we saw in learning, art, and the polity, the negotiation of ID change via the judging of performances by institutionally authorized judges. The Erindale College loss of the championship, according to O, hinged on "dirty play" by the opponents, nail gouging underwater, which was intentionally invisible to the referees, except in a cumulative sense as the pool water reddened with blood. On this basis O's team plans to appeal the outcome, so perhaps the victory as ID-transformation is not so permanent in this case after all. In any event, we can view in this occasion the entire metamorphosis, both teams being identified as "contenders" at the outset, and one winner and one loser at the end.

In N, the judges far outnumber the contestants. A democratic election empowers voters, such as N, to officially judge the performance of candidates and create the ID, through their cumulative judgments, of "winning office holder." This is how, in a democratic polity, ordinary participants in discrete, live social occasions, reproduce the state. All of the arrangements described in Exhibit N are designed to officially define and qualify N's vote to be a legitimate judgment, an authoritative part of the over-all ID negotiation constituting the election. The metamorphosis from candidate to elected official occurs by law within the specified time of polling, and those who enter an election necessarily come out of it changed, even as the structure of democratic government is reproduced and strengthened.

And finally in I, an "ordinary wedding" (documented to be ordinary by the standard wedding flower re-worn by I to this, as to other weddings), a socially foundational set of IDs is created on the spot, forged out of nothing more substantial than the good intentions of all the participants, but resulting in the most solid, most durable, most consequential structural entities in everybody's social life, the institution of kinship, the organization of a family, the relationships among kin and their circle of close friends of the family.

Symbolized by the sides of the aisle the ushers guided them to, the wedding guests arrived at the church with IDs as friends and relatives of the bride or friends and relatives of the groom. But "bride" and "groom" as social IDs were to be liquidated at the ceremony's climax, then evaporated as if there never were such people. The moment the priest "pronounced" them "husband and wife," the previously distinct IDs of all the guests, as well as bride and groom, disappeared, erased as if by magic.

In the greatest metamorphosis any of us ordinarily experiences, everyone in the church except the priest *became* members of one family and friends of one family, their intentionally permanent-from-then-on kinship and friendship relationships transformed en masse and instantaneously. From the church proceeded brand new social structure, brand new social life, brand new people who did not exist as *these* selves an hour before.

In the wedding certificates and in the photographs this miraculous metamorphosis is certified legally, economically, religiously, and commemorated as documented institutional social fact. While they pulsate before us with the new life of their creation by the participants themselves, how could anyone mistake these elements of social structure for a sui generis, externally imposed set of constraints?

These cases vigorously imply that IDs are not in any sense "facts of nature" to be simply counted and statistically analyzed. Rather, they are observably hard-won and ever-disputed negotiated achievements, acquired, sustained, and changed in live interaction. IDs tell us "who we are acknowledged to be to each other," without regard or respect for "who do I think I am"— social ID rather than personal identity.

The identification process is also an organization-building, institutional-structure-reproducing process. Through the eyes of participants, as they recalled their recent observations of live events, we have been able to witness: the creation of a new family and with it the reproduction of the institutional structure of kinship (Exhibit I); the re-assembly of a marketplace, with goods displayed and prices marked, and thus a localized reproduction of a segment of the economy (Exhibit D); the election of a new local government, the embodiment of the state, and thereby the reproduction of the institution of the polity (Exhibit N); the re-gathering of a congregation of worshippers, intentionally and freely reproducing the institutional structure of religion (Exhibit G); a seminar of students working to advance their certifiable knowledge of French literature, and as a by- product, to reproduce on the spot the institution of (higher) learning (Exhibit K); the assembly of singers practicing to meld and blend their voices into the harmonic sound judged aesthetically correct by the audience/expert, the conductress, and thus to *become* a true choir, and to reproduce the institution of art (Exhibit E); the striving of swimmers to win the intercollegiate women's waterpolo championship by means fair and foul, and around that difference reproducing the institution of sport here, in this pool (Exhibit O); and the gathering of semi-strangers in a host's house for the purpose of mutual enjoyment of each other's company, and through casual chat, jokes, and gossip, to "get to know" one another, to socialize, and thus reproduce the foundational institutional structure of friendship (Exhibit P).

It is in each case the developing set of *relationships* between participants that *is* the institutional structure, a structure in a state of dynamic change (and ever-possible dissolution) as these relationships change (and could at any moment be dissolved). The goods in D, marking the relationship between buyers and sellers in the market, may sell or not sell, which will determine continued existence of the business, which determines the continuation of the employee-employer relationships of the night crew, and so goes the economy. The relationships constituting a democratic polity are being freely *exercised* by the voters, officials, and candidates in N, and only thus does this form of state persist. Weddings like I are, of course optional, and there *need not* come into existence all of the new kinship relationships with which the participants walk out of the church.

Kinship may be a necessary institutional structure for the existence of any livable society, but that doesn't mean it cannot dissolve, or that it may not be dissolving before our eyes as the twentieth century ends. If kinship is necessary, its dissolution would not be impossible, merely insufferable. No law of nature guarantees us a livable society. And, kinship appears to have remained strong to the end in Ruanda and in Bosnia, so even if necessary, it is evidently not sufficient.

The kind of social life we get is the social life we take the trouble to build, and reproduce together, day by day, tending our sandcastles in occasions of interaction whose ordinariness is their strength, and whose appearance of ordinariness is our most artful vital achievement.

NOTES

1. The total is nineteen cases because we look at Exhibit H twice, once in terms of what happened to ID in the stadium as a whole, and again here in terms of what happened to ID on the playing field.

EPILOGUE

The present study merely begins to scratch the surface of what can be learned about everybody's social life through analysis of the testimony of participants as to what they authentically observed to have transpired during live ordinary social occasions.

A second volume in preparation re-examines the occasion descriptions transcribed in this book along three additional lines of inquiry, asking: how did the participants in the eighteen occasions described form up and then live within the temporal meaning structure of the occasion, its when dimension; how did they create and react to its spatial meanings, its where dimension; and how did they establish and live by the occasion's motivational meaning structure, its why dimension.

Together the two volumes provide a Burkean (1969) pentadic analysis of the real-life dramatic structure of these eighteen "routine dramas" (Lyman, 1990) by intensifying and asking rigorously the five journalistic questions, what, who, when, where, and why. Further studies are underway, including the continued collection of interview data, the analysis of larger numbers of cases, and the broadening of our categorical and theoretical net to capture more of the lived reality that we can observe. It seems clear already, for instance, that at least one ubiquitous activity pattern must be added to our six modes (chapter 3) in order to approach an exhaustive list. Occasions of commutation, ordinary journeys by groups of two or more who share appoint of departure and a destination, and the transitory interaction in between, probably make up a seventh major activity mode, distinct from the rest. We have begun collecting instances.

The major point that these continuing studies continue to make is that the substantiality and continuity of social structure, the reality as material fact in the world of who we are to each other and what we do together, is an artfully, freely co-produced illusion. In myriad ways, we jointly reproduce the seemingly concrete details of this illusion at the same time that we conspire to suspend our disbelief in it, day after day, during participant-generated occasions of live interaction.

Our evidence supports the existential and phenomenological arguments of Sartre (1956) that we are both completely responsible for the outcomes of our actions and/or inactions in social life and completely free to participate or not, to conform or oppose, to replicate or innovate orderliness. Social structure as meaningful organization is the product of our live interaction, so we are responsible for it, for everything there is to say about it, including its moral quality. Our genocidal horrors are as much our own productions as are our aesthetic humanistic masterpieces. And we freely choose to participate, and could choose just as freely not to participate, in either the production and rationalization of the horrors, or the production and appreciation of the masterpieces.

REFERENCES

Adato, A. (1972). "On the Sociology of Topics in Ordinary Conversation: An Investigation into the Tacit Concerns of Members for Assuring Proper Conduct of Everyday Activities." Unpublished Ph.D. dissertation, U.C.L.A.

Adato, A. (1980). " 'Occasionality' as a Constituent Feature of the Known- in-Common Character of Topics." *Human Studies* 3: 47–64.

Arendt, H. (1963). *Eichmann in Jerusalem: A report on the Banality of Evil.* NY: Viking Press.

Atkinson, P., and Heath, C. eds. (1981). *Medical Work: Realities and Routines.* Farnborough, U.K.: Gower.

Atkinson, M. and Heritage, J. eds. (1984). *Structures of Social Action.* Cambridge: Cambridge University Press.

Barker, R. (1963). *The Stream of Behavior.* New York: Appleton-Century.

Bennett, W. L., and Feldman, M. S. (1981). *Reconstructing Reality in the Courtroom: Justice and Judgement in American Culture.* New Brunswick, NJ: Rutgers University Press.

Berger, P., and Kellner, H. (1964). "Marriage and the Construction of Reality." *Diogenes* 46: 1–24.

Berger, P., and Luckmann, T. (1967). *The Social Construction of Reality: A Treatise in the Sociology of Knowledge.* New York: Doubleday.

Best, J., ed. (1989). *Images of Issues: Typifying Contemporary Social Problems.* Hawthorne, NY: Aldine.

Bocock, R. (1974). *Ritual in Industrial Society.* London: Allen & Unwin.

Boughey, H. (1968). "Blueprints for Behavior: Architects' Intentions." Unpublished Ph.D. dissertation, Princeton University.

Boughey, H. (1978). *The Insights of Sociology: A Multiperspective Introductory Text.* Boston: Allyn & Bacon.

Brannigan, A., and Lynch, M. (1987). "On Bearing False Witness: Perjury and Credibility as Interactional Accomplishments." *Journal of Contemporary Ethnography* 16 (2): 115–146.

Braudel, F. (1981). *Civilization and Capitalism, 15th–18th Century.* Volume 1: *The Structures of Everyday Life: The Limits of the Possible* (1982); Volume 2: *The Wheels of Commerce* (1984); Volume 3: *The Perspective of the World.* New York: Harper.

Brown, D. (1991). *Human Universals.* Philadelphia: Temple University Press.

Bullowa, M. (1975). "When Infant and Adult Communicate How Do They Synchronize Their Behaviors?" In Kendon, A., Harris, R., and Key, M., eds., *Organization of Behavior in Face-to-Face Interaction.* The Hague: Mouton.

Burke, K. (1969). *A Grammar of Motives.* Berkeley: University of California Press.

Cicourel, A. (1972). "Basic and Normative Rules in the Negotiation of Status and Role." In Sudnow, D., ed., *Studies in Social Interaction.*

Cicourel, A., and Knorr-Cetina, K., eds. (1981). *Analysis in Social Theory and Method-*

ology: Toward an Integration of Micro- and Macro-Sociologies. Boston: Routledge & Kegan Paul.
Counihan, C. (1992), "Food Rules in the United States: Individualism, Control, and Hierarchy. "*Anthropological Quarterly* 65: 55–66.
DaMatta, R. (1979). "Ritual in Complex and Tribal Societies." *Current Anthropology* 20: 3.
Douglas, M. (1972). "Deciphering a Meal." *Daedelus* 101: 61–81.
Douglas, M., and Nicod, M. (1974). "Taking the Biscuit: The Structure of British Meals." *New Society* (19 December).
Durkheim, E. (1912/1961). *The Elementary Forms of the Religious Life,* trans. Swain, J. New York: Free Press.
Durkheim, E. (1895/1962). *The Rules of Sociological Method.* Glencoe, IL: Free Press.
Eddy, M. (1906). *Science and Health: With Key to the Scriptures.* Boston: J. Armstrong.
Ellul, J. (1965). *Propaganda.* New York: Vintage Books.
Farb, P., and Armelagos, G. (1980). *Consuming Passions: The Anthropology of Eating.* Boston: Houghton Mifflin.
Fine, G. (1986). "Friendships in the Workplace." Chapter 10 in Derlaga, V. and Winstead, B., *Friendship and Social Interaction* (pp. 185–206). New York: Springer-Verlag.
Garfinkel, H. (1963). "A Conception of, and Experiments with, 'Trust' as a Condition of Stable Concerted Actions." In Harvey, O.J., *Motivation and Social Interaction.* New York: Ronald Press.
Garfinkel, H. (1964). "Studies of the Routine Grounds of Everyday Activities." *Social Problems* 11: 225–250.
Garfinkel, H. (1967). *Studies in Ethnomethodology.* Englewood Cliffs, NJ: Prentice-Hall.
Garfinkel, H. (1974). "The Rational Properties of Scientific and Common- Sense Activities." In Giddens, A., ed., *Positivism and Sociology.* London: Heineman.
Garfinkel, H. (1981). "The Work of a Discovery Science Construed with Materials from the Optically Discovered Pulsar." *Philosophy of the Social Sciences* 11 (2): 131-158.
Garfinekl, H., ed. (1986). *Ethnomethodological Studies of Work.* London: Routledge & Kegan Paul.
Garfinkel, H. (1988). "Evidence for Locally Produced, Naturally Accountable Phenomena of Order, Logic, Reason, Meaning, Method, etc. in and as of the Essential Quiddity of Immortal Ordinary Society (I of IV): An Announcement of Studies." *Sociological Theory* 6: 103–109.
Garfinkel, H. (1993). "A Catalogue of Investigations with Which to Respecify Topics of Logic, Order, Meaning, Method, Reason, Structure, Science, and the Rest, in, about, and as Workings of Immortal Ordinary Society, Just in Any Actual Case: What Did We Do, What Did We Learn?" Plenary session address, Society for Phenomenology and the Human Sciences annual meeting, 1993, New Orleans, Louisiana.
Giddens, A. (1976). *New Rules of Sociological Method.* New York: Basic Books.
Giddens, A. (1979). *Central Problems in Social Theory.* London: Macmillan.
Giddens, A. (1984). *The Constitution of Society.* Berkeley: University of California Press.
Glaser, B., and Strauss, A. (1964). "Awareness Contexts and Social Interaction." *American Sociological Review* 29: 5.
Goffman, E. (1959). *The Presentation of Self in Everyday Life.* Garden City, NY: Dou-

bleday.
Goffman, E. (1961). *Encounters.* Indianapolis, IN: Bobbs-Merrill.
Goffman, E. (1963). *Behavior in Public Places.* New York: Free Press.
Goffman, E. (1968). "The Neglected Situation." In Becker, H. et al., eds., *Institutions and the Person.* Chicago: Aldine.
Goffman, E. (1971). *Relations in Public.* New York: Harper & Row.
Goode, J., Curtis, K., and Theophano, J. (1984). "Meal Formats, Meal Cycles, and Menu Negotiation in the Maintenance of an Italian-American Community." In Douglas, M., ed., *Food in the Social Order.* New York: Russell Sage.
Goode, W., and Hatt, P. (1952). *Methods in Social Research.* New York: McGraw-Hill.
Gross, J. (1984). "Measurement of Calendrical Information in Food-Taking Behavior. " In Douglas, M., ed., *Food in the Social Order.* New York: Russell Sage.
Harre, R. (1979). *Social Being.* Oxford: Basil Blackwell.
Heap, J. (1981). "Verstehen, Language, and Warrants." *Sociological Quarterly* 18(2): 177–184.
Heath, C. (1984). "Participation in the Medical Consultation: The Coordination of Verbal and Nonverbal Behavior between the Doctor and Patient." *Sociology of Health and Illness* 6 (3): 311–338.
Heath, C. (1986). *Body Movement and Speech in Medical Interaction.* New York: Cambridge University Press.
Hewitt, J. (1988). *Self and Society.* Boston: Allyn & Bacon.
Hilbert, R. (1990). "Ethnomethodology and the Micro-Macro Order." *American Sociological Review* 55: 794–808.
Homans, G. (1950). *The Human Group.* New York: Harcourt, Brace.
Huizinga, J. (1952). *Homo Ludens.* London: Routledge.
Hume, D. (1738/1964). *A Treatise of Human Nature* (volume 1). London: Dent.
Irwin, J. (1987). "Reflections on Ethnography." *Journal of Contemporary Ethnography* 16(1): 41–48.
Kendon, A., Harris, R., and Key, M., eds. (1975). *Organization of Behavior in Face-to-Face Interaction.* The Hague: Mouton.
Kendon, A. (1979). "Some Theoretical and Methodological Aspects of the Use of Film in the Study of Social Interaction." In Ginsburg, G., ed, *Emerging Strategies in Social Psychological Research* (pp. 67–91). New York: Wiley.
Kendon, A. (1990). *Conducting Interaction.* New York: Cambridge University Press.
Lanigan, R. (1990). "Is Erving Goffman a Phenomenologist?" In Riggins, S., ed., *Beyond Goffman* (pp. 99-112). New York: Mouton de Gruyter.
Levy, M. (1989). *Our Mother-Tempers.* Berkeley: University of California Press.
Lyman, S. (1990). "The Drama in the Routine: A Prolegomenon to a Praxiological Sociology." *Sociological Theory* 8: 217–223.
MacAloon, J. (1984). *Rite, Drama, Festival, Spectacle: Rehearsals toward a Theory of Cultural Performance.* Philadelphia: Institute for the Study of Human Issues.
Mayhew, B. (1983). "Causality, Historical Particularism and Other Errors in Sociological Discourse." *Journal for the Theory of Social Behavior* 13.
Maynard, D., and Wilson, T. (1980). "On the Reification of Social Structure." In McNall, S., and Howe, G., eds. *Current Perspectives in Social Theory,* Greenwich, CT: JAI Press.
Mchoul, A. (1978). "The Organization of Turns at Formal Talk in the Classroom." *Language and Society* 7: 183–213.
McHugh, P. (1968). *Defining the Situation: The Organization of Meaning in Social Interaction.* Indianapolis, IN: Bobbs-Merrill.

McLaren, P. (1986). *Schooling as a Ritual Performance.* London: Routledge.
Mead, G. (1932). *The Philosophy of the Present.* Chicago: Open Court.
Merton, R. (1957). *Social Theory and Social Structure.* Glencoe, IL: Free Press.
Meyer, J., and Rowan, B. (1977). "Institutionalized Organizations: Formal Structures as Myth and Ceremony." *American Journal of Sociology* 83(2): 55–77.
Mills, C. (1959). *The Sociological Imagination.* New York: Oxford University Press.
Moerman, M. (1988). *Talking Culture: Ethnography and Conversational Analysis.* Philadelphia: University of Pennsylvania Press.
Moore, S., and Meyerhoff, B. (1977). *Secular Ritual.* Amsterdam: Royal Van Gorcum.
Murray, H. (1951). "Toward a Classification of Interactions." In Parsons, T. and Shils, E.A., *Toward a General Theory of Action.* Cambridge, MA: Harvard University Press.
Nagel, E. (1957). *Logic without Metaphysics.* Glencoe, IL: Free Press.
Nagel, E. (1961). *The Structure of Science.* New York: Harcourt.
Panofsky, E. (1955). Meaning in the Visual Arts. New York: Doubleday.
Papineau, D. (1978). *For Science in the Social Sciences.* London: Macmillan.
Pareto, V. (1935). *The Mind and Society.* New York: Cambridge University Press.
Parkes, D., and Thrift, N. (1980). *Times, Spaces, and Places.* Chichester: Wiley.
Pawson, R. (1989). *A Measure for Measures: A Manifesto for Empirical Sociology.* London: Routledge.
Pfohl, S. (1975). "Social Role Analysis: The Ethnomethodological Critique." *Sociology and Social Research* 59 (3): 243–265.
Pike, K. (1967). *Language in Relation to a Unified Theory of the Structure on Human Behavior.* 2nd rev. ed. The Hague: Mouton.
Podilchak, W. (1992). "Fun, Funny, Fun-of Humor and Laughter," *Humor* 5(4): 375–396.
Pollner, M. (1978). "Constitive and Mundane Versions of Labeling Theory." *Human Studies* 1: 269–288.
Pollner, M. (1987). *Mundane Reason: Reality in Everyday and Sociological Discourse.* New York: Cambridge University Press.
Popper, K. (1965). *Conjectures and Refutations.* New York: Harper.
Prus, R. (1987). "Generic Social Processes: Maximizing Conceptual Development in Ethnographic Research." *Journal of Contemporary Ethnography* 16(3): 250–293.
Psathas, G., ed. (1979). *Everyday Language.* New York: Irvington.
Psathas, G. (1989). *Phenomenology and Sociology: Theory and Research.* Washington, DC: University Press of America.
Rawls, A. "The Interaction Order Sui Generis: Goffman's Contribution to Social Theory." *Sociological Theory* 5: 136–149.
Rinehart, J. (1975). *The Tyranny of Work.* Don Mills, Ontario: Longman.
Robboy, H. (1988). "At Work with the Night Worker." In Clark, C. and Robboy, H., eds., *Social Interaction*(pp. 441–455). New York: St. Martin's.
Rogers, M. (1983). *Sociology, Ethnomethodology, and Experience.* New York: Cambridge University Press.
Roy, D. (1960). " 'Banana Time': Job Satisfaction and Informal Interaction." *Human Organization* 18: 156–168.
Sacks, H. (1972). "An Initial Investigation of the Usability of Conversational Data for Doing Sociology. " In Sudnow, D., ed., *Studies in Social Interaction.* New York: Free Press.

Sacks, H. (1984a). "Notes on Methodology." In Atkinson, M. and Heritage, J., eds., *Structures of Social Action* (pp. 21–27). Cambridge: Cambridge University Press.
Sacks, H. (1984b). "On Doing Being Ordinary." In Atkinson and Heritage, *Structures*, pp. 413–429.
Sacks, H. (Forthcoming). "The Inference-Making Machine: Notes on Observability."
Sacks, H., Schegloff, E. A., and Jefferson, G. (1974). "A Simplest Systematics for the Organization of Turn-Taking in Conversation." *Language* 59: 696–735.
Sacks, H., Schegloff, E. A., and Jefferson, G. (1979). "Two Preferences in the Organization of Reference to Persons in Conversation and Their Interaction." In Psathas, G., ed., *Everyday Language* (pp. 15–21). New York: Irvington.
Sartre, J. (1956). *Being and Nothingness*. New York: Philosophical Library.
Schegloff, E. A. (1979). "Identification and Recognition in Telephone Conversation Openings." In Psathas, *Everyday Language*, pp. 23–78.
Schegloff, E. A. (1986). "The Routine as Achievement." *Human Studies* 9(2/3): 111–151.
Schegloff, E. A. (1992). "Repair after Next Turn: The Last Structurally Provided Defense of Intersubjectivity in Conversation." *American Journal of Sociology* 97: 1295–1345.
Schegloff, E. A., and Sacks, H. (1973). "Opening Up Closings." *Semiotica* 7: 289–327.
Schenkein, J. N. (1978). "Identity Negotiations in Conversation." In Schenkein, J. N., ed., *Studies in the Organization of Conversational Interaction* (pp. 57–78). New York: Academic Press.
Schutz, A. (1951). "Making Music Together: A Study in Social Relationship." *Social Research* 18: 76–97.
Schutz, A. (1962). *Collected Papers, I: The Problem of Social Reality*. The Hague: Martinus Nijhoff.
Schutz, A. (1963). "Common Sense and Scientific Interpretations of Human Action." In Natanson, M., ed., *Philosophy of the Social Sciences: A Reader*. New York: Random House.
Schutz, A. (1967). *The Phenomenology of the Social World*. Evanston, IL: Northwestern University Press.
Shrag, C. (1991). "The Phenomenological Sociology of George Psathis: Appraisal and Critique." *Phenomenology and the Human Sciences* 16(3): 1–10.
Simmel, G. (1892/1949). "The Sociology of Sociability," trans. Hughes, Everett C. *American Journal of Sociology* (November): 254–261.
Simmel, G. (1950). *The Sociology of Georg Simmel*, ed. and trans. Wolff, K. Glencoe, IL: Free Press.
Simmel, G. (1955). *Conflict and the Web of Group Affiliations*, trans. Wolff, K. and Bendix, R. Glencoe, IL: Free Press.
Smelser, N. (1988). *Handbook of Sociology*. Newbury Park, CA: Sage.
Smith, D. E. (1974a). "Women's Perspective as a Radical Critique of Sociology." *Sociological Inquiry* 44 (1): 7–13.
Smith, D. E. (1974b). "The Social Construction of Documentary Reality." *Sociological Inquiry* 44 (4): 257–268.
Smith, D. E. (1990). *Texts, Facts, and Femininity: Exploring the Relations of Ruling*. New York: Routledge.
Smith, D. E. (1992). "Sociology from Women's Experience: A Reaffirmation." *Sociological Theory* 10: 88–98.
Sorokin, P. (1965). *Fads and Foibles in Modern Sociology and Related Sciences*. Chicago: Henry Regnery.

Spector, M., and Kitsuse, J. (1987). *Constructing Social Problems.* Hawthorne, NY: Aldine de Gruyter.
Speier, M. (1973). *How to Observe Face-to-Face Communication.* Pacific Palisades, CA: Goodyear.
Spencer, H. (1898). *The Principles of Sociology.* New York, Appleton.
Sudnow, D. (1972). "Temporal Parameters of Interpersonal Observation." In Sudnow, D., ed., *Studies in Social Interaction* (pp. 259–279). New York: Free Press.
Suttles, G. (1970). "Friendship as a Social Institution." In McCall, G. J. et al., eds., *Social Relationships* (pp. 95–135). Chicago: Aldine.
Tuchman, B. W. (1984). *The March of Folly from Troy to Vietnam.* New York: Alfred A. Knopf.
Turner, V. (1969). *The Ritual Process: Structure and Anti-Structure.* Chicago: Aldine.
Visser, M. (1991). *The Rituals of Dinner.* Toronto: HarperCollins.
Wallerstein, I. (1974). *The Modern World-System.* New York: Academic Press.
Weber, M. (1905/1946). *Theory of Social and Economic Organization,* trans. Henderson, A. R. and Parsons, T. New York: Macmillan.
Weber, M. (1949). *Max Weber: Basic Concepts in Sociology,* trans. Secher, H. P. New York: Citadel Press.
Whitehead, A. N. (1954). *Science and the Modern World.* New York: Macmillan.
Zimmerman, D. H. (1969). "Record Keeping and the Intake Process in a Public Welfare Agency." In Wheeler, S., ed., *On Record: Files and Dossiers in American Life* (pp. 319–354). New York: Russell Sage.

INDEX

Adato, A. 25
Agendas, generic, spoken, tacit, and written, 111–165 ff.
Alignment (reciprocity) of Perspectives, 33, 114, 121, 124, 129
Alimentation Monitoring, 114–126 ff.
Analytical Categories, 43, 161, 189
Anderson, M. 19
Anthropology, 3, 4, 5
Arendt, H. 18
Ariadne's Thread, 160
Aristotle 19, 144–147
Art, Artful, 10, 134–137, 156, 172–187 ff., 189
Assembling, 122, 123, 137–149 ff.
Athens, 158
Atkinson, P. 26, 156, 167
Audio/Video Recording, 33–36 ff., 150
Authentic Description/Observation, 13, 19, 29–43 ff., 150, 189
Authoritarianism, 134

Barker, R. 24
Beach, R. 156
Beethoven, L. 19
Bennett, W. 156
Best, J. 5
Berger, P. 5, 10, 25, 111
Bias, 29–43 ff.
Blumer, H. 25
Bocock, R. 22
Bosnia, 187
Boughey, H. 25
Brannigan, P. 45, 156
Braudel, F. 11, 12, 20, 21
Brown, D. 3, 4, 21, 27
Buddha, 19
Bulgaria, 6
Bullowa, R. 121
Burke, K. 189

Canute, 6
Caring, Concern, 114, 121, 124
Carucci, D. 25
Catharsis, 137–149 ff., 179
Causality, 13, 16, 18, 19, 111
Cellular Units, 1, 2, 9, 11, 12, 14, 16, 19, 29, 31, 33, 43, 112
Certification, 149–155 ff., 184, 186
Church, 10, 140, 143, 147, 178
Cicourel, A. 10, 20, 122
Collaboration, 18, 32, 113, 119, 125, 126–137 ff. 142, 143, 147, 155, 160, 161, 163, 182
Commemoration, 12, 124, 125, 133, 147, 148, 150, 158, 159, 186
Commensality, 5, 18, 32, 113–126 ff., 127–129, 131, 135, 137, 143, 147, 160, 163
Communication, 18, 32, 113, 142, 149–155 ff. 157, 163
Commutation, 189
Competition, 18, 32, 113, 139, 140, 142, 155–160 ff., 163, 164, 183
Confidentiality, 149–155 ff.
Congregation, 18, 32, 113, 137–149 ff., 155, 163
Constructionism, 5
Consummation, 161, 177
Contexts of Normalcy, 6, 8, 9, 13, 16, 33, 34, 36, 43, 111–165 ff., 171, 176
Conversation Analysis, 8, 33, 34, 119
Conviviality, 18, 32, 113, 118, 119, 139, 156, 160–165 ff.
Counihan, C. 114, 165, 166
Courtroom Interaction, 156
Crowds, 9, 10, 137–149 ff.
Czechoslovakia, 6

DaMatta, R. 22
Definition of the Situation, 2, 5, 9, 15, 111–165 ff., 176.

Determinism, 10
Deviance, 141, 162, 175
Disclosure, 119, 149–155 ff.
Disconfirmation, 14, 16
Dissolution of Meaning/Structure, 2, 15, 16, 121, 147, 155–160 ff., 184, 186, 187
Diversity at Erindale College, 42
Documentary Reality, 7, 124, 150, 157
Double Blind, 31, 32, 36
Douglas, M. 22, 165, 166
Drew, D. 26, 156
Durkheim, E. 24, 111, 128, 134, 138, 139, 144, 145, 147

Economy, 10, 128, 139, 172–187 ff.
Einstein, A. 19
Empirical Method, Evidence, 1, 13–16, 19, 29–43 ff., 150
Equality, 6, 117, 118, 124, 131, 164
Ethnography, 29–43 ff.
Ethnomethodology, 5, 29–43 ff., 112
Evil, 18, 19, 190
Exhibits A–R, Interview Transcripts, 46–109 ff.
Exteriorized Fact, 7, 13, 19, 170

Face to Face Interaction, 7, 19, 111–165 ff.
Family, 10, 114, 119, 125, 129, 130, 142, 172–187 ff.
Feldman, M. 156
Feminist Sociologists, 5
F–Formation, 118
Fine, G. 176
Freedom, 17–19, 116–118, 123, 124, 131, 133–135, 144, 148, 155, 164, 189, 190
Friendship, 7, 10, 129, 131, 136, 139, 164, 172–187 ff.
Fun, 119, 126, 160–165 ff.

Gandhi, M. 19
Garfinkel, H. 5, 19, 20, 22, 27, 44, 112, 114, 127, 167
Genocide, 18, 190
Giddens, A. 9, 10, 12, 14, 15, 24–26, 112, 123, 124
Glaser, B. 24
Goffman, E. 7, 9, 19, 22, 24–26, 116

Guise, 171

Harre, R. 16, 37, 39, 166
Heath, C. 8, 34, 35, 167
Hewitt, J. 20, 22, 23
Hilbert, R. 10
History, 3–5, 10
Hobbes, T. 160
Holocaust, 18, 19, 134
Homans, G. 165
Homeric Epithets, 170
Human Universals, 3–5, 14, 18, 19, 42, 115, 117, 120, 156, 159, 160, 164, 165
Humanism, 13, 16, 17, 127, 190
Hume, D. 22

ID acquisition, confirmation, continuity, creation, metamorphosis, and transformation, 169–187 ff.
Identification Process, 15, 155, 160, 169–187 ff.
Identity, 169–187 ff.
Individualism, 6–8, 133, 145, 147, 170, 178
Inequality, 117, 118, 131, 134, 160
Infant–Caretaker Interaction, 121
Institutions, Institutional Settings, 9–12, 119, 121, 169–187 ff.
Intellectual Elitism, 5
Interior Mental Experience, 6, 7, 10, 13, 170
Interludes, 6, 7
Interpretation, 7
Intersubjectivity, 7, 11, 13, 114, 120–122
Intimacy, 118, 124, 160–165 ff., 177
Introductions, 169–190 ff.
Invariant Properties, 12
Irwin, J. 44
Isomorphism, 12, 111–165 ff.

Jesus, 19
Journalism, 3–5, 39, 43, 189
Judgement, 7, 133, 134, 155–160 ff., 182–185

Kant, E. 16
Kendon, A. 12, 15, 25, 35, 113, 118, 151
King, M. 19
Kinship, 10, 114, 131, 139, 172–187 ff.

INDEX ■ 199

Kirosawa, 38
Kitsuse, J. 5
Knowledgeability, 14, 15, 121, 123, 155, 182

Labeling, 170
Learning, 10, 12, 139, 153, 172–187 ff.
LeBon, G. 144
Legitimation of Authority, 129, 131, 134, 135, 155–160 ff.
Levy, M. 20, 27
Life, Social, Mental, Organic, 1, 9, 10
Link ID versus Task ID, 171–173
Live Interaction, 1, 9, 10, 12, 14, 19, 111–165 ff., 189, 190
Luckmann, T. 5, 10, 25, 111
Lying, 41
Lyman, S. 1, 2, 19, 27, 189
Lynch, M. 156

MacAloon, J. 22, 167
Macro/Micro Scale, 10, 17
Marx, K. 10, 11, 111, 112, 127, 128, 134, 167
Massification, 137–149 ff., 178, 179
Mayhew, B. 21
Maynard, D. 10, 20, 11, 112, 119, 156
McHoul, A. 119
Meaning Construction, 1, 9, 13, 111–165 ff., 172–187 ff.
Memory Traces, 12, 137, 148
Methodology, 29–43 ff.
Meyer, J. 22
McHugh, P. 15, 25
McLaren, P. 22, 144–146
McPhail, R. 148
Mead, G. 7, 23
Merton, R. 14
Mills, C. 44
Mimicry, 141, 144, 148
Moerman, M. 24
Mohammed, 19
Moore, S. 22
Morphology, 14, 111–165 ff.
Moses, 19
Murray, H. 24
Myerhoff, B. 22

Nagel, E. 20, 21, 26, 44
Naked Senses, 9

Naming Occasions, 111–165 ff.
National Football League, 8
Natural History Approach, 29–43 ff.
Nofsinger, F. 156
Nonverbal Interaction, 34, 118, 130
Normalcy, Normalization, 2, 15, 19, 155–160 ff.

O'Barr, P. 156
Observation, Observability, 7, 9, 10, 12–14, 19, 29–43 ff.
Ontological Security, 2, 15, 120
Ordinariness, 2, 3, 14, 16, 17, 19, 112, 114, 124, 172, 187

Page, C. 20
Panofsky, E. 17
Papineau, D. 26
Pareto, V. 27
Participant Observation, 29–43 ff., 150
Patient–Doctor Interaction, 34, 150, 152, 153, 179, 180
Pfohl, S. 120
Pike, K. 12
Phenomenology, 3, 13, 17, 189
Polity, 10, 139, 156, 172–187 ff.
Pollner, M. 156, 170
Potter's Object, 127
Prefabrications, 6, 144, 156, 158
Procrustean Bed, 6
Professionals, 149–155 ff., 179, 180, 182
Prompting, 133, 144, 150, 155–157, 159
Prus, R. 29, 43
Psathis, G. 23

Racism, 5
Rashomon Effect, 38
Rawls, A. 10, 15, 16
Realization, 7, 15, 111–165 ff.
Recurrence, 12
Reification, 10, 111–165 ff., 170
Relationships, 9, 10, 121, 139, 151, 169–187 ff.
Religion, 10, 139, 142, 172–187 ff.
Representativeness, 29–43 ff.
Reproduction of Structure, 2, 10–12, 14, 111–165 ff., 169–187 ff., 189
Revel, P. 115
Rogers, M. 17
Role, 170

Rooting, 141
Routine, Routinization, 15, 111–165 ff.
Rowan, B. 22
Roy, D. 132, 166
Ruanda, 187
Rules of Sociological Method, 29–43 ff.

Sacks, H. 2, 5, 26, 30, 31, 33, 34
Salutations, 151
Sandcastles, 1, 2, 10, 16, 114, 121, 147, 156, 170, 177, 187
Santayana, G. 2, 6
Sartre, J. 189
Scheff, T. 144, 145
Schegloff, E. 11, 26, 27,34,
Schutz, A. 4, 19, 26, 27, 112, 114, 166
Secret Societies, 153, 154
Self, 7–9, 169–187 ff.
Sexism, 5, 116
Shakespeare, W. 19
Shrag, C. 23
Sideline Activity, 127, 129, 130, 132
Simmel, G. 112, 116, 117, 131, 134, 138, 147, 153, 161, 165–167
Slavery, 134
Smelser, N. 10
Smith, D. 5, 7, 11, 44
Sociability, 160–165 ff.
Social Issues, Problems, 4, 5
Social Object, 9, 112, 123, 136
Social Occasion Defined, 9, 111
Sociology, 3–6, 8, 12, 13, 17, 19, 29–43 ff., 128, 134, 138, 156
Solidarity, 127, 128, 137–149 ff.
Solitude, 6, 7, 116, 117, 127
Sorokin, P. 3
Spector, M. 5
Speier, M. 2, 9, 12, 25, 26, 29–31
Spencer, H. 6
Sport, 10, 119, 125, 134, 139, 141, 148, 158, 172–187 ff.
Standard Operating Procedures, 5, 111–165 ff.
State, 10, 156, 172–187 ff.
Stefan, F. 20
Strauss, A. 24
Subjective Meaning, 7
Subordination/Superordination, 117, 128, 130, 131, 133–135, 154, 155, 174, 175, 179, 180, 182

Sudnow, D. 35
Supervision, 128, 129, 131–135, 175
Synchronization, 116–133

Table Manners, 115, 119
Tacit Knowledge, 14
Taken for Granted, 121, 123, 132
Talk, 8, 33, 34, 119, 123, 130, 162, 163
Tarde, G. 144
Teamwork, 126–137 ff.
Teresa, M. 19
Thomas, W. 2, 19
Thrift, N. 6
Truth Seeking, 41
Trust, 114, 121, 122, 124, 129
Tuchman, B. 21
Turner, V. 19, 22, 140
Turn Taking, 34

Uncertainty, 155–160 ff., 180, 181
Unintended/Unanticipated Consequences, 14, 148, 178

Verstehen, 114
Visser, M. 22, 115, 119, 166

Waiting, 122, 123, 125, 179
Wallerstein, I. 11
"We" and "Us", 7, 115, 122, 132, 136, 159, 164, 165, 172–187 ff.
Weber, M. 7, 8, 22, 24, 114, 128, 134
Whitehead, A. 20
Wilson, T. 10, 20, 111, 112, 119
World–Economies, 129, 132, 135
Worship, 140

Zimmerman, D. 125